Shaping a
Maritime
Empire

Commodore Perry Meets the Imperial Commissioners at Yokohama, 1854

Shaping a Maritime Empire

The Commercial
and Diplomatic
Role of the
American Navy,
1829–1861

John H. Schroeder

Contributions in Military Studies, Number 48

GREENWOOD PRESS
Westport, Connecticut · London, England

Library of Congress Cataloging in Publication Data

Schroeder, John H., 1943-
  Shaping a maritime empire.

  (Contributions in military studies, ISSN 0883-6884 ;
no. 48)
  Bibliography: p.
  Includes index.
  1. United States—History, Naval—To 1900.
2. United States. Navy—History—19th century.
3. United States—Commerce—History—19th century.
I. Title II. Series.
E182.S36 1985   973   85-942
ISBN 0-313-24883-4 (lib. bdg.)

Library of Congress Catalog Card Number: 85-942
ISBN: 0-313-24883-4
ISSN: 0883-6884

First published in 1985

Greenwood Press
A division of Congressional Information Service, Inc.
88 Post Road West
Westport, Connecticut 06881

Printed in the United States of America

10 9 8 7 6 5 4 3 2 1

Copyright Acknowledgment:

Chapter 2 appeared in somewhat different form in *New Aspects of Naval History: Selected Papers
from the Fifth Naval Symposium* (Baltimore, 1985).

To my mother, Azalia,
and the memory of my father, Herman

Contents

Acknowledgments

I wish to thank the College of Letters and Science of the University of Wisconsin-Milwaukee for helping to support the research which led to this book. I owe a considerable debt of gratitude to the professional staffs of UWM's Golda Meir Library, the American Geographical Society Collection now housed at UWM, and the Library of the Wisconsin State Historical Society. Librarians at the National Archives, the Manuscript Division of the Library of Congress, and the Chester W. Nimitz Library of the U.S. Naval Academy provided valuable assistance with my research. I also want to thank the UWM Cartographic Services for preparing the maps in this book.

The preparation of this book was also assisted by the special efforts of several individuals. Professors David Healy and David Long provided detailed critiques of the manuscript and significantly improved the final product. Professor Reginald Horsman encouraged the project from beginning to end, shared his extensive knowledge of the period, and enhanced the manuscript through his detailed editorial and substantive criticisms. Ms. Eunice Kepp faithfully typed the several versions of the manuscript with care, accuracy, and good cheer. I am indebted to my wife, Sandra, for her encouragement and patience with this project and for her assistance in helping to excise stylistic gremlins from the text. My sons, John and Andrew, contributed nothing to the book and, in fact, frequently interrupted the progress of the manuscript. In so doing they added a personal perspective which made the entire project more worthwhile to me.

*Shaping a
Maritime
Empire*

1.
Introduction

In the three decades before the Civil War, the peacetime role of the U.S. Navy increased dramatically. Although the primary peacetime mission of the navy remained the protection of American overseas commerce, accelerating American economic activity around the world transformed the operational definition of that responsibility by creating additional demands and pressures for increased naval support. In the 1820's the protection of commerce meant that the navy combatted pirates, policed smuggling, showed the flag in major ports around the globe, maintained a continuous presence on various overseas stations, and performed limited diplomatic duties. Government officials and most politicians, regardless of their partisan faction, believed the navy should play a limited peacetime commercial role and defined that mission in a rather narrow and defensive manner. Americans also assumed that most of the navy's activities would occur in the Caribbean, the Mediterranean, and the Atlantic. To perform its role, the Navy Department maintained a small, active force of fewer than two dozen warships and existed on a budget that averaged less than $4 million per year.[1]

By the 1850's the protection of commerce had been redefined and meant a great deal more than it had three decades earlier. The navy now played a positive and expansive role in the nation's burgeoning overseas commerce and in its emerging American maritime empire. The navy not only protected and defended American lives, property, and trade overseas, it now also helped identify new markets, collected valuable commercial and nautical information, concluded diplomatic agreements, and opened new areas to American enterprises. In the navy, the Mediterranean Squadron continued to be the most prestigious duty station, but American naval forces in Latin America, the Pacific, and the East Indies now carried out activities that were more challenging and more valuable to American overseas commercial interests.

By the 1850's the varied diplomatic and commercial activities of the navy had become an important factor in helping to shape the growing American maritime empire. In the Caribbean and Central America, the navy carried the burden of ineffective American efforts to end British hegemony and replace it with American power. American naval officers also led exploring expeditions intended to hasten American commercial penetration of the Amazon Valley, the La Plata Basin, the Isthmus of Panama, West Africa, and the North Pacific. In 1853–1854 Commodore Matthew C. Perry commanded a naval expedition which established formal commercial and diplomatic relations with Japan. In Asia, the nation's efforts to place commercial and diplomatic relations with China on a stable basis rested heavily on the navy. Elsewhere around the world, American naval forces carried out punitive actions against people who had attacked American citizens or their interests. These far-flung activities required an active force of between forty and fifty warships and an annual budget which averaged more than $12 million a year between 1853 and 1860. Although the navy still had fundamental problems on the eve of the Civil War, the nation's staggering overseas commercial expansion had redefined the peacetime mission of the navy. In the process, the navy had assumed an important role in shaping the nation's overseas commercial development and its maritime empire.

The navy's growing commercial importance in the antebellum period had neither been planned nor envisioned by the great majority of government officials, politicians, or naval officers. Little serious or sustained discussion seems to have been devoted to the navy's expanding peacetime mission. The debates that did occur usually centered around questions of the navy's capacity to defend the republic in wartime and the extent to which the navy should attempt to match the navies of Europe and Great Britain and challenge them on the high seas. In Congress, discussion of naval questions usually focused on specific appropriation items or on the internal problems of the navy and was dominated by partisanship and sectional jealousy.

The Cabinet and the Navy Department seem rarely to have addressed the need to redefine the navy's peacetime commercial role, nor did the conservative Board of Navy Commissioners which was comprised of senior naval officers with very traditional views. In addition, the level of civilian leadership in the Navy Department was weak or mediocre through most of the period. Partisan political considerations, not interest or experience in naval affairs, almost invariably dictated the selection of the Secretary of the Navy. Lieutenant Matthew F. Maury summarized the situation well in 1841 when he observed that the Secretary "is usually selected from among politicians, who have never made Naval affairs any part of their study. Neither is the selection made on account of any peculiar fitness or qualifications . . . for the duties of his office." As a result, the new Secretary "goes to work in the dark, and, of course, blunders and mismanagement ensue." Although a number of men who served as Secretary proved to be competent administrators and managed the department efficiently, few had any real understanding or conceptual vision of the navy's changing peacetime commercial role. And the few individuals, such as Abel P. Upshur and John P.

Kennedy, who attempted to address this question served briefly and enjoyed only limited influence.[2]

In the absence of a clearly defined peacetime naval policy, the nation's overseas commercial expansion and the national policy which supported that growth were primarily responsible for the navy's developing role as an arm of American commercial diplomacy. In the three decades before the Civil War, American foreign commerce grew at a staggering pace. Total American foreign trade expanded from $134,523,566 in 1829 to $687,192,176 in 1860, an increase of 411 percent. These figures included an increase in total exports from $67,434,651 to $333,576,057, or 395 percent, and an increase in total imports from $67,088,915 to $353,616,119, or 427 percent. In the same period, the registered tonnage of the U.S. merchant marine expanded from 592,859 to 2,379,396 gross tons while the total American tonnage which entered and cleared U.S. ports grew from 1,817,748 to 12,087,209 net tons. Rather than surprise or astound most Americans, these dramatic figures only confirmed existing American assumptions about the ultimate commercial destiny of the republic. "When I contemplate the ardor with which the Anglo-Americans prosecute commerce, the advantages which aid them, and the success of their undertakings," Alexis de Tocqueville had written in 1835, "I cannot help believing that they will one day become the foremost maritime power of the globe. They are born to rule the seas, as the Romans were to conquer the world." By the 1850's the United States was well on the way to proving the accuracy of this prediction.[3]

In fact, the great proportion of the nation's trade continued to be with the nation's traditional markets. In 1855, 77 percent of the nation's imports came from Europe, Canada, and Cuba while 84 percent of the nation's exports went to these same markets. In contrast, the entire Pacific trade including that of China accounted for less than 9 percent of the nation's imports and a bare 4 percent of its exports. In South America, trade with Brazil and the Argentine accounted for smaller percentages of the nation's total. But the reality of these figures meant little to a generation of Americans who believed that the nation's ultimate commercial destiny lay in the vast reaches of the Pacific and, to a lesser extent, in South America.[4]

By acquiring Texas, California, and Oregon, the United States had created a huge continental empire which not only provided enough land to guarantee economic prosperity and living space for future generations but also established the geographic base for a worldwide commercial empire. As they studied the globe, expansionists concluded that the United States occupied a strategic central position between Europe and Asia. "The world contains no seat of empire so magnificent as this," declared William Henry Seward, which "offers supplies on the Atlantic shores to the over-crowded nations of Europe, while on the Pacific coast it intercepts the commerce of the Indies. The nation thus situated . . . must command the empire of the seas, which alone is real empire."[5] Once Oregon and California could be connected to the Mississippi Valley and to the eastern seaboard by the transcontinental railroad and isthmian canal, the United

States could command the trade of Asia, the Pacific, South America, and the Caribbean and serve as the passage for European trade to Asia and the Pacific. In spite of the fact that the United States had created a loosely knit but impressive maritime empire by the 1850's, most Americans believed that their nation's commercial destiny had not yet been realized. Confident expansionists were already pressing for an isthmian canal, overseas coaling stations and naval bases, and territorial acquisitions in the Caribbean and the Pacific. Most Americans, then, viewed their commercial destiny as unfulfilled and their maritime empire as an unfinished product in the 1850's. They confidently anticipated the day when their commerce would encircle the globe and command the trade of the Western Hemisphere, the Pacific basin, and Asia.

The creation of a commercial empire had been a primary objective of American foreign policy since the early republic, but by the late 1820's accelerating American interest in and penetration of new or undeveloped markets demanded greater naval support. Specifically, the expansive overseas commercial activities of the nation created two general kinds of pressures for increased commercial and diplomatic support from the navy. Within the United States, those interest groups most directly involved in the extensive whale fishery and foreign trade pressed for a stronger and more active peacetime navy. A variety of individual entrepreneurs, adventurers, politicians, publicists, and naval officers also presssed for greater naval support. In advocating their own interests, they argued that the navy needed to expand its protection of specific American interests overseas, to help open new markets, to augment American diplomatic initiatives, and to collect the nautical, commercial, and geographic information needed to encourage American trade with remote, but potentially rich, areas of the globe. Given the diversity of interests they represented, these advocates of a strong, commercially oriented navy never constituted a unified political lobby in the United States. Instead these groups and individuals tended to come forward in turn to advocate a specific interest or project. Once their need had been met or rejected, most retired and turned their attention from the navy to other concerns.

Overseas, American economic activities and the growth of the nation's maritime empire created an array of situations that required a naval presence or a specific naval response. The very slowness of oceanic travel and the length of time required to transmit and receive a reply to diplomatic communications meant that naval officers often could provide the only response for various problems that arose in areas far removed from the continental United States. Warships had to be available to insure that American merchant ships remained unmolested, that American residents were not harassed, and that shipwrecked American sailors received friendly treatment. When pirates became active or when individual outrages occurred, only the navy could respond adequately. When American interests overseas required a punitive action or a show of force, the navy provided the necessary military might. Moreover, the actual conduct of diplomacy required the presence of the navy in most areas of the nonwestern world. American warships not only conveyed American diplomats to their destinations, but they also helped create the environment of respect necessary to conduct diplomatic and commercial relations with local authorities. In China, commercial privileges could neither be established nor maintained without a naval presence. With Japan, the establishment of formal diplomatic and commercial relations would not have been possible without an overwhelming naval squadron. And through its warships around the world, the United States maintained an international presence which helped hundreds of Americans carry on their commercial enterprises.

Given the uncoordinated nature of American commercial activity abroad, the navy's antebellum development occurred in a rather haphazard and unsystematic manner. Most Presidents, Secretaries of the Navy, politicians, lobbyists, and naval officers did not recognize or advocate the type of peacetime navy required by the republic's emerging overseas empire, but the nation's very commitment to continental expansion and commercial growth inevitably enhanced the navy's role. In many respects, naval development accurately mirrored American commercial growth abroad, which itself was erratic and unsystematic, but simultaneously relentless and dramatic. In short, the growth of an American maritime empire prior to the Civil War resulted largely from private enterprise and individual initiative, not from a well-planned or coordinated policy of the federal government. Although American leaders had dreamed of a commercial empire for decades, they had not committed the government to the type of imperial policies pursued by European nations. Instead, the United States had attempted to gain equal commercial access to the mercantile empires of Europe through various diplomatic agreements and, when necessary, retaliatory legislation. In undeveloped commercial areas, the nation had concluded numerous agreements to open the commercial door to American initiative and enterprise. The web of a commercial empire, then, was spun by hundreds of American entrepreneurs and adventurers, merchants and dreamers, sea captains and whalers, consuls and naval officers, missionaries and explorers. In a similar way, the navy's peacetime growth was shaped by an array of opportunities, problems, pressures, and crises which demanded direct but often unrelated naval responses. Erratic, uncoordinated, and unplanned, American antebellum naval development was nevertheless persistent and substantial.

In such an atmosphere, the ideas, dreams, and initiatives of various individuals had a substantial impact on naval activity. In the Navy Department, Abel P. Upshur and John P. Kennedy each had short tenures as Secretary, but their enthusiasm and vision augmented the navy's peacetime role. Among naval officers, Matthew Maury and Matthew C. Perry understood the potential commercial role of the navy and worked effectively to realize that goal. In spite of the fact that he spent most of his career behind a desk at the Naval Observatory in Washington, Lieutenant Matthew Maury enhanced the navy's peacetime activities as he worked tirelessly throughout the 1840's and 1850's to collect valuable information on the tides, currents, and prevailing winds in the Atlantic and the Pacific. By the early 1850's, he produced charts which showed the most productive whaling areas in the Pacific. Maury was also instrumental in launching the Amazon exploring expedition of the early 1850's and in encouraging naval participation in other explorations of commercial and scientific importance. Undramatic as they were, his activities helped create an important commercial responsibility for the peacetime navy. Commodore Matthew Perry is best remembered for his dramatic expedition to Japan in 1853–1854 which illustrated the central role the navy could play in the building of a commercial empire. However, Perry had also long been involved in efforts to modernize and reform the navy and establish it as an aggressive instrument of an expansive American foreign policy overseas. As such, Perry stands as a distinct precursor to Alfred T. Mahan and his influential ideas on seapower.

In addition to government officials and naval officers, individual promoters and lobbyists had a significant influence on naval activity between 1829 and 1861. In spite of considerable support, the United States Exploring Expedition of 1838–1842 probably would never have been launched without the indefatigable efforts of Jeremiah N. Reynolds, who publicized and lobbied the project through Congress and then prodded reluctant government officials to insure its departure. Promoters Aaron H. Palmer and Edward A. Hopkins played similar key roles in stimulating naval expeditions to the North Pacific and to the La Plata Basin, respectively, in the early 1850's. Through their New England representatives in Congress, China merchants demanded and received increased protection and support from the navy in the early 1840's and again the 1850's. Spokesmen for the extensive Pacific whaling industry pressed for and received naval support for whaling ships in the Pacific; in fact, the standing orders of virtually every American Commodore dispatched to the Pacific in the period carried specific instructions to protect American whaling interests there.

The development of the navy's commercial role between 1829 and 1860 occurred in two roughly equal fifteen-year periods divided by the mid–1840's. At the outset, the navy's restricted peacetime place seemed to have been confirmed when Andrew Jackson declared in his 1829 message to Congress, "In time of peace we have need of no more ships of war than are requisite to the protection of our commerce."[6] As an agrarian Democrat from an interior western state, Jackson viewed the militia as the bulwark of the nation's defense and advocated limited federal expenditures. Accordingly, the navy should be as small as possible and confined to a narrow role. The problem for Jackson, as for every other President in the next thirty years, was that he needed the navy much more than he initially anticipated. The tremendous growth of American trade overseas and the expansive thrust of American foreign policy dictated an active and expanded navy, not a reduced one. From 1829 to 1837 Jackson worked to increase American trade, conclude new reciprocity agreements, open new markets, and retaliate against attacks on American commerce. To achieve these goals, he relied heavily on the navy; by the end of his administration, Jackson had become its strong advocate.

Undaunted, Martin Van Buren ignored the lessons of his predecessor and effectively resisted both naval reform and expansion during his single term as President. However, Van Buren also turned to the navy to protect American economic interests in China during the Opium War in spite of the fact that the President did not wish to pursue an aggressive foreign or commercial policy. In response to appeals from American merchants at Canton, the Van Buren Administration dispatched Commodore Lawrence Kearny to China in 1841 to protect American lives, property, and commercial interests. Although the President was indifferent, the navy's presence in China was acknowledged as a permanent necessity by the time Van Buren left office.

After the mid–1840's the navy's expanding commercial role accelerated as a result of important developments in the decade. The rising popular ideology of Manifest Destiny, the acquisition of Oregon and California, and the emergence of an expansive gospel of commerce all combined to place new pressures on the navy. Advocates of Manifest Destiny envisioned the development of a powerful commercial and continental empire for the United States. As such, their ideology demanded, by implication, a stronger navy to facilitate American expansion in the Caribbean, the Pacific, and ultimately the East Indies and Asia. In reality, the acquisition of Oregon and California required a continuous naval presence on the nation's long Pacific coastline. These acquisitions also confirmed the United States as a Pacific power with vital interests in the vast Pacific Basin. Only an effective navy could protect existing commercial interests and facilitate the growth of American economic power in the region. Finally, the proponents of the American "gospel of commerce" realized that strong naval support was essential to a vast overseas maritime empire. If American commerce was ever to penetrate the far corners of the globe, as they believed it would, an effective navy was a prerequisite to that commercial destiny.

By the 1850's these factors created a part for the navy which far surpassed its traditional function of protecting and defending American interests from threats in the Caribbean, the Atlantic, and the Mediterranean. The navy now engaged in the expansion of commercial opportunity and the creation of the American maritime empire. It had become a positive and aggressive arm of American commercial and diplomatic policy. The exploring expeditions of the 1850's charted remote seas, surveyed important river basins, searched for a canal route in Central America, and collected a wealth of commercial information about potential new markets. American activity in the Caribbean, South America, and the Pacific also dictated a larger diplomatic role for the navy. In China and Asia, where diplomacy could not be conducted without a continuous naval presence and frequent intervention by naval officers, the effect was to diminish the primacy of the State Department representatives and to elevate the importance of the naval officer in conducting diplomatic and commercial relations.

Ironically, this increased but uncoordinated level of naval activity produced an anomalous position for the navy in the 1850's. On the one hand, the navy played the type of commercial and diplomatic role which foreshadowed its responsibilities a half century later. On the other hand, this development had not been accompanied by the rise of a more modern navy or a body of appropriate strategic thought. Although the actual size of the navy had increased by the 1850's, most of its ships remained old, inefficient, and technologically backward. The introduction of steam power, iron armament, and explosive ordinance, technologies which were then revolutionizing the navies of Europe, lagged in the United States. On their distant stations, American naval officers also found that the vessels assigned to them often restricted their ability to perform their peacetime commercial and diplomatic functions. Most naval vessels then were unfit for war with the newer ships of Europe and poorly suited for many of the commercial peacetime duties in the Caribbean, along the coasts of Asia, or the river ports of China.[7]

In addition, the United States had not yet developed a systematic body of naval thought which envisioned or outlined a comprehensive peacetime commercial and diplomatic role for the navy. Some politicians and editors advocated such a role, but their arguments remained undeveloped. In the navy itself, no Alfred T. Mahan or Stephen B. Luce emerged. Those officers, like Commodore Perry, who envisioned such a role had neither the forum nor the opportunity to develop and present their thoughts. On the eve of the Civil War, the U.S. Navy found itself in a position which was both flattering and frustrating. The navy now played an undeniably vital role in the defense and extension of the nation's interests overseas, but it did not have the resources or the national support or direction to accomplish its mission effectively.

Prior to 1815 the navy's role in American foreign policy had been defined largely by the defensive posture of the nation. Although committed to territorial expansion and the increase of foreign trade, the United States was unable to extricate itself from European affairs and was preoccupied with the protection of its independence and territorial integrity. Dreams of continental and commercial empire had to be subordinated to the pressing need for national security at home and neutral rights on the high seas. In North America, American leaders believed that their political freedom required the removal of the Indians from the frontier, the Spanish from the Floridas, the French and Spanish from Louisiana, and the English from the Great Lakes and the far Northwest. Overseas, a succession of Presidents struggled to maintain American neutrality, prevent various depredations on American commerce, resist the impressment of American sailors, and defend American neutral rights on the seas. For the U.S. Navy, these national objectives meant the role of defender of existing American trade and protector of American neutral rights. Established in the 1790's, the navy struggled valiantly in its early years to combat various English, French, and Spanish privateers, to fight the French in the undeclared naval war of 1798–1800, and to protect American neutral commerce against French and English violations. At the same time, the navy tried to protect American shipping in the Mediterranean region by waging war against the Barbary corsairs.

During the War of 1812 the republic's tiny navy attempted to protect the American coast from invasion, guard American commerce overseas, and maintain control of the Great Lakes against the overwhelming superiority of the British Navy. The task was an impossible one, and the war came close to being a disaster for the United States as the British rampaged the Chesapeake, threatened invasion from Canada and the Caribbean, and swept American commerce from the seas. In spite of the dismal American war effort, news of the Treaty of Ghent and Jackson's stunning victory at New Orleans in early 1815 created the illusion of an American victory and produced an immediate upsurge of postwar nationalism. Although its efforts had not altered the strategic balance or the course of the war, the navy had achieved dramatic victories. On the high seas, American frigates defeated British warships in several single-ship encounters. Oliver Hazard Perry stunned the British on Lake Erie in 1813, and, on Lake Champlain, the Thomas MacDonough victory in 1814 checked a British invasion from the North. Such exploits kindled an intense popularity for the navy and its fighting heroes in a young nation without a long military tradition. That national support was further enhanced in May, 1815, when Stephen Decatur sailed from New York with ten ships on a mission to chastise the Dey of Algiers for continued attacks on American commerce in the Mediterranean. By August, Decatur had defeated several Algerian warships and exacted a settlement from the Dey as well as indemnity from Tunis and Tripoli. The appearance of another squadron under the command of Commodore William Bainbridge effectively ended the long-standing hostilities with the Barbary powers.

After the War of 1812 the United States experienced a brief era of intense nationalism during which the federal government attempted to strengthen the nation's defense and economy. In 1815, the regular army was enlarged and the Board of Navy Commissioners was created to improve administration of the Navy Department. Appointed by the President with the consent of the Senate, the three-man Board of Captains was to provide professional advice and assistance in the administration of the Department. Actual control of policy was to remain with the civilian Secretary of the Navy. In December, 1815, President James Madison proposed a program to strengthen the nation's economic self-sufficiency. Congress should create a new national bank, approve a protective tariff, and establish a federally financed road and canal system under national authority. In Congress, Jeffersonian Democrats now found themselves supporting measures that many had long opposed. As a result, Congress soon chartered the second Bank of the United States and passed the Tariff of 1816, which established protective duties on most woolen, cotton, and iron manufactures. The federally financed system of internal improvements also seemed imminent.

As part of the nationalists' program, Congress also approved the Revenue Bill of 1816. This measure specified that the direct wartime tax of $6 million be continued after the war but reduced to $3 million to provide additional peacetime revenue. Although the measure did not specify how the additional funds were to be spent, debate on the bill centered on its possible uses and indicated a clear understanding that the funds would be used in part to augment the peacetime military establishment and finance internal improvements.[8] Opponents of the measure denounced levying a direct tax to build roads and canals as well as to support "expensive Military and Naval establishments." Such "chimerical projects," charged one critic, only increased demands on the government for the purpose of "extending public patronage, and running the road of power in the same way that President Adams did." Congressmen John Randolph of Virginia and Benjamin Hardin and Samuel McKee of Kentucky argued that the direct tax should be terminated because a large army and navy served no useful purpose in a peacetime republic. They were particularly scornful of the assertion that a large peacetime military establishment would enhance the stature and rising glory of the young republic. Ridiculing the "prosecution of wild schemes of erratic chivalry," Federalist William Gaston of North Carolina urged the republic not to "run in the race of glory, nor to divert the citizens of the Republic from the occupations of honest industry to military pursuits." To Representative Hardin, national glory consisted not in a large army or navy but rather in the reduction of the national debt and government expenditures so "that every citizen should be enabled to enjoy the fruits of his industry. . . . The national glory consists in the pristine principles of this Government, in the blessings of tranquility and comfort at home, and peace with all foreign powers."[9]

Proponents of the Revenue Bill argued that continuation of the direct tax was essential to the economic strength and military defense of the republic. To them, the recent war with England had demonstrated the need for a strong peacetime military. "I would act seriously, effectively act," declared Henry Clay, "on the principle, that in peace we ought to prepare for war. . . . These halcyon days of peace, this calm will yield to the storm of war; and when that comes, I am for being prepared to breast it." In peacetime, the nation could depend on a strong navy "not only for protection but for negotiation," according to Massachusetts Representative Albion Parris. As the nation's power grew, its commerce expanded, and its wealth burgeoned, John C. Calhoun emphasized that the hostility and jealousy of the European powers would grow. Such a prospect required that the United States have a strong peacetime navy, "not for the purpose of conquest, but to maintain our essential rights."[10]

In addition to their desire to strengthen the republic's defenses and to use the navy in support of diplomatic objectives, supporters of the measure were anxious to enhance the nation's prestige. To them a strong peacetime navy was a most effectual way of achieving national glory. Henry St. George Tucker of Virginia summarized this attitude when he observed that the Revenue Bill would "permit us gradually to increase our navy—the glory and boast of the nation. I am not ashamed, Mr. Chairman, to speak of national glory. I love national glory." Unlike Hardin, Tucker did not define this concept in terms of a small national debt or low federal expenditures. Labelling "foreign wars and foreign conquests" as a wretched kind of "false glory," Tucker praised the true "glory of being able to protect our country and our rights from every invader. . . . There is no glory in a nation's submitting to every invasion of its rights, because it wants the spirit to defend them, or the liberality to pay for their defense. This is not national glory—it is national disgrace. . . . "[11]

Opponents of the Revenue Bill were placed in a difficult position in regard to the peacetime navy. In the intense nationalistic afterglow of the War of 1812, the heady concepts of national greatness, national glory, and national defense were more than a match for simple old Republican principles. In addition, the navy's stirring wartime victories and recent dramatic success against Algiers rendered its service and value above reproach. Even opponents who in the previous decade would have questioned the need for a strong peacetime navy now praised the valor and gallantry of the nation's navy and acknowledged the need to maintain and strengthen the postwar navy. In this atmosphere, opponents of the bill failed to defeat it or to restrict the manner in which the additional revenue was to be used. On February 6, 1816, the House passed the bill by a vote of 86 to 67. The Senate soon followed suit.[12]

Once additional revenue was assured, the path was clear for an increased navy. "An Act for the Gradual Increase of the Navy of the United States" became law on April 19, 1816. The measure provided that $1 million be spent in each of the next eight years to construct nine ships of not less than seventy-four guns each and twelve ships of not less than forty-four guns each. The act represented a triumph for the navalist viewpoint and seemed to insure a large permanent peacetime navy. "The act is one of the most important in the legislative history of the Navy," observed one historian, "as it committed the United States for the first time to a policy of building up a fleet in peacetime which was comparable to those of European powers."[13] The terms of the act represented a victory for the proponents of a large European-style navy in that the bill, as recommended by the House Naval Affairs Committee, specified the construction of large capital ships rather than smaller, more versatile, and swifter vessels of fewer than forty-four guns. In addition, the report of Secretary of the Navy Benjamin Crowinshield, on which the bill was based, clearly anticipated the concentration of these ships into one or two large squadrons. Such a fleet of ships-of-the-line represented an unprecedented source of national pride and might be used to influence the European balance of power and to provide the foundation of a formidable naval defense. The way now seemed clear for the United States to develop a navy which would be used in the way that European powers had always attempted to use theirs.

In fact, the Naval Bill of 1816 did not represent a lasting victory for navalist objectives. Within several years, questions about the size, composition, and cost of the peacetime navy resurfaced with significant effect. Unfortunately for such nationalists as Henry Clay and John Calhoun, the postwar atmosphere of patriotism, confidence, and unity which made their nationalistic program possible soon changed. The Panic of 1819 effectively ended the so-called Era of Good Feeling, jeopardized the programs of 1816, and set the nation on a course of rising sectionalism, political tension, and government retrenchment. Caught in this reaction was the program of the naval expansionists. By the beginning of 1820 opponents of a large navy had begun to question the annual expenditure of $1 million to increase the navy in a time of financial distress. Although supporters of the navy prevented immediate reduction of naval expenditures, the supporters of naval retrenchment could not be deterred. In 1821 Congress reduced the 1816 annual appropriation by half, from $1 million to $500,000 per year, and extended the program three years. Defeated by a single vote was a motion that would have prevented the commissioning of any of the new vessels.

In the debates on the navy during the 16th Congress in 1820 and 1821, supporters of naval retrenchment emphasized two arguments. First, the United States could not afford a program of continued naval expansion in a time of fiscal crisis and declining government revenues. Second, the utility of large warships for peacetime purposes was questionable. Questions about the usefulness of a fleet of ships-of-the-line and large frigates in peacetime with no threat of war underlined a growing inconsistency in postwar naval policy. The large ships authorized by the Act of 1816 were poorly designed to discharge the responsibilities which had devolved on the postwar American navy. With the end of the Napoleonic Wars, the United States had little need for a fleet of large warships. One of the prime objectives of the navalists had been the creation of a European-style navy which could affect the European balance of power, protect American neutral shipping against the vicissitudes of European politics, and prevent the republic from being drawn into another conflict like the War of 1812. In effect, the navalists sought a navy that could prevent recurrence of the difficulties, damages, and humiliations which had plagued the republic from the early 1790's to 1815. With Europe embarking on a century of peace, however, those conditions were not repeated.[14]

Peace in Europe permitted the United States to pursue a different type of foreign policy. Although the nation maintained close diplomatic ties to England and the nations of Europe, the focal point of those relations shifted from the Old World to the New. American leaders now focused on the territorial and commercial expansion of their republic, and the nation's foreign policy reflected that orientation. Under the diplomatic leadership of Secretary of State John Quincy Adams, the United States acquired the Floridas and established a transcontinental corridor to the Pacific through the treaty with Spain. At the same time, Adams worked effectively to preserve American interests along the Canadian border, in the Oregon Country, and on the far Northwest Coast of the continent. In 1823 the Monroe Doctrine warned against further intervention or colonization in Latin America while asserting American interests there. As "the manifesto of an American empire," Monroe's statements embodied the republic's long-range determination to be the primary commercial and political power in both North and South America.[15]

Overseas, the United States attempted to expand commercial opportunities through its shipping policies. Congress reversed the traditional practice of imposing discriminatory duties on foreign shipping by passing the Reciprocity Act of 1815, which empowered the President to establish complete reciprocity in direct trade. Foreign ships could enter American ports under the same terms as were extended to U.S. ships in the ports of those same nations. Soon after the act became law, the United States and Great Britain eliminated all discriminatory duties in direct trade between the two countries. Two years later, Congress passed the Navigation Act of 1817, which prohibited foreign vessels from carrying imports which did not come from the ship's home country. However, the prohibition was removed if a similar prohibition was not enforced against American ships by the foreign nation. In the next twelve years, the United States signed more than a dozen agreements for shipping reciprocity including those with every major nation of Europe. These reciprocity treaties proved so effective that American ships traded directly with the chief ports of the world by 1830 without appreciable hindrance from discriminatory regulations.[16] The most significant exception to this success occurred with the indirect trade of the British West Indies. The British made some initial concessions, then refused Adams' demands for complete reciprocity, and finally excluded American ships from the British West Indies in 1826. Here the matter stood until the Jackson Administration reached a new agreement for partial reciprocity in 1830.

For the navy, the postwar orientation of American foreign policy created new responsibilities which the Naval Construction Act of 1816 had not anticipated. After the Barbary powers capitulated in 1815, the need for a fleet of large ships with massive firepower virtually disappeared. Increasingly, the navy had to be dispersed over an extended area as its primary duties now included policing the African slave trade (outlawed in 1808), combating pirates in the Caribbean, and protecting American merchant ships from privateers on both coasts of South America. Unfortunately, the ships of the existing navy and those authorized by the Naval Act of 1816 were poorly equipped to perform those duties. Slavers operated in small ships which could sail in shallow water to avoid apprehension. Likewise, privateers and pirates in the Western Hemisphere operated close to shore in a variety of small vessels which could fully utilize the innumerable shallow inlets, coves, and bays of regions like the Caribbean. To operate effectively, the navy needed small, fast ships which had the speed and versatility to penetrate the hideaways of pirates and slavers, not the heavy firepower offered by large deep-draught warships.[17]

Congress responded to these problems with a number of measures. In 1818 it authorized the President to use the navy to suppress the slave trade and, then, in 1820 declared slave trading to be an act of piracy punishable by death. Congress also approved measures in 1819, 1820, and 1823 which authorized the President to use the navy to suppress piracy and protect American commerce in the Caribbean. Confronted by the reality of large ships which could not discharge the navy's primary peacetime duties, Congress had no choice but to authorize more small ships. In 1820 it approved construction of five schooners of not more than twelve guns each, and, in 1821, approved acquisition of an unspecified number of additional vessels to combat piracy. Ultimately, the navy purchased thirty four ships under this legislation.

Although naval forces captured some slavers and helped to found Liberia, the navy's main challenge in the early 1820's came from pirates in the Caribbean. According to one estimate, almost 3,000 pirate attacks occurred against merchant ships in the region between 1815 and 1823.[18] The frequency of these assaults and the brutality of the marauders presented a serious threat to American commerce and lives in the Caribbean. Newspapers carried gruesome accounts of the pirates' murderous activities. In response, the United States strengthened its naval forces and dispatched a succession of squadrons to rout the pirates. Commodore James Biddle and then Commodore David Porter led expeditions against the elusive enemy. But the task proved to be tedious, difficult, and dangerous. The scattered pirate lairs were hard to locate and destroy. In addition, the constant threat of yellow fever made the work hazardous and forced American naval forces to suspend operations on a number of occasions.

The reluctance of some local officials to cooperate fully with American naval efforts also helped to shield the pirates and created several sensitive diplomatic situations.[19] The most dramatic occurred in November, 1824, after Commodore David Porter was informed that an American officer had been temporarily imprisoned while ashore to confer with the Mayor of Fajardo on the east coast of Spanish Puerto Rico. On November 14, Porter landed with 200 armed men from three American warships and demanded an apology. After being threatened with the total destruction of Fajardo, the Mayor conferred with and apologized to Porter. However, Porter's action displeased American officials, and they ordered him back to the United States, where he was court-martialed and suspended for six months. In anger, Porter resigned and joined the Mexican Navy.[20] Finally in 1825, Commodore Lewis Warrington took command of the squadron in the West Indies and along with British naval forces effectively eradicated the pirate problem in the next two years. By the end of the 1820's, piracy in the Caribbean had been reduced to an irritating, but minor threat to American trade.

The postwar navy also confronted threats to American commerce posed by political upheavals in Latin America. As Spain's colonies struggled for independence, American merchant ships and whalers were often caught between the conflicting authority of imperial officials and of local patriots. Depending on the specific time and country, royalists and patriots commissioned privateers, established blockades, seized neutral shipping, and harassed American citizens in South American ports in various ways. American naval officers were dispatched to the coasts of South America with instructions to protect the lives and property of Americans, to defend American commerce, and to preserve American neutrality. Although most officers were sympathetic to the patriotic cause, they often found themselves in sharp conflict with rebel leaders as well as royalist officials because both violated American neutral rights in pursuit of their own political objectives. Along the Chilean and Peruvian coasts, the declaration of illegal paper blockades, the inordinate delays in adjudicating ships accused of violations, and the desertion of American merchant seamen during these delays created frustrating obstacles for American officers. Still, only rarely did they intervene forcefully to protect merchant ships.[21]

More often from 1817 to 1825 in the Pacific, American naval officers protected American commerce in less dramatic but substantive ways. They provided convoys between ports and escorted American ships in and out of illegally blockaded ports. The presence of American warships in port helped to minimize harassment and maintain discipline among merchant crews. Assisting with repairs and supplying needed equipment, American naval vessels also acted as a depository for money and specie collected by American merchantmen and transported that specie safely back to the United States on a regular basis.

To meet the demands of protecting American commerce, the Navy Department developed a policy of scattering its ships around the world to distant stations. Although proponents of a large navy preferred a concentration of warships to exert the most influence on political situations, the postwar situation dictated the dispersal of existing ships. Conceived by Secretary of the Navy Benjamin Stoddert in 1801, the distant station policy developed fully after 1815 to provide some measure of protection to the republic's far-flung whaling and commercial interests. In the eleven years after 1815, the navy created stations in the Mediterranean (1815), the West Indies (1821), Africa (1821), the Pacific (1821), and Brazil (1826). To each of these stations the Department dispatched warships singly or in small numbers. Generally, a frigate was joined by several sloops or schooners in patrolling one of the stations. Although a frigate or a ship-of-the-line was more useful in the Mediterranean or the Pacific than in the Caribbean, the smaller warships were essential to the variety of tasks of the peacetime navy because of their versatility.[22]

By the administration of John Quincy Adams, the navy's place in the republic seemed to have been clarified. The proponents of a large European-style navy had been defeated since the republic had neither the resources nor the need for such an expenditure. At the same time, Adams was committed to a foreign policy which required an effective peacetime navy. The republic's long-term interests on the Pacific coast had to be protected against European encroachment to permit the eventual development of a continental empire in North America. Overseas, the nation's far-flung maritime interests and commercial rights also had to be guarded. Viewing commerce as one of the natural rights and duties of mankind, Adams believed commercial expansion essential to the future of the United States as well as to the general improvement of civilization.[23] In spite of these views, Adams did not press for a program of further naval construction during his Presidency. Instead he expected the peacetime navy to be a limited force which would protect American commerce. He realized that a large navy might well involve the United States in European affairs, a prospect he sought to avoid as he concentrated on the nation's territorial growth and commercial expansion. Rather than build more warships, the Naval Act of 1827 provided $500,000 for each of six years to purchase navy materials and supplies. In the event of a national emergency, these materials could quickly be used to build the necessary warships, but until then some large warships could be taken out of commission and placed in ordinary.[24]

At the same time, the decline of piracy in the Caribbean and the end of the wars for independence in Peru and Chile permitted some limited initiatives in behalf of America's Pacific interests. As Secretary of the Navy from 1825 to 1829, Samuel L. Southard of New Jersey advocated a number of naval reforms, proposed a thorough survey of the nation's coast, and recommended creation of a naval academy.[25] In the Pacific, he ordered Commodore Isaac Hull in the *United States* to cruise into the western Pacific from the coast of South America. Although Hull remained close to the South American coast, he dispatched Master Commandant Thomas ap Catesby Jones in the *Peacock* to the Society Islands. Here Jones arranged a treaty before proceeding to Hawaii, where he negotiated a more elaborate treaty. Although the United States never ratified the treaty, Hawaiian officials observed the terms of the agreement for years in their dealings with Americans. As Secretary, Southard joined Adams in supporting the proposal for a full-scale American exploring expedition to the South Pacific. In 1829 Southard also ordered the sloop *Vincennes* under Master Commandant William B. Finch to return from the Pacific station to the United States via the western Pacific and the Cape of Good Hope. In the process the *Vincennes* was to touch at the Society Islands, the Sandwich Islands, and Canton as well as to render whatever assistance possible to American commerce and whalers along the way.[26]

But these were isolated efforts. By the end of the 1820's most government officials accepted a sharply limited role for the navy. Overseas, the growth of American trade had not yet created pressure for a more aggressive peacetime navy. The 1820's were years of uneven foreign trade for the United States. In 1828, total U.S. imports and exports remained below the levels for 1819. As Adams prepared to leave the White House in March, 1829, few observers would have predicted the extraordinary expansion of American foreign commerce or the nation's growing reliance on the navy that characterized the next three decades.

2.

President Andrew Jackson: Advocate of an Expansive Navy*

The increase of our commerce and our position in regard to the other powers of the world will always make it our policy and interest to cherish the great naval resources of our country.

Andrew Jackson, message to Congress, December 5, 1836

In his Inaugural Address Andrew Jackson conceded that "prudence" dictated the continued "gradual increase of our navy," but emphasized that "the bulwark of our defense is the national militia, which in the present state of our intelligence and population must render us invincible." Old Hickory warned of the danger of standing armies to free government in peacetime and of the need to maintain civilian over military authority in the government. As long as "our government" is worth defending, he declared, "a patriotic militia will cover it with an impenetrable aegis."[1]

Nine months later Jackson outlined to Congress his views on the peacetime navy. Although it constituted "the best standing security of this country against foreign aggression," the navy in peacetime required "no more ships of war than are requisite to the protection of our commerce." Because large ships were not useful for this responsibility and decayed quickly once they were out of commission, the best policy was to build no more "ships of the first and second class." Instead, the navy should accumulate an ample stock of timber and shipbuilding materials so that, in the event of war, these materials could be fashioned quickly into needed battleships by the skilled hands of American shipbuilders.[2]

*This chapter appeared in somewhat different form in *New Aspects of Naval History: Selected Papers from the Fifth Naval Symposium* (Baltimore, 1985).

In essence, the new President had accepted the existing narrow definition of the navy's peacetime role. Precluded from a role in international politics, the navy would concentrate on the "protection of our commerce." Like his Presidential predecessors, Jackson interpreted this term to mean that the navy would combat pirates, police the African slave trade, and discourage various threats to American commerce. To achieve some measure of protection for a far-flung commerce with a small navy, available naval vessels would have to be dispersed to cruise singly or in small groups around the world. Once in a distant ocean, navy captains were expected to stop at major ports, contact the American consul there, pay their formal respects to local officials, and collect pertinent economic and political information for government officials in Washington. Occasionally, naval officers protected American commerce by resolving local disputes in which American merchants were involved or by defending the rights of Americans abroad from arbitrary local officials or foreign competitors.

In addition to accepting existing national policy, Jackson's naval sentiments reflected his party's agrarian orientation and its commitment to such traditional old Republican ideas as a limited federal government, narrow construction of the Constitution, strict economy in government expenditures, and opposition to a large professional military establishment. With the exception of Martin Van Buren, Jackson's closest and most influential advisors in the White House were men such as Kentuckians Francis Blair and Amos Kendall who shared their chief's western agrarian outlook and Jeffersonian attitudes.[3] In addition, Jackson himself was the nation's foremost military hero of the day, but he was also an amateur soldier and militia captain *par excellence*. He was without formal military training, and his terms of service were of very brief duration for an individual who achieved such tremendous military glory.

In fact Jackson's 1829 statements did not accurately forecast the navy's role during his Presidency. His administration did not attempt to redefine the peacetime role of the navy nor to place it on a competitive footing with the navies of Europe. Old Hickory did, however, use the navy more aggressively than his two predecessors to preserve the nation's honor, to expand the republic's overseas commerce, and to implement his administration's commercial diplomacy. The center of the nation's increased naval activity was the Pacific Ocean where the Jackson Administration dispatched several naval cruisers, initiated significant diplomatic contacts through the navy, began an almost continuous naval presence in the Far East, and approved a far-reaching naval exploring expedition. By the end of his Presidency, Jackson acknowledged the value of such an expanded role for the peacetime navy and took steps to enhance that role.

The President had not foreseen such a development in 1829. Nor was the navy's expanded part one that had been envisioned by any one of Jackson's three Secretaries of the Navy, his closest political advisors, or by the Board of Navy Commissioners. No serious debate over the role of the peacetime navy seems to have occurred in either the Cabinet or Congress between 1829 and 1837.[4] Likewise, one searches the messages of Jackson's three Naval Secretaries in vain for any recognition or vision of the navy's role as an arm of peacetime American diplomacy. Each Secretary had little experience and few qualifications for the position; each was selected primarily for political and personal reasons; and each played an unimaginative role as head of the department.

Jackson's first Secretary of the Navy, John Branch, was a wealthy North Carolina planter and politician who served in the state legislature, as Governor, and as U.S. Senator prior to his selection as Secretary of the Navy. Political considerations rather than any consideration of interests or naval experience led to Jackson's appointment. As an avid state rights politician Branch was concerned primarily with reform and efficiency during his two years in office. Of particular concern to Branch was the navy practice of saving funds appropriated for ship repairs and then using them, in effect, to construct new ships. In 1830, after he visited the Norfolk Navy Yard, Branch reported such a procedure being used to construct the sloop *John Adams*. Because not "one cent" had been appropriated to build such a vessel, Branch reported to Jackson that he disliked "very much to practice such a deception" which had only occurred in two or three instances under "the late Dynasty." Branch's days, however, were numbered in Jackson's Administration. Because he was never close to Jackson and was one of those who lined up against Jackson in the Peggy Eaton Affair, Branch was forced to resign in the Cabinet reorganization of 1831. At best, he had been a competent administrator who did not grasp the potential peacetime importance of the navy.[5]

In naming Levi Woodbury as Branch's successor, Jackson was moved again by political considerations. Woodbury was a loyal party man, a strong personal supporter of the President, and had served as U.S. Senator from New Hampshire since 1825. Like his predecessor, Woodbury proved to be a competent and unimaginative administrator who recommended various internal reforms, spent funds cautiously, did not challenge the conservatism of the Navy Board, and did not press for a larger navy. Although Woodbury's annual reports evinced little awareness of the potential role the peacetime navy could play, his interest in commercial expansion helped create the need for more naval vessels. He was married to the daughter of a wealthy Maine merchant, Asa Clapp, and had extensive contacts with New England merchants such as Edmund Roberts who were deeply involved in trade in the Pacific. This personal interest in commercial expansion resulted in an influential role for Woodbury in formulating the mission to chastise the Quallah Batoo pirates and in the 1832 mission of Edmund Roberts to the Far East. In recognition of his role, Roberts dedicated his account of his first mission to the Secretary of the Navy.[6]

In June, 1834, when Woodbury became Secretary of the Treasury, Mahlon Dickerson replaced him in the Navy Department. Dickerson came from a wealthy New Jersey family, owned a large iron works, and had served as the Governor and a Senator from his home state. In addition to his lack of experience or knowledge of naval affairs, Dickerson proved to be an indecisive and ineffective administrator. At a time when the need for an increased navy was obvious, when the federal government enjoyed a surplus, and when support for naval expansion in Congress was increasing, Dickerson provided little leadership or direction for his department. He was actually opposed to the United States Exploring Expedition, failed to understand the need for a larger navy, and did little to build support for various naval reforms he proposed in spite of the fact that his annual reports in 1835 and 1836 recommended increases in the navy to protect the nation's commerce.[7]

The navy's expanded role during the Jackson Administration, then, arose not from any theoretical belief in the need for an expanded navy but from the practical demands which a burgeoning overseas trade placed on an intensely nationalistic President. By 1830 the United States was in the process of developing a rich and far-flung commercial empire. Extensive American trade with Europe, the Mediterranean, and the Caribbean had long been, and continued to be, essential to the nation's prosperity and economic growth. In addition, long-standing commercial contacts in the Pacific were fast maturing into a vital part of the nation's commercial empire. The growth of American foreign trade was particularly dramatic during Jackson's Presidency. Between 1828 and 1836 total U.S. exports rose by 94 percent, from $64 million to $124 million. The vast majority of this growth resulted not from the so-called reexport trade but from the export of domestic goods from $50 million to $106 million, a jump of 112 percent. Of the domestic exports, the greatest increase and the largest share consisted of such agricultural products as cotton, tobacco, wool, and livestock.[8]

As President, Old Hickory recognized the importance of the nation's foreign trade, the need to expand it, and the necessity of using the navy to protect the commercial rights of Americans overseas. Although he came from a frontier agrarian background and led a political party with a strong agrarian orientation, Jackson and the Democratic Party were neither indifferent nor hostile to American commercial interests. Significantly, the Jacksonian political coalition consisted of entrepreneurs as well as southern planters, businessmen as well as farmers, and rural capitalists as well as self-sufficient yeomen. Jackson himself was an acquisitive and upwardly mobile frontier lawyer, businessman, and land speculator. Pursuing a general policy of liberal capitalism, the Jacksonian Democrats broadened their initial attack on political privilege into an assault on economic privilege as they attempted to open the avenues of economic opportunity to the creative enterprise of business and agriculture. The Jacksonian maxim, "The best government is that which governs least," applied as much to economic freedom as it did to political liberty. Accordingly, Jackson did not outline a program of positive government action. Instead he attempted to reduce the role and privileges which the federal government was extending to segments of the economy. In addition to his attack on the Second Bank of the United States, Jackson vetoed the Maysville Road Bill and ended government subsidies to small arms manufacturers.

At the same time, various agricultural interests manifested an increasing preoccupation with foreign trade and overseas markets. Tobacco and cotton planters had long understood the importance of the European market to their prosperity. So too had wheat and corn producers east of the Appalachians understood the value of the West Indies and European markets. By the late 1820's and early 1830's two significant developments whetted the interest of farmers in the Northwest to new markets. First, the transportation advances of the 1820's accelerated the transformation of these states from a condition of "pioneer self-sufficiency to a market oriented agriculture." Second, the trade of the region was being redirected from the South to the East and to Europe. Increasingly during the 1830's, western politicians expressed their concern about adequate markets at home and abroad for their wheat, corn, beef, and pork.[9]

An increasing number of western politicians also understood the importance of territorial expansion to their commercial interests. In addition to fulfilling the republic's continental destiny and adding huge amounts of rich soil, Oregon and upper California promised the unlimited potential of the Pacific trade. Throughout the 1820's supporters of congressional proposals to occupy Oregon advanced the fabled commercial wealth of the Orient as a key argument in favor of occupation. In the House in 1821, Representative John Floyd of western Virginia urged the occupation of Oregon in a report which stressed the commercial potential of Oregon for the United States. The leading proponent of this view was Missouri's Thomas Hart Benton, who would be one of President Jackson's closest political allies and strongest defenders in Congress. Beginning in 1819, Benton urged American acquisition of the Columbia River as the American portal to the trade of Asia. Once open, this "Passage to India" would directly link the commerce of the Pacific to the agrarian states of the Ohio and Mississippi River Valleys.[10]

Support in both major parties for continued commercial expansion and the tremendous increase in American commercial activity overseas, particularly in the Pacific, created two types of pressure on the President during these years of additional naval support. At home the growth of whaling and shipping interests produced increased pressure from private individuals, various firms, and politicians for a greater naval presence in the Pacific, for more active naval protection of American interests overseas, and for information from the federal government which would facilitate whaling, navigation, and commercial opportunities around the world. Overseas the nation's ever expanding commercial activities inevitably produced various incidents and insults which required some type of military or diplomatic response from the U.S. government. When such incidents arose, only the navy could provide the power to respond effectively overseas.

As President, Jackson paid close attention to the nation's commercial development and took pride in his ability to promote American trade overseas. When he was inaugurated, Jackson confronted a number of disputes with European nations involving the claims of American merchants against illegal ship seizures and damages to American property by European nations. These unsettled claims stood against France, Denmark, Naples, Spain, and Portugal and in some cases dated back to the administration of Thomas Jefferson. Between 1829 and 1837 American diplomats settled these disputes and also extended the nation's policy of shipping reciprocity by concluding agreements with ten additional nations.[11]

In addition, the Jackson Administration signed a number of important commercial treaties with powers such as Russia, Turkey, Muscat, and Siam. The most important of the agreements occurred with Great Britain in 1830 and applied to the British West Indies. After granting limited concessions in the British West Indies in 1822, the British resisted American pressure for further privileges, staunchly defended the principle of colonial preference within their empire, and excluded all American ships from the British West Indies in 1826. In response the Adams Administration closed American ports in 1827 to ships coming from any of Britain's possessions in the Western Hemisphere. There the matter rested until 1829. As a significant issue in his election victory, Jackson was anxious to resolve the deadlock. In addition, the West Indies trade had traditionally been an important market for American foodstuffs, and the expectation in the late 1820's was that American farmers and merchants needed to have access to the British West Indies.

After some initial delays the Jackson Administration, with the support of Congress, abandoned the demand that Britain relinquish her colonial preference system prior to the removal of discriminatory duties by the United States. In October, 1830, Jackson proclaimed the end of retaliatory duties and opened American ports to British ships on the same terms as American ships. In response, the British issued an Order-in-Council opening the direct trade of the British West Indies to the United States subject to whatever duties it might choose to impose. Although he had not won the right of free trade for the United States in the British West Indies, Jackson had restored direct trade between American ports and the British Islands.

In the eastern Mediterranean, Jackson faced another unresolved diplomatic situation. Although Americans had traded in the area since the 1780's a formal commercial agreement had never been signed with the Ottoman Empire. Since the 1790's a succession of administrations had tried and failed to negotiate such a treaty. Turkish officials treated a succession of American diplomats and naval officials with respect, seemed interested in a formal commercial treaty, and somehow always declined to conclude such an agreement. In the spring of 1829 Jackson renewed American diplomatic efforts. To assist the U.S. Consul in Smyra, David Offley, Jackson named Navy Captain James Biddle and New York merchant Charles Rhind as commissioners. In early 1830 Rhind left Offley and Biddle at Smyra and proceeded alone to Constantinople. Here, in an atmosphere of diplomatic intrigue and European hostility, Rhind managed to persuade his vacillating counterparts to sign a treaty on May 7, 1830. The agreement granted the United States ''most-favored-nation'' status regarding tariffs, right of extraterritoriality, the power to appoint consuls to Turkish ports, and trading privileges in the Black Sea equal to those of other nations. A secret article provided minor concessions to Turkey regarding the construction of warships in the United States.

Rhind's unilateral course and the resulting treaty with its secret article produced criticism from his fellow commissioners. In the United States similar objections were expressed in the Senate where the treaty was ratified but the secret article deleted in February, 1831.[12]

In his annual messages to Congress Jackson noted these agreements with pride and attributed economic significance to them. In 1832 he observed that the treaty with Turkey opened "New markets . . . for our commodities and a more extensive range for the employment of our ships." Four years later he spoke of the "great advantages to our enterprising merchants and navigators" promised by the commercial agreements with Siam and Muscat. In his *Thirty Years' View* Thomas Hart Benton staunchly defended Jackson's diplomatic achievements and cited a "grand and impressive" list of Jacksonian commercial agreements to prove that "the foreign diplomacy of General Jackson [was] on a level with the most splendid which the history of any nation has presented." In fact, such praise was overly extravagant because the settling of commercial disputes and the concluding of new commercial agreements had little immediate impact on American trade. At the same time, these agreements were important to Americans in the 1830's because of the stature they seemed to accord to the young republic and the promise they held for the future. The real significance of these treaties rests with the foundation they provided for increased trade and additional commercial activity over the long term. As such, these agreements also held important long-term implications for increased commercial activity by the American Navy around the world.[13]

In practice Jackson's desire to extend the nation's burgeoning commercial empire combined with his strong determination to protect American rights and honor overseas and compelled him to rely much more heavily on the navy as an arm of his policies than he had intended in 1829. After 1831 the President made regular use of the navy in an aggressive way to defend and expand the nation's commerce. In addition to dispatching naval vessels to retaliate against attacks on American trade and rights abroad, Jackson used the navy to facilitate commercial negotiations overseas, and to gather information essential to commercial expansion in the Pacific. Old Hickory's impetuous and pugnacious diplomatic style made predictable his use of the navy to respond to outrages on American commerce. Whether his bellicose style was attributable to his personality, his frontier sense of honor, or his lack of diplomatic experience, Jackson tended to react chauvinistically. In response to separate incidents at Quallah Batoo in Sumatra and the Falkland Islands off the coast of Argentina, Jackson dispatched warships to retaliate promptly rather than seek diplomatic solutions to attacks on American trade.

In the East Indies, Americans had long engaged in the profitable pepper trade and, by the early nineteenth century, had come to dominate trade with the so-called pepper coast which included northern Sumatra. Although northern Sumatra was politically unstable and the coast was infested with pirates, Americans engaged in the pepper trade enjoyed relatively friendly relations with the Atjehnese who ruled the region. However, by the late 1820's, American-Atjehnese relations deteriorated as a result of an increasing number of individual grievances and the general decline of the pepper trade. For example, American traders frequently used false weights just as local inhabitants added rocks and sand to the bags of pepper.[14]

After various threats, the situation erupted early in 1831 at the small pepper port of Quallah Batoo. Although nominally under the control of the Atjehnese sultan, Quallah Batoo enjoyed almost complete independence and was ruled erratically by several local rajahs. On February 7, 1831, Captain Charles M. Endicott of the *Friendship* went ashore to buy pepper.[15] Owned by the firm of Silsbee, Pickman, and Stone, the 316 ton vessel carried a crew of seventeen men. In the absence of Endicott, several armed Sumatrans were permitted onto the *Friendship*. They then attacked, killing three Americans, wounding three others, and capturing the ship. In the meantime, Captain Endicott and the shore party spotted the attack, eluded capture, and rowed 25 miles to the port of Mukee. There Endicott enlisted the support of three American merchantmen, returned to Quallah Batoo two days later, and recaptured the *Friendship*. Unfortunately, the ship had been plundered and "bore ample testimony of the scene of violence and destruction with which she had been visited." Lost was $41,054 in specie, opium, and other goods.[16]

Reports of the outrage preceded Endicott to the United States and various New England merchants, shipowners, and politicians joined the owners and demanded an immediate response. Senior partner Nathaniel Silsbee, a Senator from Massachusetts, wrote directly to the President, but Jackson and Secretary of the Navy Levi Woodbury needed no pressure. After investigating, the administration dispatched a warship to secure restitution of the property losses and punishment of the murderers. On August 9, 1831, Secretary of the Navy Woodbury instructed Captain John Downes in command of the frigate *Potomac* to sail "at once to Sumatra, by way of the Cape of Good Hope." Once at Quallah Batoo, Downes was to investigate further and if his findings confirmed what was already known, he was to demand "restitution of the property plundered, or indemnity therefor . . . and the immediate punishment of those concerned in the murder of the American citizens. . . ." If the local officials did not comply in a "reasonable time," the Secretary instructed Downes and his men "to seize the actual murderers, if they are known . . . to retake such part of the stolen property as can there be found and identified; to destroy the boats and vessels" used in the piracy as well as the forts and dwellings near the scene, and to inform the population there that additional punishment would be inflicted unless "full restitution" was made and further acts of piracy ceased.[17]

Although he was a capable and experienced officer, Downes was not well suited to this assignment. He had served under Captain David Porter on the *Essex* during his famous cruise in the Pacific during the War of 1812 and had developed a close relationship with Porter. As a flamboyant officer who used excessive force against natives on a number of occasions, Porter had demonstrated to Downes that natives deserved little respect and that a naval officer could readily exceed his instructions if he determined that the situation warranted it.[18]

The *Potomac* sailed from New York on August 26, 1831, carrying fifty mounted guns and a crew of 500 men. Two months later the ship put into Cape Town where British officers warned Downes about the residents of Quallah Batoo.[19] When the *Potomac* reached Sumatra in February, 1832, Downes apparently had decided already to ignore his specific instructions because of the information he received at Cape Town and the fact that no vessels were present along the coast to provide him with the further information specified in his orders. In addition, Downes did not demand satisfaction at Quallah Batoo because he "was satisfied, from what knowledge I had already of the character of the people, that no such demand would be answered, except only by refusal. . . . " Instead he organized a landing party of 250 midshipmen and marines and ordered an attack on February 6th, the day after he arrived. The party landed early in the morning, marched toward the several small strongholds at Quallah Batoo, and attacked immediately. Two and one-half hours of intense fighting resulted in the destruction of the forts, the burning of the town, and the death of more than 100 natives. Although only two Americans were killed and several wounded in the attack, the Americans were unable to recover any of the stolen property or secure any indemnity.[20]

The next day Downes bombarded the village for more than an hour before a white flag was raised. In subsequent negotiations, Downes determined that any restitution of the lost property was impossible but emphasized that further attacks on American commerce would bring prompt American reprisals. From Quallah Batoo, he sailed along the pepper coast, received other rajahs, and accepted their assurances of friendship for the United States. On February 18th, his mission completed, Downes departed the pepper coast for a cruise to Java, China, Hawaii, and Tahiti before returning to the United States in 1834.[21]

News of the attack on Quallah Batoo reached the United States in the early summer of 1832. With Congress in session, a Presidential campaign underway, and Jackson's veto of the bill to recharter the Second Bank of the United States imminent, partisan feelings ran high in Washington. In such an atmosphere the Quallah Batoo incident provided ready ammunition for Old Hickory's enemies after it became known that Downes had acted precipitously, that women and children had been killed in the action, and that neither indemnity nor restitution had been secured. On July 10th, the day Jackson sent his bank veto message to Congress, the *National Intelligencer* opened the attack. The anti-Jackson paper defended the gallantry of Downes and his men and affirmed the right of the United States to punish those who violated American commercial rights. However, the *Intelligencer* criticized the absence of any negotiation by Downes prior to the assault and condemned Jackson for abusing his executive power by making war at Quallah Batoo without a formal declaration from Congress. "If the President can direct expeditions against the Malays, we do not see why he may not have the power to do the same in reference to any other power or people."[22]

When the official administration paper, the *Washington Globe*, responded the next day, a political controversy was underway. The *Globe* vigorously defended Jackson's defense of American commerce, praised the courage of Downes' force, and condemned the unpatriotic and legalistic arguments of the *Intelligencer*. "These learned Puffendorffs" had now put forth the incredible doctrine that a President could not strike against pirates "without special act of Congress. . . . Shame upon such unmanly and disingenuous subterfuges for party effect."[23]

The matter surfaced in Congress on July 13th when the House passed a resolution asking the President to deliver copies of Downes' instructions and his correspondence concerning the incident. Jackson complied on the same day with a letter asking that the communications remain secret until Downes returned to the United States. Further turmoil over the incident was averted when separate motions to print all the documentation and Downes' instructions respectively failed. Both supporters and opponents joined to defeat publication because of what the documents revealed. Once anti-Jacksonians such as Edward Everett realized that Downes had clearly violated his instructions, they were anxious to terminate the matter lest it result in the condemnation of a popular naval officer and the exoneration of their hated political opponent, the President.

In spite of the fact that Downes had disobeyed his orders, the administration praised the mission. Jackson was not about to reprimand Downes publicly or to publish his official instructions. In his December, 1832, message to Congress, Jackson avoided the question of whether Downes had exceeded his order or not and instead emphasized that this "chastisement" would deter a "band of lawless pirates" from further aggression. The result of the mission, according to the President, "has been an increased respect for our flag in those distant seas and an additional security for our commerce." In his own annual report, Woodbury also ignored the issue of Downes' instructions and commended the lasting benefits which the action had produced.[24] Privately, both the President and the Secretary were upset with Downes' conduct. On July 16, 1832, Woodbury had written to Downes, requested a full explanation for his actions, and explained that the "President regrets that you were not able before attacking the Malays at Quallah Batoo, to obtain fuller information on the particulars of this outrage on the *Friendship*." Woodbury also indicated that Downes should have made "a previous demand . . . for restitution and indemnity" because such a step "would have furnished the most favorable opportunity for success in obtaining redress and would have tended to remove any complaint in any quarter, on account of the nature and consequences of the attack." Although Woodbury also commended Downes and his men for the actual attack and a court-martial was never convened, the incident seriously affected Downes' naval career. He never again commanded an American warship, and he spent the remainder of his career performing shore duties.[25]

The Jackson Administration responded in similar fashion to another incident in the South Atlantic almost five months after the *Potomac* had sailed for Sumatra. The Falkland Islands are located about 300 miles east of the Straits of Magellan and 1,200 miles south of Buenos Aires. Although barren and unsuited for colonization, the islands contain a number of good harbors and had been important to American seamen since the Revolution because of their proximity to furbearing seals and whale fisheries. The British had a long-standing claim to the islands, and they had been an issue of international contention for decades, but sovereignty of the islands apparently passed to the government of Buenos Aires in the early 1820's. To strengthen its claim, the government attempted to encourage colonization of the islands by issuing a number of land grants to individuals. The most successful of these individuals was Louis Vernet, a naturalized citizen of Buenos Aires who had been born in France and had resided in both Germany and the United States. In 1820 the Governor of Buenos Aires appointed Vernet Military Governor of the islands, affirmed Argentine sovereignty over the islands, placed them under control of a political and military governor, and declared that restrictive regulations protecting the seal fisheries would be enforced. In 1829 and 1830 Vernet warned several American vessels, including the *Harriet*, against the killing of seals on the shores of the islands. When he discovered the *Harriet* again violating the regulations in July, 1831, he arrested the Captain and held the crew and ship at Port Soledad, or East Falkland. Soon thereafter, two other American ships were seized although one escaped. Subsequently, the *Harriet* was taken by Vernet to Buenos Aires for trial as a prize.[26]

In Buenos Aires an unfortunate situation existed. The absence of capable American diplomatic representation compounded the existing unstable political climate. The death of American Chargé John M. Forbes left only Consul George W. Slacum as an official American representative. To make matters worse, Slacum was an inexperienced and tactless diplomat whose attitudes and behavior rendered him incapable of dealing effectively with a sensitive diplomatic situation. One day after the *Harriet* arrived in Buenos Aires, Consul Slacum launched a series of formal dispatches which inquired into the grounds for seizure, protested the acts of Vernet, denied the right of Argentine officials to restrain American citizens from using the fisheries, and protested the decree of June 10th, 1829. In response, Argentine officials refused to accept Slacum's position as the official stance of the United States, expressed their desire for a peaceful settlement, and asserted that the United States held no rights to the fisheries.

Although he was without diplomatic rank and had no instructions on the question from his government, Slacum pressed on. When the *U.S.S. Lexington* arrived in Buenos Aires in December, Slacum conferred with its commander, Captain Silas Duncan, and then issued a virtual ultimatum on December 6th. Unless the government of Buenos Aires suspended the right of capture and promised restoration of the *Harriet* and its property, the *Lexington* would leave in three days for the Falklands. Captain Duncan, an aggressive, young officer eager to defend American rights and honor, also communicated directly with the foreign minister and demanded the trial of Vernet as a pirate and a thief.

When the Argentine foreign minister refused to comply with Slacum's deadline, the *Lexington* sailed for the Falklands, where it arrived on December 28th.

Duncan and his men promptly spiked the cannon of the fort, destroyed the arms and ammunition of the colony, arrested several colonists, and seized property taken from the *Harriet* and another American ship. Duncan also posted a decree declaring that anyone who interfered with American fishing rights was a pirate. In effect, these actions had destroyed the colony as a viable settlement. On February 3rd the *Lexington* returned to Montevideo with its prisoners. Although they were later released, an uproar ensued with Argentine newspapers condemning Duncan's action and defending the position of Vernet. In Buenos Aires the government issued a public declaration denouncing the *Lexington*'s raid and informed Slacum that he would no longer be recognized as an official representative of his country. Slacum responded by refusing to designate a successor.[27]

In the United States Jackson proceeded in characteristic fashion. In his annual message to Congress in December, 1831, he reported that he had dispatched a naval vessel to protect trade in the area because an American ship "engaged in the pursuit of a trade which we have always enjoyed without molestation has been captured by a band acting, as they pretend, under the authority of the Government of Buenos Aires."[28] In fact, the naval and special instructions did not arrive until after Duncan had acted under his general standing orders to protect American commerce and fisheries. Once Duncan had filed a full report, the administration hastened to approve his actions. In instructions to the new diplomatic representative, Secretary of State Robert Livingston wrote that the President "entirely approves of his [Duncan's] conduct, under the circumstances, which he details." At the same time, the administration ordered all available warships to protect American rights in the area and dispatched Francis Baylies to Buenos Aires as the American chargé d'affaires.[29] Baylies, who was a Massachusetts lawyer and politician, carried instructions which authorized him to defend American fishing rights in the Falklands, and to demand restitution of the captured ships, reparation for the lost property, and disavowal of Vernet's actions.

Once he arrived in Buenos Aires in June, 1832, Baylies proved no more tactful or effective in dealing with Argentine government officials than Slacum had been. As a result, a diplomatic break occurred and Baylies departed in September. The British further complicated the picture by reoccupying the Falklands in January, 1833. As far as the United States and Buenos Aires were concerned, however, the matter would rest for a decade until diplomatic contact was renewed in 1844.

In the Falklands, as he had at Quallah Batoo, Jackson used the navy in an aggressive manner to protect American commercial rights. His failure to acknowledge or consider seriously the legitimacy of Argentine sovereignty in the islands was typical of his chauvinistic diplomacy when dealing with weak states and his aggressive defense of American commercial interests overseas. At Quallah Batoo, the right of the United States to respond to the piratical outrage was not in question, only the form and nature of that response was. In the Falklands, both the right of the United States and the violent precipitous nature of that naval response were questioned. Jackson, however, ignored both issues. It is also instructive of Jackson's use of the navy that he sent strong orders for Duncan to respond and then fully approved of his actions when he learned that Duncan had not waited for specific instructions from the Navy Department.

In a minor incident in 1832 the administration sustained the Captain of the *Grampus* when it seized a Mexican government vessel, the *Montezumas*, held it as a prize, and imprisoned its crew for alleged piracy. Here again neither specific instructions nor a reasonable investigation had preceded the act. In September, 1832, the New York *Journal of Commerce* questioned Jackson's diplomatic style and methods by asking whether the President had not carried "his summary process a little too far" in regard to Quallah Batoo, the Falklands, and the *Montezumas*. The United States was at peace with each people and enjoyed regular diplomatic relations with the governments of Buenos Aires and Mexico. Yet, the administration had secured "by a short process, that which otherwise might require long and tedious negotiation." What, asked the *Journal*, would occur when an American vessel suffered a similar outrage or indignity at the hands of a "British or French cruiser, or the Governor of a British or French colony." Would the administration then eschew diplomacy, exact retribution. and explain to England or France that "we exacted no more than was right, . . . in the shortest and simplest method of obtaining justice . . . in accordance with the genius of our institutions." This article pinpointed a key element of Jackson's chauvinistic diplomacy, that is, the President's determination to define American rights in the broadest terms, act militarily to defend those rights, and rely on regular diplomacy in a secondary manner. Such a diplomatic style dictated reliance on the navy as an immediate arm of American foreign policy and had generally been avoided by previous Presidents.[30]

Closer to home, the administration used the West Indies Squadron during the last two years of Jackson's Presidency to protect American commerce during the Texas revolution by maintaining strict U.S. neutrality in the Gulf. Naval officers were instructed to insist that full rights as neutral carriers be granted to American ships in spite of the fact that such a position hurt the Texans. In addition, American naval officers intervened with both Mexico and Texas on different occasions to insure that legitimate American trade was not interrupted.[31]

In addition to using the navy to respond to alleged outrages on American commercial rights, Old Hickory relied on the navy to open new markets and to facilitate maritime diplomacy. The navy, of course, had long played a significant role in negotiating diplomatic agreements.[32] Under Jackson that role continued in the Mediterranean, but it was extended to the Far East as well. In many parts of the Pacific Basin traditional diplomatic and commercial practices were not effective in dealing with local rulers. Here the presence of a warship created respect for American power and facilitated commercial diplomacy. Continuous cruises by naval vessels were also the only means by which some measure of protection for American commerce could be maintained in the far-flung islands and ports of the Pacific and East Asia.

In 1832 negotiations with the Kingdom of the Two Sicilies stalled over the question of claims owed to American commerce for damage during the Napoleonic Wars. At the request of the American chargé d'affaires in Naples the administration authorized the use of the Mediterranean Squadron. The commander of the squadron, Commodore Daniel T. Patterson, entrusted the mission to Master Commandant Matthew C. Perry. In concert with the frigate *Constellation* and sloops *John Adams* and *Concord*, Perry sailed the frigate *Brandywine* to Naples in July, departed in August, and reappeared in September. The presence of the American warships had the desired effect, and a treaty was signed on October 20.[33]

In the same year, Secretary of the Navy Levi Woodbury ordered Master Commandant David Geisinger in the sloop *Peacock* to visit Quallah Batoo, to cruise in Chinese waters, and to visit ports in East Asia, Arabia, and East Africa. Serving as secretary to the commander of the *Peacock* was New Hampshire merchant and ship owner Edmund Roberts, who carried orders as a special diplomatic agent to negotiate commercial treaties with Muscat, Siam, Annam, and Japan. Having travelled and done business extensively in the Far East, Arabia, and Africa, Roberts knew first hand that the absence of formal commercial treaties with local rulers often resulted in higher duties for American merchants than for their European competitors. Roberts conveyed his concern for commercial protection to a sympathetic Senator Levi Woodbury in the 1820's. Once he became head of the Navy Department, Woodbury was instrumental in formulating and winning administration support for a diplomatic mission to the Far East. In fact, the choice of Roberts resulted from Woodbury's influence, and the Navy Department paid one-third of his salary. Having suffered a series of financial setbacks, Roberts accepted the position eagerly. In the Far East, Roberts was unable to establish diplomatic negotiations with Cochin China, but he did sign treaties of amity and commerce with Siam and with the Sultan of Muscat in 1833.[34] Since the Sultan also ruled Zanzibar, the latter agreement gave the United States trading rights in East Africa as well as the Middle East.

In retrospect these agreements mark a significant milestone in American diplomatic and commercial relations because they were the first such agreements concluded with rulers in the Far East and the Indian Ocean. The agreement with Siam specified duties to be charged American merchantmen in Siamese ports, abolished certain penalties for debts, and contained a clause protecting shipwrecked American sailors. The treaty with the Sultan of Muscat went further by granting a reduction in import and export duties, placing American trade on a most-favored-nation basis and containing a generous clause on the treatment of shipwrecked sailors. Although neither of the treaties represented a particularly dramatic commercial breakthrough, they did pave the way for additional diplomatic and commercial initiatives in the Far East and thereby helped create the need for greater naval activity in the area.[35]

Once the Senate ratified the agreements, the State Department commissioned Roberts in 1835 to exchange ratifications and authorized him to negotiate with

Cochin China and Japan. He sailed on the *Peacock* under the command of Edmund P. Kennedy, who had orders to assist Roberts' mission in any way that he could. Unfortunately, the crew of the *Peacock* was plagued by serious sickness in the Far East. After exchanging ratifications with Muscat in 1835 and Siam in 1836, the *Peacock* proceeded to Macao to nurse her sick. There on June 12, 1836, Roberts died. Since Captain Kennedy had no orders to conduct diplomatic negotiations himself, he returned to the United States without stopping at Japan.[36]

In addition to using the navy in the Far East to expand diplomatic and commercial contact, the Jackson administration supported an unprecedented role for the navy in overseas exploration. The idea of an exploring expedition into the Pacific actually dated back to the Madison administration and had gained considerable support in Congress during the administration of John Quincy Adams. As President, Jackson was not interested initially in the proposal. Not only did interest in the project center in Adams' native New England, but also such a scientific undertaking in an area far removed from American shores conflicted sharply with basic Jacksonian ideas about the limited sphere of federal activities. Support and pressure, however, continued to build during the early 1830's due largely to the unceasing efforts of Jeremiah N. Reynolds, a former newspaper editor from Ohio. During the mid–1820's, Reynolds met fellow Ohioan John Symmes and became enamored of his theory that the earth was a hollow sphere which contained several concentric spheres and had openings at each pole. According to Symmes, an exploring party could penetrate the ice at one pole, sail into an open polar sea, and explore the hollow end of the earth.[37]

Beginning in 1825 Reynolds joined Symmes to lecture frequently on the theory of "Symmes Hole" in an effort to build support for an exploring expedition. Soon Reynolds established himself as the more compelling speaker and publicist of the two. After Symmes died in 1829, Reynolds dissociated himself from the Symmes' theory but not from the idea of an expedition to explore the South Pacific and test the prevalent idea of an open polar sea. In his efforts, Reynolds broadened support for the project beyond the circle of whaling captains and curious scientists. He worked hard to collect a vast amount of information which he used to demonstrate the scientific, commercial, and national value of an exploring expedition to the South Seas. By the mid–1830's he had won the support of numerous politicians, young naval officers such as Matthew F. Maury, Thomas ap Catesby Jones, Charles Wilkes, and John Downes, various merchants and ship captains, and a growing number of scientists in the United States.[38]

On April 3, 1836, Reynolds' lobbying efforts culminated with an evening address in the House of Representatives. He argued that the time had come for the United States to make a contribution to human knowledge through a voyage of discovery and exploration. Although undertaken "for the sole purpose of increasing our knowledge of the Pacific and Southern Oceans," the expedition would extend "commercial research" and thereby add "more to our national resources, than to discover mines of diamonds, or heap our treasures with coined gold." "I do not believe," stated Reynolds, "that there is a record of a single voyage since . . . Columbus . . . which does not contain . . . the evidence of some contribution to the knowledge of mankind, worth vastly more than the cost of the enterprise!'' Given ''extensive interests in those seas,'' the nation's ''dignity and honour'' dictated such an expedition as the ''best possible employment of a portion of our naval force. . . .'' In short, ''Commerce, science, [and] patriotism'' rendered the expedition essential.[39]

Although Reynolds spoke at length about the value of scientific discovery, he also viewed the expedition as a means of strengthening American naval presence in the Pacific. From 1832 to 1834 he had sailed with Captain John Downes on the famous voyage of the *Potomac*. In his published account of the voyage, Reynolds' title page carried the inscription ''Naval Power is National Glory.'' In the book's ''Dedication,'' Reynolds emphasized the need to have ''an effective navy'' bear ''our flag . . . to every portion of the globe, to give to civilized and savage man a just impression of the power we possess. . . .'' The theme of naval presence and power in the Pacific was one Reynolds returned to, albeit in muted tones, in his address in the House of Representatives.[40]

Reynolds' sentiments well suited the national mood of pride and confidence and coincided with a prosperous economy. In the Senate, legislation authorizing the expedition had been introduced and now won approval in both houses. By May 10, 1836, $300,000 had been approved to underwrite the exploration. The only real debate came in the House where several westerners led by Democrat Albert Gallatin Hawes of Kentucky challenged the project. Hawes asked why the navy would take ''vessels and seamen of the United States, and send them to the South Seas, exposing them to all the diseases, hurricanes, and mishaps of that climate, and for what? For nothing on the face of the earth.''[41]

Significantly, the most comprehensive response to Hawes came from Jacksonian Democrat Thomas Hamer of Ohio. In response to charges that the expedition was a ''chimerical and hairbrained notion'' comparable to an ''expedition to the moon,'' Hamer labelled the proposal ''one of the most practical affairs that had been proposed during the present session of Congress.'' The numerous merchants, mariners, and captains who endorsed the voyage ''were not likely to be carried away by wild and visionary schemes. . . .'' Hamer also emphasized that the ''West had a deep interest in it. It was well known . . . in the great grain-growing States of the interior, that our principle difficulty was to find a market for the surplus productions of our fertile soil. . . . This trade, which we now propose to foster, is daily increasing, and it furnishes a market already for a large amount of our surplus produce.'' The large majorities in each house indicated bipartisan support for the exploring expedition. Once passed, Jackson signed the bill and then wrote to his Secretary of the Navy Mahlon Dickerson of his ''lively interest'' in the project. In fact, the exploring expedition well suited Jackson's competitive nationalism and his desire to expand commercial opportunities in the Pacific.[42] By the time he left office, preparations seemed to be well underway for the departure of the expedition.

By the end of 1835 Jackson had learned first hand that the demands of an expansive overseas commerce made a larger navy essential, and he acknowledged that lesson in his annual message to Congress. A year earlier, the President had reported that a "force sufficient to guard our commerce" existed and that a gradual increase of our navy material insured the prompt construction of a navy large enough "for any exigency." Now in December, 1835, Jackson admitted that the navy was "inadequate to the protection of our rapidly increasing commerce" and acknowledged that the navy, not the militia, represented "our best security against foreign aggressions. . . . " The navy, then, needed "a speedy increase of the force" as well as an apprentice system to serve as "a nursery of skillful and able-bodied seamen" for boys between thirteen and eighteen years old.[43]

Jackson's 1835 naval recommendation was hastened by two developments. First, the American economy was booming. Rising government revenues and a strict economy in government expenditures combined to produce an operating surplus for the federal government in the early 1830's. By 1835, the government had eliminated the national debt, and the President was able to report a federal surplus of $19 million to Congress.[44] Second, the crisis with France over the payment of outstanding claims to Americans intensified the President's concern for national defense. France had appropriated 25 million francs in April to be paid on the condition that Jackson apologize for previous statements he had made about France in the dispute. When Jackson bluntly refused to apologize in December, the crisis worsened. In January, 1836, the President recommended reprisals against the French, the completion of coastal defense, and a large increase in naval appropriations. At the same time he opened the door to conciliation with the French. Subsequently, the United States accepted an offer of mediation from England, and the dispute was on its way to a peaceful settlement in May, 1836.

The termination of the French claims dispute, however, did not diminish Jackson's desire to increase the size and effectiveness of the navy. While the crisis provided a handy argument for increased naval expenditures, the President's basic reasons for enlarging the navy went beyond the dispute with France and were not changed by the end of the crisis. In December, 1836, Jackson reported ratification of the commercial treaties with Siam and Muscat, noted the huge federal surplus, and urged "the necessity of further appropriations to increase the number of ships afloat and to enlarge generally the capacity and force of the Navy." The "increase of our commerce and our position in regard to the other powers of the world," Jackson argued, "will always make it our policy and interest to cherish the great naval resources of our country."[45]

Three months later, in his Farewell Address, Jackson repeated his appeal for the nation to strengthen the navy each year: "our local situation, our long line of seacoast, indented by numerous bays, with deep rivers opening into the interior, as well as our extended and still increasing commerce, point to the Navy as our natural means of defense. . . . It is your true policy, for your Navy will not only protect your rich and flourishing commerce in distant seas, but will enable you to reach and annoy the enemy and will give to defense its great efficiency by meeting danger at a distance from home.'' Such sentiments were a far cry from those of the President who in 1829 had spoken of the militia as the bulwark of the nation's defense and acknowledged only in passing the navy's role in the protection of American commerce.[46]

During 1836 and 1837 Jackson's recommendations were translated into increased appropriations and expenditures for the navy. From 1829 to 1835 naval expenditures had remained at a relatively stable level of between $3.2 million and $4 million. From a level of $3,865,000 in 1835, naval expenditures jumped by 52 percent to $5,808,000 in 1836 and by another 14 percent to $6,647,000 in 1837. The annual amounts spent in 1836 and 1837 not only surpassed naval expenditures for any year since 1815, but also averaged almost 20 percent of total federal expenses in 1836 and 1837. In contrast, during the first six years of Jackson's administration, naval expenditures averaged only about 14 percent of total federal expenditures.[47]

Andrew Jackson—Tennessee planter, agrarian, Democrat, and militia captain—left the Presidency as an advocate of a steadily increasing navy which would play an expanded role in American foreign policy. There is no evidence that Jackson and his supporters devoted a substantial amount of time, reflection, or discussion to naval policy. Certainly, the Jacksonians did not intend to rethink or redefine the peacetime role of the navy, but Jackson employed an aggressive diplomatic style and responded to the pressures of a growing commercial empire. With an extensive commercial diplomacy came an increased role for the navy on an expanding overseas stage.

3.

Commercial Pressures and Naval Presence: The Emerging East India Squadron

---

The presence of a fleet of United States ships appearing here would do more to obtain a favorable treaty than any other measure; for unless the Emperor and officers of the Chinese government are convinced of our power, they will not fail to be governed by that policy which the British . . . will be inclined to carry out in opposition to the interests and trade of the United States.

Commodore Lawrence Kearny to the Secretary of the Navy,
September 23, 1842

The period from 1837 to 1842 well illustrates an important characteristic of naval development in the United States prior to 1860. The administration of Martin Van Buren did not support an expanded commercial role for the peacetime navy. And unlike his predecessor the Little Magician did not pursue the type of active foreign and commercial policy which might have forced him to rely directly on the navy overseas. Moreover, the Panic of 1837 and the ensuing depression embroiled the administration in a debilitating debate over economic policy. At the same time sectional tension increased as Congress and both major parties struggled with the problems created by the rise of radical abolitionism. The late 1830's, then, were not propitious years for the advocates of naval growth. Yet, in spite of the growing federal deficit, naval expenditures did not decline sharply and the size of the navy even increased slightly. More important, developments overseas combined to expand the navy's role in the Far East. In spite of the government's official indifference, various pressures created by the situation in China forced consolidation of the infant East India Squadron. Although Van Buren did not endorse the development of a new squadron, he conceded its importance when he acknowledged its permanent status as a separate entity in

1840. The growth of the squadron is both ironic and significant because it demonstrates the extent to which overseas commercial pressures could dictate naval development even in the face of official indifference or hostility.

When he assumed Jackson's mantle of leadership, Van Buren repeatedly endorsed the true republican principles and policies of Old Hickory's administration. Once in office, the Little Magician moved to insure continuity by means of a Cabinet which included only one new appointee and an inaugural address which affirmed his desire to maintain the status quo.[1] However, events quickly shattered Van Buren's hopes for leading a unified Democratic Party and cooperating with Congress. Overspeculation, the death of the Second Bank of the United States, the Specie Circular of 1836, and a depression in England converged in 1837 to produce a severe panic and a serious depression in the United States. For the next four years economic issues preoccupied the administration and dominated national politics. At the same time, the slavery issue further weakened the Democratic Party and the administration as politicians in Congress argued over a flood of abolitionist petitions and the imposition of the so-called Gag Rule.

Van Buren proved to be more effective in his foreign policy than in his domestic policy. As a cautious man, Van Buren pursued a less aggressive and less crisis-prone diplomacy than Old Hickory. With serious political problems, Van Buren did not press for the annexation of Texas, the occupation of Oregon, or the claims of Maine in the New Brunswick border dispute. He also sought to avoid confrontation during the diplomatic crisis created by the *Caroline* affair and other Anglo-American differences in the late 1830's. After Canadian rebel leaders began to use the New York side of the Niagara River as a base for their operations, Van Buren refused to bow to Anglophobic pressures in the United States to support the insurrection. Instead in January, 1838, a neutrality proclamation warned Americans not to engage in hostile acts against Canada, dispatched General Winfield Scott to the border to maintain neutrality, and adopted other measures to prevent border violations by the rebels. Van Buren followed a similar course in the northeastern border dispute between Maine and New Brunswick. During the bloodless Aroostock War in the winter of 1838–1839, the President dispatched Scott to the area and he prevented actual hostilities by arranging a truce. Overseas the administration avoided confrontation when France imposed a blockade on Buenos Aires in 1838 during a diplomatic dispute with the Argentine government. Although American trade with Buenos Aires suffered and American officials there urged action, the administration largely ignored the situation until the blockade was lifted in 1840. At the same time, the administration pursued traditional diplomatic objectives by concluding commercial and navigation agreements with Greece, Sardinia, the Netherlands, Hanover, Equador, and Portugal as well as resolving several claims settlements.[2]

Van Buren's own political ideology, his political problems at home, and his desire to reduce international tensions resulted in an administration opposed to the expansion of the nation's peacetime military establishment. During the diplomatic crisis with Great Britain, Van Buren did not contemplate war, nor did he request a defense buildup. In regard to the navy Van Buren did not attempt to continue the expansive policies of his predecessor. In his Inaugural Address, Van Buren did not even mention the navy. And in his annual messages to Congress the President dealt with the navy in only a perfunctory manner. Although he acknowledged the "absolute necessity of a naval force" to protect the "rapid increase and wide expansion of our commerce," Van Buren interpreted that role in traditional terms. He maintained naval expenditures at more than $6 million per year and supported construction of only a few additional small warships.[3]

The President's two Secretaries of the Navy well illustrated the importance he ascribed to the department. Mahlon Dickerson remained as Secretary in spite of his demonstrated administrative inertia.[4] Although Dickerson recommended some internal reforms, he remained insensitive to technological developments of long-range significance to the navy. Moreover, his procrastination continued to delay the departure of the United States Exploring Expedition. As a result, the expedition still had not sailed when Dickerson resigned in June, 1838, more than two years after Congress authorized the project. For a replacement the President named James K. Paulding of New York. Known primarily as a literary figure, Paulding nonetheless had served as Secretary to the Board of Navy Commissioners and as Naval Agent for New York.[5] As Secretary from 1838 to 1841 Paulding proved to be more diligent, interested, and capable than his predecessor. He urged a larger navy, recommended that more men and ships be maintained on active duty, requested the establishment of a naval academy, and proposed a number of needed reforms. In urging a navy "in full vigor and activity," Paulding observed that because "Commerce makes neighbors of all nations . . . the conflicts of interest or ambition between any two, can scarcely fail of involving many others. Against such imminent contingencies, an adequate naval force . . . is our most effectual security." Paulding's advocacy of a stronger and more efficient navy, however, was both narrow and conservative. Along with the old naval officers on the Board of Navy Commissioners, the Secretary viewed the navy's role in traditional terms and remained committed to a navy of wooden sailing ships and solid shot cannon.[6]

In addition to the administration's basic indifference and conservatism on naval matters, the President and his naval advisors did not understand the necessity of an expanded commercial role for the peacetime navy. They acknowledged the need to protect the nation's growing overseas trade, constructed some additional ships, and maintained the department's budget at over $6 million in a time of fiscal crisis. Yet they adhered to a traditional view that the navy was responsible for combating pirates, preserving neutral rights, and responding to the periodic outrages rather than an active force assisting in the expansion of American commercial interests overseas. Although Jackson's political and military attitudes were very similar to Van Buren's, Old Hickory's aggressive foreign policy compelled him to rely on the navy and to revise his attitudes on its role by the end of his Presidency. No such transition would occur during Van Buren's Presidency. In practice the administration's basic naval attitudes were demonstrated by the manner in which the Navy Department dealt with the United States Exploring Expedition and responded to the nascent revolution in naval technology of the late 1830's.

Preparations for the Exploring Expedition began soon after Congress authorized the project in May, 1836, and within three months the Navy Department had completed most of the planning. The Department dispatched Lieutenant Charles Wilkes to Europe to purchase needed equipment, contacted scientific and learned societies for advice on the project, and appointed Captain Thomas ap Catesby Jones as commander of the expedition. A long-time supporter of the project, Jones was a highly regarded officer whose service under Jackson at the Battle of New Orleans had earned him the President's lasting confidence. As commander, Jones received considerable authority to select the men and ships which he believed would best serve the expedition.[7]

However, the Navy Department could not sustain its initial momentum. Jones' broad authority and personal self-confidence led him into direct conflict with Secretary of the Navy Dickerson over the number and type of ships needed, their specifications, and the officers selected for the expedition. Confusion and rivalry also existed over a variety of other issues including the selection of the civilian scientists and their role. In addition, serious jealousies surfaced among naval officers as they objected to the appointment of junior officers such as Charles Wilkes to accompany the expedition and the inflated role assigned to the civilians in what was a naval expedition. Under Jackson's prod, and occasional intervention, preparations proceeded. But once Jackson left office, the situation deteriorated. Van Buren was willing to implement congressional legislation in this case, but nothing more. Moreover, the new President's attitude permitted Dickerson's indecision, indolence, and pettiness to compound the delays.

Indicative of the problem was the confusion which existed over the precise objectives of the expedition. Since neither Congress nor the President had defined the specific purpose of the expedition in 1836, that task remained for the Secretary of the Navy. Finally in November, 1837, eighteen months after Congress authorized the project, Dickerson declared the "primary object of this expedition" to be "the promotion of the great interests of commerce and navigation. The advancement of science is considered an object of great, but comparatively of secondary importance."[8] At the same time, Jones asked to be relieved of his command after endless months of bickering with Dickerson. Several months later, President Van Buren transferred responsibility for the expedition to Secretary of War Joel Poinsett, who selected Lieutenant Charles Wilkes in 1838 to replace Jones. Although Wilkes had solid scientific qualifications for the position and no senior officer would accept the command, the decision created an uproar in the navy. The crew of the expedition's flagship, the *Macedonian*, at first objected to being assigned to a junior rank officer. At the same time, junior and senior naval officers protested Wilkes' selection to the Van Buren Administration, albeit without effect. In Congress opponents of the project criticized the decision and attempted to restrict the expedition to a routine coastal survey. In spite of the furor Wilkes worked assiduously and effectively to get the project underway. With final details complete the six-vessel squadron put to sea in August, 1838— more than two years and two months after Congress had approved the expedition.[9]

Responsibility for the inordinate delay rests largely with Secretary of the Navy Dickerson. Although he was an amateur botanist and a member of the American Philosophical Society, Dickerson evinced little interest in the commercial or scientific potential of the expedition. The situation deteriorated to such an extent that the new President was finally forced to take the extraordinary step of transferring responsibility for this naval expedition to the Secretary of War. Admittedly, preparing the expedition posed a difficult and demanding challenge, but a tough-minded, energetic, and resourceful Secretary could have insured that the expedition would sail within a reasonable time period. Obviously, Mahlon Dickerson was not that man. Of greater significance than Dickerson's incompetence is the low priority which President Van Buren assigned to the expedition. For almost a year he refused to replace his Secretary or to intervene directly himself. Even after a year of inaction on the project Van Buren chose not to remove his Secretary but to reassign this naval function to another department. His course indicated that the President cared little about the commercial potential of the navy because the Exploring Expedition offered an excellent opportunity for the navy to demonstrate its commercial value to the nation.

The Van Buren Administration also resisted the basic technological revolution which was beginning in naval science. For decades, massive wooden sailing ships with rows of smooth-bore cannon had been the symbol of naval power, and superior seamanship in these complicated sailing vessels had represented the epitome of naval leadership. By the late 1830's, however, steam power had begun to challenge the sailing ship. Once the submerged screw propeller proved workable and superceded the cumbersome amidship paddle wheel, the process accelerated in the 1840's and 1850's. Similarly, the introduction of explosive shells necessitated changes in naval ordnance and rendered the wooden hull obsolete within a generation. In Europe with its climate of diplomatic rivalry, the major navies had already begun to experiment seriously with steam power, iron hulls, and explosive shells.[10] But in the United States, the Van Buren Administration and the Board of Navy Commissioners remained committed to the wooden sailing ship and the smoothbore cannon. Although the Board and Secretaries Dickerson and Paulding acknowledged the introduction of steam power and acquiesced in a very limited application to the U.S. Navy, their collective view was very conservative and hostile to technological innovation. At most, naval authorities believed that steam could be used to power coastal defense batteries to repel invasions, but not to power the navy's ocean-going warships. Authorization by Congress in 1839 and 1841 to construct several steam warships came as the result of congressional concern, not initiative from the

Navy Department. "I am *steamed* to death," complained Paulding. "I am willing
. . . to go with the wind," wrote Paulding after Congress had approved the
steamers, "and keep the steam enthusiasts quiet by warily administering to the
humour of the times, but I will never consent to let our old ships perish, and
transform our Navy into a fleet of sea monsters."[11]

Such arch-conservative attitudes rendered those responsible for naval policy
in the late 1830's insensitive to the progressive ideas of an energetic and farsighted group of younger career officers. Such men as Matthew C. Perry, Alexander Slidell [MacKenzie], Franklin Buchanan, and Robert Stockton were
experienced officers whose further advancement had been stifled by the navy's
seniority-based promotion system and the tenacious occupation of the most influential positions by older officers in their sixties and seventies. Unfortunately,
men like John Rodgers and Isaac Chauncey had served as senior officers in the
War of 1812 and held traditional ideas about the nature of naval power. Although
willing to concede a limited role for steam power in the navy, they detested the
idea of a navy dominated by cumbersome steam vessels which did not demand
a high level of seamanship and created endless noise and dirt.

The younger group advocated extensive reforms to improve the quality of
naval service and urged the implementation of steam power and other technological innovations. They also endorsed a more aggressive peacetime commercial
role for the navy. In the decade which preceded congressional approval for the
Exploring Expedition, such officers as John Downes, Thomas ap Catesby Jones,
Matthew C. Perry, Charles Wilkes, and Midshipmen Matthew F. Maury and
Sylvanus Gordon endorsed the project because of its scientific and commercial
value. After a cruise to the Pacific, Jones acknowledged that the naval expedition
"would open to our commercial and, of course, national interests sources of
great wealth, which cannot be brought into action without the protecting aid of
Government." When he returned from the Pacific, Downes also endorsed the
expedition, noting that no argument should be needed "to prove that a portion
of our commerce might be rendered more secure, and probably greatly increased,
by vessels sent, properly prepared, to examine such islands" in the South Seas.
These sentiments clearly demonstrated the presence of a group of officers who
wanted to stake out an active and integral role in the extension of the nation's
overseas commercial empire.[12]

The most outstanding member of the group was Matthew C. Perry who came
from a distinguished naval family. His father had served with distinction on a
privateer in the Revolution and later commanded a frigate in the Quasi-War with
France. His brother, Oliver Hazard Perry, won honors as the hero of the Battle
of Lake Erie in the War of 1812. Born in 1794, Matthew Perry served in the
War of 1812 as a midshipman and rose through the officer ranks after the war
to become a captain by the late 1830's. During his naval career Perry also
developed a wide variety of intellectual interests and became an able linguist,
literature student, amateur botanist, and avid conchologist. Wherever he travelled
he collected specimens and shells. With his active mind and commitment to a
naval career, Perry constantly sought ways to improve the service.

As commandant of the Brooklyn Naval Yard in the 1830's Perry worked to improve the recruiting of seamen and to provide better naval education. In 1833 he was instrumental in the founding of the Naval Lyceum, an organization designed "to promote the diffusion of useful knowledge, [and] to foster a spirit of harmony and a community interest in the service." For officers stationed at Brooklyn, the Lyceum held regular meetings and lectures, recorded weather data, and maintained a library. Perry also helped found the *Naval Magazine*, served on its editorial board, and contributed a number of articles.[13]

Perry always maintained a great interest in technological innovation. Long interested in steam power, Perry wanted to develop a steam warship rather than the floating steam batteries authorized by Congress and favored by some senior officers. After construction of a steam warship was authorized in 1834, the Department placed Perry in charge of construction of the *Fulton II* which was launched in 1837. Although serious problems existed with the vessel, Perry worked to prove the practicality of a steam warship. In 1838 he sailed the *Fulton II* to Washington where the President and numerous congressmen toured the ship. Although resistance to steam power remained intense in the navy, this venture helped convince numerous politicians of the importance of steam power and was one factor in congressional authorization in 1839 for three war steamers. For his efforts, Perry is often credited with being the "father of the steam navy" and the founder of the navy's engineering corps. At the same time, Perry experimented during these years with different cannons and types of shells. As a result, he demonstrated the superiority of the Paixhans-type 64 pound shell artillery and the inaccuracy of grape shot. Perry also advocated the use of iron warships and endorsed construction of the propeller-driven, steam frigate, the *Princeton*, built under the supervision of Robert Stockton.

Many of the ideas of the navy's progressive young officers were embodied in the 1837 article, "Thoughts on the Navy," published in the *Naval Magazine*. Although written by Alexander Slidell, the article carried many of Perry's ideas, and argued the need for a more modern, efficient, and powerful navy. Asserting that "all of our misfortunes as a nation, from the day we became one, have proceeded from the want of a sufficient navy," the article urged the nation to learn from the "mistakes and disasters of the past" and establish the principle that attacks on our commerce and "our national honor shall be prevented at the time by a prompt display of power. . . . " To accomplish this, the United States needed to build a navy commensurate to the "extent and value" of its commerce and in "relative proportion" to what the navies of other maritime nations had with respect to their foreign trades. The navy could then "follow the adventurous trader, in his path of peril, to every sea with cruisers ready to spread over him the protecting flag of the republic!" As the eighth ranked naval power, the United States would have to expand the navy to three times its current size, a goal which Slidell and Perry endorsed enthusiastically.[14]

As long as Van Buren remained President, he largely ignored calls for a larger navy and for the application of technological innovations to the navy's wooden sailing ships. In Washington, D.C., the advocates of change and reform did not receive a sympathetic hearing from the administration. But events and attitudes in the U.S. capital did not completely determine American naval developments between 1837 and 1841. Overseas, pressures for naval support persisted and intensified. In California, Commander French Forrest of the *St. Louis* arrived in Monterey in June, 1840, to discover that more than one hundred foreign residents of the Mexican province had been jailed since April on charges of plotting to overthrow the government. Among the arrested were a large number of Americans including the alleged leader of the plot, Isaac Graham. For the next several weeks Forrest investigated, asked questions, and conferred with local officials to convey his concern and dismay. On June 30, 1840, local residents thanked Forrest for his efforts and appealed for an American naval presence in California. Although Forrest sailed in July the prisoners were subsequently freed and Forrest given much of the credit for their release. In his December, 1841, report the Secretary of the Navy praised Forrest's "prompt and spirited interposition" which "vindicated and secured the rights" of Americans and British alike in upper California.[15]

Events halfway around the world were underway which would transform the East India Squadron from a footnote to an essential part of American naval and commercial policy.[16] The East India Squadron had actually been created in 1835 when the Department selected Commodore Edmund P. Kennedy to command two ships to the Far East and authorized him to fly the broad pennant of a squadron commander. Kennedy's primary responsibility was to escort Edmund F. Roberts with the *Peacock* and the *Enterprise* back to Asia to exchange treaty ratifications and to negotiate new commercial agreements with China and Japan.[17] The limitations on Kennedy's authority were underlined when Roberts died in June, 1836, and Kennedy returned to the United States immediately because he lacked authority to conduct any diplomatic negotiations. After the squadron returned to the United States in October, 1837, it was replaced several months later by another squadron consisting of the frigate *Columbia* and her consort, the *John Adams*, under the command of Commodore George C. Read.

Born in Ireland in 1787, Read had migrated to the United States and later joined the navy in 1804. He rose steadily, achieved the rank of Captain in 1825, and subsequently commanded the *Constitution* and the *Constellation*. The most serious blemish on his record occurred in 1835 when he was court-martialed and received a one-year suspension for his harsh treatment of a young officer. Dated April 13, 1838, Read's instructions directed him to sail around the Cape of Good Hope, touch at several ports in the Indian Ocean and the East Indies, and visit other ports where his "appearance might promote the interests of our commerce." Absent were any orders which dealt with China or American commercial interest there.[18]

En route to China, Read learned of another attack on an American merchant ship along the pepper coast of Sumatra. In that incident, the captain and crew of the *Eclipse* had been killed or wounded and a cargo of Spanish dollars and opium stolen. When he reached Sumatra in December, 1838, Read proved fully capable of invoking gunboat diplomacy. At Quallah Batoo Read contacted the local rajah who promised to produce the culprits. When he failed to do so after two days, the American ships shelled the village into surrender with a one hour assault on Christmas Day. At Mukkee local officials also failed to produce any of the pirates and again the two American warships bombarded the village. The American force then landed, burned the town, and returned to the ships. At Soo Soo Read found the village and its inhabitants in such deplorable condition that he exacted a promise of safety for American ships and seamen without an attack. After receiving similar assurances from other local rajahs, the two-ship squadron sailed on January 2, 1839.[19]

When he finally reached China in April, 1839, Read carried no specific instructions regarding China and was not prepared for the unstable and changing commercial situation he found there. By the 1830's, American trade with China dated back more than one-half century to the voyage of the *Empress of China*. Although lucrative for those few firms willing to take the risk, commerce with China was limited because the Chinese imposed restrictions, limited all foreign trade to the foreign "factories" outside the walled city of Canton, and specified that all trade had to be conducted with authorized Chinese, the so-called Hong merchants. Prior to the 1820's American merchants relied on sea otter, pelts, sealskins, sandalwood, and specie to exchange for the tea, silks, and other luxuries of China. With the decline of the fur and sandalwood trades in the 1820's, American merchants depended on such items as cotton goods, but increasingly on opium and specie as the commodities for which the Chinese would exchange their goods. During the 1830's American imports from China averaged more than $6 million annually while American exports to China averaged more than $1.2 million.[20]

In fact the China trade represented only a tiny portion of the foreign trade of the United States that decade, but the importance of the trade is to be found in the great profits it yielded to those willing to participate and in the seemingly limitless potential it offered for the future. Since the time of Thomas Jefferson, Americans had dreamed of a "passage to India" and the commercial opportunities offered by trade with the people of China. By the 1830's a substantial body of geographic descriptions, travel accounts, commercial information, and economic predictions fed the nation's fascination with China and the Far East. The huge "heathen" population of China also offered a formidable challenge to Protestent missionaries. Although their evangelical success was limited, missionaries such as Peter Parker, Samuel Wells Williams, and Elijah Bridgman generated additional information on and interest in China.

To a great extent, commercial and religious activity was conducted without formal diplomatic agreements or the official sanction of Chinese authorities. Although an American consul had resided irregularly at Canton since the 1790's, these officials provided virtually no real assistance for American commerce because they were neither recognized officially by the Chinese nor respected by American merchants. Instead, the consul's duties included reporting to Washington on trade, administering estates of the dead, disciplining mutinous sailors, and caring for needy Americans.

American merchants, then, pursued their trade very much on their own and at the mercy of the Chinese. Acquiescing to all Chinese restrictions, however petty, they accepted their status as "inferior" barbarians. The nature of the situation was well illustrated by the Terranova incident. In 1824 Chinese officials accused Francis Terranova, an illiterate Italian seaman from the *Emily* of Baltimore, of causing the death of a woman who had come to the *Emily* to trade. Although the American consul offered a payment to the woman's family, the Chinese demanded the arrest and trial of the sailor. When the captain of the *Emily* refused to surrender Terranova, American residents met and appointed a committee of merchants and sea captains to resolve the issue. The committee decided not to surrender Terranova but to permit the Chinese to try him on board the *Emily*. Having concurred, the Chinese held a summary trial, declared Terranova guilty, and demanded his surrender. When the Americans refused, the Chinese stopped trade. Under pressure from American merchants, a new compromise was reached whereby Chinese officials were permitted to seize Terranova on the condition that a second trial would be held. This trial was no fairer than the first, and Terranova was tried, convicted, sentenced to death, and executed summarily.[21] In presenting their side of the case, American merchants presented a petition which termed the Chinese laws as unjust, but acknowledged that the Americans had no choice but to submit to the "overwhelming force" of the Chinese. This admission and the incident itself underline the determination of the American community at Canton to maintain trade even at the cost of national honor. In the estimation of one scholar, the incident "shows how completely the Chinese held the foreigners in their power by means of one weapon—stopping the trade."[22]

In such an atmosphere, the presence of American warships created an awkward situation at best for Americans, and between 1819 and 1839 few naval vessels touched at Macao. In 1819 the Navy Department appointed Captain John Henley to command the frigate *Congress* and instructed him to sail for the "protection of commerce of the United States in the Indian and China Seas." The *Congress* was ordered to sail to Canton, pay respects to the Chinese authorities there, gather information about American commerce, and offer to convoy American merchant ships safely through the pirate infested China Seas. Between November, 1819 and September, 1820, Henley sailed to Macao on three occasions. Ignoring standard Chinese orders for the *Congress* to depart immediately, Henley travelled to Canton, insisted on procuring supplies for his ship, and actually sailed the *Congress* into the forbidden waters of the Bogue, a mouth of the Canton (Tigris) River, on his last visit to insure that he received his supplies. At Canton American merchants responded with apprehension to the appearance of the *Congress* and Henley's actions because they understood that their commercial privileges could not be guaranteed by a single warship. Fearing retribution by Chinese officials, they refused Henley's offers of convoy for American merchant ships and expressed relief when the *Congress* departed for good in October, 1820.[23]

Ten years later the sloop *Vincennes* touched briefly at Macao during its voyage to become the first American warship to circumnavigate the globe. During his two-week stay at Macao Master Commandant William Finch inquired of the American community about the state of trade and the need for periodic naval visits. In response the merchants expressed their appreciation for Finch's visit, noted the "many local grievances and impositions to complain of," and acknowledged that frequent naval visits would benefit the nation's commerce as well as enhance our national "character in the estimation of the whole Chinese empire and the neighboring governments. . . . "[24] At the same time, the merchant community manifested its continued apprehension by urging naval officers to observe Chinese laws and not sail beyond Lintin Island because an "interruption of trade can arise from their noncompliance with the customs of the country." Subsequently, the *Potomac* in 1832, the *Peacock* and *Boxer* in 1832 and 1836, and the *Vincennes* in 1836 visited Macao briefly. In each case, the brevity of the visit was occasioned by the problem of sickness among American sailors at Macao, the lack of specific instructions to make a prolonged stop, and the general anxiety which an American naval presence created in the American merchant community at Canton.[25]

However, a dramatic rise in the opium trade during the 1830's changed the commercial atmosphere in China. Although banned since the 1790's, opium continued to be smuggled into China by various means until it reached levels that alarmed the Chinese. In 1834 an estimated 34,000 chests of opium entered China and by 1840 the total reached 40,000. Although Americans participated in the illegal trade, the British were much more heavily involved. According to British sources, the value of British opium imports into China between 1818 and 1833 totalled more than $104 million compared to less than $5 million for Americans in the same period. Out of total American imports into China of $3,678,000 during the 1836–1837 trading season, only $275,921 was in opium.[26]

In China vast quantities of the drug seriously debilitated an increasing number of Chinese people and alarmed officials. The opium trade also created an unfavorable balance of trade and drained specie from China. Imperial edicts had little effect because corruption and involvement ran deep among the very officials responsible for controlling the trade. At the same time, the Chinese were not capable of policing their coastline against smugglers. Finally, the imperial government appointed Lin Tse-hsu as a special commissioner with full authority to do what was necessary to end the trade. In March, 1839, Lin demanded that all opium in possession of foreigners at Canton be surrendered and that all foreign merchants sign bonds guaranteeing the end of the opium trade. To enforce his edict Lin stopped all foreign trade and declared the foreign merchants at Canton prisoners in their own factories. Lin placed a guard around the factories, removed all foreign servants, shut off all communication with the outside world, and placed armed ships in the river. At the same time, Lin pressed the American and British to sign the bonds. Although he was prepared to pledge an end to opium imports by American merchants, Peter Snow, the American consul, found the bond presented to him particularly offensive because it specified that all opium found on any American vessel would be subject to confiscation, that the entire crew of the guilty ship would be subject to death, and that the signers of the bond would be held responsible for all smuggling. The British agreed with Snow, and their Superintendent of Trade, Captain Charles Elliot, also refused to sign the bonds presented by Lin.

It was during the confinement of the foreigners at Canton and the impasse over the bond that Commodore George C. Read arrived at Macao in the *Columbia* in late April, 1839. After consulting with Peter Snow, Read decided that the situation was not dangerous and that he would avoid a show of force or an attempt to rescue the hostages at Canton. The crisis eased in early May when the British surrendered 20,280 chests of opium, of which 1,540 were held on English account by Americans. Lin then lifted the quarantine of the factories but renewed his demands that the bonds be signed by foreign merchants. Here the British and Americans parted company. Refusing to sign the bonds, the British withdrew to Canton and appealed to the Americans to do the same in the hope of demonstrating that the Chinese were as dependent on the opium trade as were the foreigners. The Americans, however, refused and remained at Canton where they eventually signed a milder form of the bond and resumed trade. During the summer of 1839 the Americans enjoyed a booming business occasioned by the British absence. Able to charge freight rates between Hong Kong and Canton that exceeded the rates between Hong Kong and America, Americans employed every available vessel to carry a heavy volume of goods to and from Canton for the British. At first miffed, British merchants adjusted and came to realize that trade with Canton through American merchants was better than no trade at all.

Against the objections of the American merchants, Read proposed to sail as conditions improved. Although they applauded his restraint at Macao, the merchants could not understand Read's determination to depart, and they appealed for the squadron to remain until the situation was resolved and thereby "for a favor done to this branch of our national commerce." In response, Read explained that he could not remain indefinitely because his instructions did not authorize him to intervene in commercial affairs or to conduct diplomatic negotiations. Instead the health of his crew, their limited terms of service, and supply problems dictated that he continue his cruise. "Their interest requires that I should stay," reported Read to the Navy Department, but "my duty demands that I should go." Accordingly, the tiny squadron finally sailed for the Sandwich Islands on August 6, 1839.[27]

Unable to convince Read to remain, the merchant community resolved to persuade the American government to alter its policy and maintain a permanent naval presence in East Asia. As he witnessed the deterioration of conditions in China before Read's arrival, American consul Peter Snow emphasized the "importance of always keeping on this station a naval force . . . for the protection generally of our commerce, and the persons of our citizens. . . . '' Noting that the navy's appearance had saved Macao and done "honor to our country," Snow reiterated his recommendation to the Navy Department after Read sailed. In August the consul wrote "that a naval force is of the utmost importance on this station, the visit of the *Columbia* and *John Adams* has demonstrated to all; for the hostile movements on the part of the high commissioner against Macao were suspended on the arrival of those ships, and immediately resumed on their departure.'' Snow also recommended the appointment of a diplomat with powers greater than those of a consul. Such an official could best determine the movement of naval vessels because a naval commander would be "unable to form a correct judgement on the course proper for him to pursue for the general good" when confronted with a "flood of private communications from interested men. . . . ''[28]

Independent of Snow, the American merchants at Canton also requested government assistance in a petition to the House of Representatives received there in January, 1840. In addition to urging appointment of a diplomat to negotiate a commercial treaty, the petition requested a "naval force for the protection of the persons resident" at Canton and emphasized that such a force was required to place American commerce on a stable basis. This and other petitions signalled a change in the attitude of American merchants in China. Previously, they had accepted their tenuous position in the hong trading system. Accordingly, they had been willing to acknowledge the value of brief periodic visits by the American Navy and the need for a consul to perform perfunctory duties, while realizing that they were dependent on the mercy of the Chinese and not on the strength of the navy or the ability of American diplomats. Now that situation had changed dramatically.[29]

American merchants and the American consul appealed for the establishment of a permanent naval force in the East Indies and for the appointment of a diplomatic official with powers to negotiate an agreement. In other words, the merchants now sought what they had long avoided, namely, to place American commerce in China on the same stable basis that it enjoyed with most of the nation's other commercial partners. For this reason, Read's voyage and his brief stay at Macao during the spring and summer of 1839 is very significant. His presence at Macao, even though it was part of a general cruise around the world, underlined the need for and importance of a permanent naval squadron in the East Indies, a fact which Read himself realized before he sailed from Canton. In his report to the Secretary of the Navy explaining why he had decided to sail, Read appealed for the dispatch of a naval force to be "constantly in these seas." American men-of-war would no doubt have "a salutary effect, in preventing the sacrifice of life for" smuggling. Once the Chinese were made to understand that the navy would retaliate in all such instances, "I do not think there would be any cause for serious apprehension.''[30]

Relations between the Chinese and English continued to deteriorate during

1839 and 1840. British merchants still refused to sign the bonds demanded by Lin. In September, 1839, the British declared, then lifted, a blockade of Canton. In November, 1839, Lin sent a fleet of Chinese war junks to Hong Kong and demanded the surrender of English seamen allegedly responsible for the death of a Chinese in an incident on the Kowloon Peninsula between British sailors and Chinese villagers. When Captain Elliot refused to cooperate, the Chinese junks advanced on English ships anchored off Hong Kong. The British ships responded by firing, destroying three junks, and forcing the rest to retreat.

Although neither country declared war officially, the conflict expanded in 1840 as the English dispatched a fleet of sixteen warships, four steamers, one troopship, twenty-seven transports, and 4,000 troops to China. The armada arrived in June, quickly imposed a blockade on Canton, and pushed the war northeast along the coast to the mouth of the Yangtze River. A temporary convention was signed in January, 1841, but it pleased neither the English nor the Chinese and the war resumed. Although the Chinese merchants of Canton saved the city from attack and capture by paying a $6 million ransom, the British pushed north and captured several cities. Finally, after Shanghai fell and the British prepared to attack Nanking, the Chinese bowed to the inevitable and accepted British terms. On August 29, 1842, the Treaty of Nanking was signed on board the *H.M.S. Cornwallis*. The agreement created a new commercial order by ending the old Canton system of trade. The terms provided for the cession of Hong Kong to England, the opening of trade at the four additional ports of Amoy, Foochow, Ningpo, and Shanghai, an indemnity of $21 million to England, the abolition of the hong trading system, the establishment of British consuls at each trading port, and the recognition of absolute equality between England and China.[31]

The First Opium War naturally placed the commerce and safety of American merchants in jeopardy. As the British blockade disrupted American trade and the American merchants had left Canton in 1841, American imports from China fell to less than half of what they had been in 1840. Meanwhile, considerable interest and concern had been generated in the United States. The dispatches of Peter Snow detailed the deteriorating situation and carried recommendations for the presence of a naval force and a high level diplomat. Petitions from merchants in China and New England confirmed the gravity of the situation and called for government action to guarantee American commercial rights. News from England also aroused suspicion in the minds of some politicians concerning British designs in China. In response to the outbreak of war there and the imposition of the British blockade, the Van Buren Administration decided to dispatch another naval squadron, but the comparative indifference of the government was demonstrated by the fact that the new squadron was no larger than the previous one, no diplomat was commissioned to accompany the squadron, and the commander was not himself authorized to conduct diplomatic negotiations or conclude commercial agreements.

After Commodore John Downes refused the command, Captain Lawrence

Kearny, then in command of the *Potomac* on the Brazil Station, was selected.[32] The fifty-one-year-old Kearny had been born in New Jersey and joined the navy in 1807. During the 1820's he captured several pirate ships on a patrol in the Caribbean and served in the Mediterranean before being promoted to Captain in 1832. His squadron consisted of the forty-three-year-old frigate *Constellation* and the sloop-of-war *Boston*. After a number of delays Kearny finally sailed from Rio de Janeiro in March, 1841, with instructions drafted by outgoing Secretary of the Navy James Paulding the previous November. Kearny's orders emphasized that "the leading objects" of his cruise were the protection of "the interests of the United States and their citizens on the Coast of China" during the war with England and the protection of the "Whale Fisheries on the coast of New Zealand, New Holland, and other places lying near the track of the Squadron. . . . " American interests in China, however, were to be his top priority. The Commodore was to observe any legal British blockade, to inform the Chinese that he could not escort American ships through the blockade without additional specific orders, and to protect American property and lives against illegal actions by the British, while at the same time impressing on the Chinese the "friendly disposition" of the American government, its commitment to encourage only lawful trade, and its determination that Kearny try "to prevent and to punish the smuggling of opium. . . . " Although Kearny's instructions did not authorize him to negotiate with the Chinese or to try to expand American commercial privileges in China, they did represent a milestone for the American Navy in the Far East. For the first time a naval commander's orders dealt with China in detail and identified American commercial interests there as the squadron's primary concern. Only after peace was concluded and the situation permitted was Kearny to proceed to New Zealand and New Holland.[33]

By the time Kearny reached Macao in March, 1842, the war was near an end and the center of military activity was now more than a thousand miles northeast at Shanghai and on the Yangtze River. At Canton the blockade had been lifted and trade, including the smuggling of opium, had resumed. In accord with his orders, Kearny moved promptly against the opium trade. On March 31st, he informed the American consul at Canton that "the United States does not sanction the 'smuggling of opium' on this coast, under the American flag, in violation of the laws of China." Nor would the U.S. government protect any American apprehended while smuggling opium. Although he did attempt to apprehend ships flying the American flag illegally while carrying opium, Kearny was unable to combat the trade effectively and his warnings and threats were ignored. Since American smugglers had never received the protection of the navy, Kearny's notice did not deter them. The Chinese may have been impressed by his good intentions, but he received no assistance from them, much less from American merchants or the British officials who were most cynical of his motives. His greatest success came more than a year later when he seized the schooner *Ariel*, near Amoy, deprived the ship of its American papers, and ordered the ship back to Canton.[34]

Kearny had more success in dealing with a number of outstanding American claims and grievances against the Chinese which had developed during the war. American merchants at Canton were particularly anxious to settle the grievances and the American vice consul forwarded a list to the Commodore soon after he anchored at Macao. Included was an incident from May, 1841, when an American merchant ship, the *Morrison*, had been fired upon by Chinese soldiers en route from the Canton factories to Whampoa. One American was killed, several wounded, and the survivors taken prisoner for several days. To obtain satisfaction Kearny decided to deal directly with the Chinese authorities and sailed the *Constellation* past the Bogue to Whampoa where he anchored on April 13, 1842. Here she was joined by the *Boston* in early May. This show of naval force marked the first time that an American warship had entered Chinese inland waters.

Next Kearny sent Lieutenant J. C. Reynolds to Canton with a letter for the Governor-General of Kwangtung and Kwangsi provinces. Again Kearny had broken new ground in relations with the Chinese by becoming the first American official to deal directly, rather than through the Co-hong, with an imperial official. Kearny's communication detailed the various grievances, and requested punishment for the guilty and redress for the American losses. Surprisingly, the Governor-General responded in a conciliatory manner, assured greater security for Americans in the future, and asked the Commodore to determine the amount of damages to be paid. Although the Chinese did not attempt to punish the guilty individuals, the hong merchants were ordered to pay the damages determined by Kearny. Kearny's visit to Whampoa and Canton was marked by unprecedented Chinese good will as they praised the Commodore for his "clear understanding, profound wisdom, and great justice" and lauded the Americans for their legitimate and honorable trade. Although the politeness of the Chinese could be attributed partially to their desire not to offend a neutral nation, their attitude reflected their new appreciation of western naval and military power. To this extent the presence of the *Constellation* and *Boston* had a direct effect on the development of American diplomacy in China.[35]

Having settled the grievances Kearny returned to Macao with his squadron in June. Here he learned of impending negotiations between the British and Chinese and then the Treaty of Nanking in September. Kearny immediately understood the tremendous significance of the agreement and its implications for the commercial rights of other foreigners in China. He dispatched three copies of the treaty and a letter to the Secretary of the Navy by separate routes. In it, he urged that a diplomatic agent be sent to China along with additional American warships: "the presence of a fleet of United States ships appearing here would do more to obtain a favorable treaty than any other measure; for unless the Emperor and officers of the Chinese government are convinced of our power, they will not fail to be governed by that policy which the British . . . will be inclined to carry out in opposition to the interests and trade of the United States."[36]

In the meantime Kearny resolved to gain rights for American merchants similar to those won by the British. Although his instructions did not specify that he should do more than protect existing American interests, Kearny sought to extend and increase American commercial opportunities. In October he reported that his "good understanding" with Chinese officials offered a "propitious moment for the U. States to enter upon some understanding in regard to commercial privileges with the Chinese." On October 8, 1842, Kearny sent a communication to the Chinese Governor-General expressing his hope that American trade would "be placed upon the same footing as the merchants of the nation most favored."[37] From Macao Kearny went again to Canton where he received an October 15 reply which was cordial and encouraging. The Governor-General reminded Kearny that Americans had been well treated in the past and that he would deliberate on their commercial privileges once matters with the British were settled. He assured Kearny that "it shall not be permitted that the American merchants shall come to have merely a dry stick (that is, their interests shall be attended to)." Although encouraging, the response neither guaranteed nor promised specific rights for American merchants equal to those of the British. "This answer," observed Consul Snow, "evinces a disposition . . . to grant every reasonable call on them . . . particularly when backed by a heavy man-of-war." Accordingly, Kearny and ships would have to remain until matters were settled. "Should it become necessary to make demands in favor of equal rights and commercial privileges, it [the squadron] cannot fail to have a beneficial effect."[38]

After a brief cruise to Manila Kearny returned to Macao on January 1, 1843, where he confronted bad news. In early December a Chinese mob had attacked the foreign factories at Canton and done considerable damage to the American firm, Augustine Heard and Company. Again Kearny sailed the *Constellation* to Whampoa, proceeded to Canton, and corresponded directly with the Governor-General. In the five weeks that he remained at Canton Kearny was unable to resolve the claims of the American company, but he did secure assurances from the Governor-General that the Chinese would pay the claims.

More disturbing was the news that the Chinese had rejected Kearny's request for equal commercial privileges. In December, while Kearny was in Manila, the Emperor issued an edict rejecting the extension of commercial privileges to other nations by instructing Chinese officials at Canton "in everything conform to the old regulations, which cannot be added to or changed." If the Americans "dare to covet the establishment of ports and so forth, be sure to stop them with earnest and sincere orders. Let there be no compromising." Additional edicts issued on the 15th and 25th of December, 1842 specified that American ships entering other Chinese ports were to be ordered to Canton and that American trade was to be prohibited outside of Canton. Clearly, the Chinese intended to restrict trade with the barbarians as much as possible. Although forced to surrender to English demands, the Chinese resolved not to extend those concessions to other nations voluntarily.[39]

Rebuffed and disappointed, Kearny renewed his efforts to secure equal commercial privileges. On January 16, 1843, he reported to the Navy Department that unless the United States concluded a treaty with China, "the trade of the United States would be subject to being cut off, until a treaty could be entered into. . . . " In the meantime, however, he would "attempt to secure the commercial interests of the United States." In spite of the fact that he carried no diplomatic credentials or instructions, American merchant support for Kearny strengthened his position considerably.[40]

Fortunately, the Chinese had already begun to alter their position. Although they remained opposed to extending the commercial privileges won by the British to other nations, the Chinese recognized that the other western nations might well unite and demand greater concessions. Consequently, the Emperor issued an edict on January 19th authorizing his commissioners to extend to all nations the new trade regulations regarding the five treaty ports. In fact, the formulation of the new regulations with the British was not completed until a supplementary treaty was signed on July 22, 1843. In the meantime, the Chinese did not inform Kearny of the Emperor's edict and continued to hope that the new privileges would not have to be extended immediately to western nations other than the British. Unaware of the shift in the Chinese position, Kearny remained pessimistic but continued to press for commercial equality. On April 13, 1843, Kearny wrote to the Governor-General praising the good will of the Chinese, noting that Americans traded in China legally, and declaring that Americans caught smuggling opium would not be protected. Kearny emphasized that the question of commercial equality was a "very weighty matter" which could "cause much unfriendly feeling" in the United States if not granted: "what his Imperial Majesty grants to the traders from other countries, his own sovereign [the President] will demand for his merchants." To prevent "further difficulties," Kearny suggested that both countries "appoint high officials to negotiate . . . and settle the terms of a lasting treaty. . . . " [41]

Three days later, the Governor-General acknowledged partial commercial equality for the Americans by assuring that the specific "commercial duties to be paid by each country are all to be regulated uniformly by one rule, without the least partiality manifested towards any one." At the same time, however, the Chinese refused to guarantee that the ports of Foochow, Ningpo, and Shanghai, newly opened to the British, would be open to other nations and emphasized that a formal treaty would be "an unnecessary and circuitous act" as long as the Americans and Chinese maintained peace and trade as usual. Further progress between the Americans and Chinese was stalled in the spring of 1843 by a delay in negotiations between the Chinese and the British on the supplemental treaty which was not completed until July.[42] In the meantime Kearny had sailed in May for the Sandwich Islands. When he left China the Commodore believed that American commercial interests were as secure as he could make them given the size of his squadron and his limited official instructions which did not authorize him to conclude a treaty even if the Chinese had been willing to negotiate one. He also believed that he needed to provide some attention to American whaling interests in the Pacific after a cruise of more than two years during which he had largely ignored this part of his instructions.

Events in the summer of 1843 bore out Kearny's optimism and his decision to sail. After the Supplementary Treaty of the Bogue was signed on July 22nd, American merchants tested the promises of the Chinese. When the *Mary Chilton* arrived at Whampoa, Edward King, the American consular agent, requested that this American merchantship be subject to the new tariff duties. The Chinese Imperial Commissioner agreed and added that all foreign nations would be permitted to trade at the five treaty ports. By September, Edward King could report to the State Department that "the American trade in China is placed on the same footing as that of any other foreign nation."[43] Clearly, the Americans had achieved a considerable triumph.

Historians have long debated whether this represented the beginning of the Open Door in China and the extent to which Lawrence Kearny can be given credit for the achievement. Certainly, a complex mixture of factors accounted for the ultimate Chinese decision to extend commercial equality to the United States. There is no question, however, that Kearny's activities in China in 1842–1843 represented a significant expansion of the peacetime role of the East India Squadron.[44] The uncertain situation in China and the needs of the American merchant community in China demonstrated the necessity of continuous American naval presence in the East Indies and frequent appearances at Canton. But Kearny went far beyond protecting lawful American commerce by showing the flag, going through the motions of combatting opium smuggling, and facilitating the settlement of American claims. As commander of a small squadron, he proved to be an officer of exceptional judgment as he used the prestige and power of his naval position to expand American commercial opportunities. In the absence of effective diplomatic representation, Kearny assumed an aggressive diplomatic role after the Treaty of Nanking was signed. Although he did not reflect on the peacetime role of the navy in the republic's commercial empire, Kearny clearly understood and embraced the use of the navy to expand commercial opportunity. The fact that his instructions had not anticipated or authorized such a role demonstrated the fact that the navy's expanding role in the development of the American commercial empire could not be tightly controlled by officials in Washington, D.C. Fortunately for Kearny his role was both understood and appreciated by the administration which came to power shortly after his instructions were drafted.

4.

Abel P. Upshur and the Rejuvenation of the Navy

With a small commerce, a small Navy was required; but now, with a commerce full-fledged, spreading her wings on every sea and sailing before every breeze on the ocean, a larger Navy with a new organization is loudly called for.

Lieutenant Matthew F. Maury,
"Scraps from the Lucky Bag," 1840

Although the election of 1840 presaged better times for the navy, the Whig victory did not promise to transform the navy's existing peacetime diplomatic role. The navy had not been an issue in 1840, and Whig attention after the election centered on national economic policy. Neither the inaugural message of William H. Harrison in March, 1841, nor that of his successor, John Tyler, barely a month later had mentioned the need for a larger or more active peacetime navy. In fact, Tyler was a state rights Whig, Virginia planter, and ex-Jacksonian Democrat who believed in strict government economy and a limited role for the federal government. The new Secretary of the Navy, George Badger, was also an ex-Jacksonian from North Carolina with no record of interest or experience in naval affairs. And the presence of an influential, pro-navy, commercial faction from the upper Atlantic seaboard in the Whig Party did not create immediate presssure from party leaders for naval expansion.

However, the international situation had a direct impact on the nation's naval policy in the spring and summer of 1841 as a series of unresolved issues increased Anglo-American tension. The Northeastern border dispute remained unresolved, and the pending trial of Alexander McLeod in New York for his role in the 1837 *Caroline* affair promised to inflame sentiment in the United States, Canada, and England. War seemed not only possible but imminent to some observers in the

United States. In the face of such a prospect, it became apparent that the U.S. coastline was extremely vulnerable to British naval action. In addition to being greatly outnumbered by the British Navy, available American warships were dispersed over several distant stations in the Mediterranean, the Atlantic, and the Pacific. The British, on the other hand, could readily concentrate large numbers of warships close to the United States at naval stations in the British West Indies. The British Navy also contained a number of new shallow draft, steam warships that would make it possible to penetrate the numerous shallow bays, inlets, and rivers which dotted the American coastline with virtual impunity from a tiny American Navy dependent entirely on sail power.

In response to this situation, Secretary of the Navy Badger recommended that the existing West Indies Squadron be increased, that a separate Home Squadron be created, and that at least two steam warships be constructed for coastal defense. In the House of Representatives, the Committee on Naval Affairs supported the request for a Home Squadron in a report drafted by Thomas Butler King, a state rights Whig from Georgia. The report noted the woeful condition of American coastal fortifications and acknowledged the rapid changes which the "introduction of steam power" had already effected in the "naval armaments of the maritime powers of Europe." In the event of war with Great Britain, the enemy's steam warships would seize American merchants' ships along the coast, insult the republic's flag, and endanger the entire American coastline. Particularly vulnerable was the southern coastline where "not a fort, from Charleston to Mobile, [was] in a condition to fire a gun." Here a fleet of enemy steamships "loaded with black troops from the West Indies" could "annoy and plunder the country." Accordingly, the committee endorsed Secretary Badger's recommendation for funds to create a Home Squadron and further recommended that the Secretary inquire into the expediency of establishing a line of private American merchant steamers which could be converted to military vessels during a war. After a brief debate, the House passed the measure by a vote of 184 to 8 and the Senate without either a debate or a recorded vote.[1]

Although primarily a national defense measure, the creation of the Home Squadron marked a significant shift in southern attitudes on the navy. Traditionally, the great majority of politicians south of the Chesapeake had been either indifferent or hostile to the need for a strong peacetime navy. The lack of many large harbors or deep rivers providing access into the interior of the south accorded a sense of security. In addition, the control of the nation's overseas commerce by northeastern merchants had long rendered the peacetime navy a sectional concern to the upper Atlantic seaboard. The war scare with England, however, began to change southern indifference to the navy. Rising southern fears over the slavery issue and the realization that the South was vulnerable to attack by English steamships combined to create anxiety over the prospect of war with England. In his report King noted that the British had given orders to increase the number of black troops in the British West Indies from 10,000 to 25,000. "These troops are disciplined and commanded by white officers, and, no doubt, designed to form a most important portion of the force to be employed in any future contest that may arise between Great Britain and the United States. . . . '' As one southerner put the fear directly, Great Britain could ''throw her black regiments from Jamaica into the Southern Country, and . . . proclaim freedom to the slaves.''[2]

The strength of the navy, then, was of immediate concern to the South. One indication of this concern is reflected in the fact that nine of the twelve Secretaries of the Navy from 1841 to 1861 came from slave states. In the previous twenty years only one of six Secretaries of the Navy had come from a southern state. Although concern over southern vulnerability did not convert a majority of southern politicians, it did provide additional support for naval expansion and create additional sympathy for the navy in a section which had heretofore consistently denied the need for a strong peacetime navy. During the Tyler Administration this change in attitude was reflected in the fact that southern state rights Whigs such as Badger, King, Tyler, and Abel Upshur spearheaded the movement to reform and modernize the navy.

Within several months of Harrison's death, President Tyler found himself in severe political difficulty. Unable to cooperate with a domineering Henry Clay and the Whig majority which the Kentucky Senator controlled in the House and Senate, Tyler vetoed a bill creating a new national bank in August and a revised version of that bill in September. The second veto led to an irreparable split between Tyler and the Whig Party and resulted in the resignation of all but one member of the cabinet on September 11, 1841. Only Daniel Webster remained as Secretary of State in an attempt to resolve the complicated and troublesome difficulties which threatened war with England. Unlike the previous Cabinet which had been dominated by Clay partisans, Tyler's new Cabinet reflected his own state rights attitudes and his hatred of Clay.

Ironically, the cause of naval reform and naval expansion benefited immensely from the cabinet shake up. After navy officer Robert F. Stockton declined the position, the President selected his longtime friend and political ally, Abel P. Upshur, as Secretary of the Navy. The fifty-one-year-old Upshur was a Virginia planter, state justice, state rights politician, and outspoken southern apologist with no experience in naval affairs. Understandably, Tyler's appointment of a political crony brought a barrage of disdainful criticism from the Whig press. Only a few journals such as *The Army and Navy Chronicle* and the *Southern Literary Messenger* approved the appointment and urged the new Secretary to initiate changes. ''Never was there a time, when this department has more abounded, than it now does, with abuses, nor when it stood more in need of reform. . . . There is no department which has been so miserably mismanaged, or so much abused as the Navy,'' observed the *Messenger*.[3]

In fact Upshur proved to be an able administrator committed to a comprehensive program of reform. The fact that his brother George had been a career naval officer for two decades made Upshur sensitive to the neglected state of the navy and the need for drastic changes. He began by working long hours during the autumn of 1841 to remove the massive backlog of work in the department and to impose some semblance of efficiency on the department's administrative "mess." During November he consulted with his brother George, Marine Colonel Archibald Henderson, Captain Beverley Kennon, Captain Charles Stewart, Captain Thomas ap Catesby Jones, Lieutenant Matthew Fontaine Maury, and numerous junior officers interested in naval reform.[4]

Upshur was also familiar with Maury's influential series of articles entitled "Scraps from the Lucky Bag," which appeared in the *Southern Literary Messenger* in 1840 and 1841.[5] In spite of his use of the pseudonym "Harry Bluff," Maury's authorship was well known, and the articles were widely read and reprinted. By 1841 a movement was even afoot to have the thirty-five-year-old proponent of naval reform resign his commission and become Secretary of the Navy. In "Scraps from the Lucky Bag," Maury spoke for many junior naval officers in arguing the need for comprehensive naval reform. In addition to an improved rank and promotion system, the navy needed better training and education, a more efficient system of ship construction, technological innovations, and a restructured organization in which separate bureaus would replace the Board of Navy Commissioners.[6]

None of these recommendations was new in the early 1840's. These and other suggestions had appeared periodically in the annual reports of Naval Secretaries for years. What Maury had done in his articles was to restate the case for naval reform in a comprehensive manner from the first-hand perspective of an experienced and knowledgeable naval officer. Maury also placed his recommendations in a broad national context by arguing that the nation's vital overseas economic interests required an efficient modern navy. "The maintenance of a Navy is no longer a matter of doubtful expediency," asserted Maury in his initial article, "With a small commerce, a small Navy was required; but now, with a commerce full-fledged, spreading her wings on every sea and sailing before every breeze on the ocean, a larger Navy with a new organization is loudly called for." Currently, a force of only 600 guns afloat was charged with the protection of one million tons of shipping manned by 100,000 seamen and valued at over $400 million. "Never since the war," noted Maury, "has the force afloat been so disproportionate to the commerce of the country. And never have the calls for a large Naval force been more urgent, [as] State after State has been added to the Confederacy; population has been multiplied; resources developed and commerce increased. . . . "[7] American commercial interests stretched from "the Cape of Good Hope to Cape Horn—from the North West coast to New Holland—from America to China and Japan—from the Eastern to the Western Hemisphere—and almost from the Arctic to the Antarctic Circle." Of particular concern to Maury was the Pacific Basin where an extraordinary empire awaited development by the "commercial and enterprising people" who inhabited North America. From the Columbia River lay the rich markets of Spanish America, Asiatic Russia, China, New Holland, Polynesia, and "all the groups and clusters of islands that stud the ocean, from Cape Horn to the Cape of Good Hope, from Asia to America."[8]

As a southerner interested in commercial activity, Maury stressed the importance of foreign trade to all Americans. It was the republic's vast overseas commerce "which diffuses health and vigor through this happy republic; which exempts you and every citizen . . . from direct taxation—filling the treasury with revenue; supplying the wants of the government; ministering to the comforts as well as to the necessities of every member of society, from the seaboard to the Rocky Mountains—from St. John's and the Lakes to the Gulf of Mexico and the Sabine." Accordingly, "every citizen is directly concerned, that ample protection should be afforded to that commerce," reminded Maury, "in a time of profound peace, its channels should be unmolested—kept free and open to the American flag; and that flag should, in all seas, and in every port, enjoy all the immunities and privileges of the most favored."[9]

As Secretary of the Navy, Upshur embraced Maury's concept of the peacetime navy as the ever present protector of the republic's burgeoning maritime empire. In his annual report of December 4, 1841, Upshur presented a comprehensive program of reform, expansion, and modernization. The report recommended a new code of rules and regulations, a bureau system of organization for the department to replace the Board of Commissioners, and three new officer ranks at the level of Admiral to improve the existing promotion system. Upshur also detailed ways to improve the training and education of officers and urged the creation of an engineering corps to run new steam warships. In addition, the Secretary recommended the creation of a depot for charts and nautical instruments and the construction of various navy facilities on the Atlantic and Gulf coasts as well as on the Pacific coast and in the Sandwich Islands.[10]

The effective size of the navy also needed to be increased rapidly, argued Upshur, by enlarging the Marine Corps, placing more existing ships in commission, and constructing new naval vessels. Although Upshur believed that the proper size for the American Navy was one-half the size of the English Navy, he recognized that this goal was unrealistic and instead proposed the immediate construction of a "large number" of first class frigates as well as ten smaller warships. Upshur also wanted to build one large steam warship, but thought it useless to construct more because they were still in the experimental stage. Instead, the federal government should assist private companies by constructing steam packet ships which could be converted to warships in the event of war.

The Secretary acknowledged that development of an "efficient navy" would require a "very great expense," but argued that extraordinary expenditures in a time of economic depression were required by the need to defend the nation and protect its overseas commerce. He warned that European warships of light draft could now "invade us at almost any point of our extended coast . . . penetrate the interior through our shallow rivers, and thus expose half our country to hostile attacks." Since such assaults would invariably array the "hostile elements of our social system against one another,'' the effect of such warfare ''in the southern portion of our country . . . probably would be disastrous in the extreme.'' The ''single question,'' then, was whether we shall ''meet the enemy upon the ocean . . . or suffer him to land upon our shores. . . .''[11]

At the same time, the nation's valuable overseas commerce required the navy to expand as rapidly ''as the means at its disposal will admit.'' Already the United States stood ''far behind all the considerable nations of the world'' in protecting its commerce. England with a foreign tonnage much less than twice that of the United States had eight times as many warships; France with a foreign tonnage only one-third that of the United States had more than five times as many warships. ''Trade is never secure unless it can, at all times and in all places, appeal for support to the national flag,'' emphasized Upshur, ''and it ought to feel that it is safe wherever that flag is displayed.'' In addition, the presence of an adequate naval force to promptly redress injuries to commerce was one of the ''best means of preventing'' disputes between rival commercial nations. American commerce seemed especially vulnerable in the Pacific where a squadron of just three sloops and one schooner was responsible for protecting American interests in the vast area. With a $40 million whaling interest in the Pacific, American trading concerns spread throughout the Pacific Basin, and American settlers moving into the unsettled Pacific coast, the American squadron there needed to be doubled to provide any measure of reasonable protection.[12]

In his brief for commercial protection, Upshur stressed the importance of these interests to the entire republic. ''The farmer, the planter, the mechanic, the manufacturer, and even the day laborer, depends in a greater or less degree, upon this for the success of his own peculiar branch of industry; and even the fine arts themselves are not exempt.'' According to Upshur, ''commerce may be regarded as our principal interest, because, to a great extent, it includes within it every other interest.'' Virtually every American, then, had a direct and vital stake in the strength of the navy and the security of American commercial enterprises being conducted thousands of miles from the United States in remote corners of the globe. Admittedly, an ''efficient navy'' could not be built and maintained without ''very great expense,'' but Upshur reminded Congress that the cost ''is more than repaid, even in time of peace, by the services which such a navy can render.''[13]

Unlike the usual annual reports of federal department heads, Upshur's report received widespread attention and evoked a strong positive response. Editors who had scorned Upshur's appointment less than three months earlier now praised the vision, statesmanship, and competence of the new Secretary.[14] In Congress reaction was less positive and the prospect for extensive naval expansion complicated by several factors. First, the danger of war with England had abated after the government in England headed by Sir Robert Peel replaced that of Lord Melbourne in September, 1841. Second, the U.S. economy continued to stagnate, and the federal debt reached the alarming level of $13,594,000 by the end of 1841.[15] At the same time, federal receipts for 1841 had declined and a precipitous drop in tariff duties was predicted for 1842. Third, resentment and bitterness continued to run high as the administration and the Whig majority in Congress battled over the need for a higher tariff and the wisdom of distributing proceeds from the sale of public lands to the individual states in a time of economic emergency.

Finally, the Secretary of the Navy became embroiled in sectional animosities when he was accused in the House on January 17, 1842, of being "an open, avowed, undisguised advocate of the immediate dissolution of the Union" by John Minor Botts, a Clay Whig from Virginia. In the month-long controversy that ensued, Upshur responded effectively to Botts' charges of disunion, but the widely publicized incident did nothing to help the Secretary's naval program. In addition, a number of anti-slavery politicians led by John Quincy Adams charged the Tyler Administration with using the navy as an arm of southern sectional policy, presumably to provoke war with Mexico and facilitate the annexation of Texas.[16]

Given traditional congressional attitudes toward the navy, Upshur's expansive program would have faced difficulty under any circumstances, but it was now drawn into a maelstrom of personal, sectional, and partisan tension. Once introduced, Upshur's recommendations won quick but misleading endorsement from the naval committees in the House and Senate. These committees were comprised of sympathetic politicians from maritime states and their recommendations did not reflect accurately the sentiments of the whole Congress. Debate itself centered on the bill to increase naval expenditures and evoked sharp opposition to a rapid increase in the navy. A succession of Democrats and Whigs argued that an expanded navy was unnecessary because the threat of war with England had passed. Opponents noted the federal deficit and expected decline in revenue to emphasize that the nation could not afford a large peacetime military establishment. Citing well-known inefficiency in the navy, critics contended that additional funds were hardly necessary when the navy wasted the money it had, took existing ships out of commission, and left many officers on shore without duty for long periods of time. More alarming to Georgia Democrat Mark A. Cooper was the threat posed by a large peacetime military to the nation's "republican simplicity, if not . . . to our very existence as a free people." Such a military establishment was "oppressive and dangerous" in a republic, charged Joseph Fornance of Pennsylvania, and "might be used by some aspiring chieftan to forward his ambitious views. . . . Liberty could not live where bayonets bristle in time of peace."[17]

Local interests also surfaced continually in the debate. Western congressmen questioned the need for a larger navy to protect overseas commerce when the nation could not afford more urgently needed internal improvements in the West. Also at issue was the relative merit and efficiency of navy yards at Brooklyn, Norfolk, and Philadelphia as well as the lack of a large naval yard in the Gulf at Pensacola. More debilitating was the "spectre of abolition" raised by charges that the Tyler Administration was pursuing a policy of sectional favoritism in packing the navy's officer ranks with a disproportionate number of midshipmen from the South. When a succession of speakers felt compelled to substantiate or refute these charges, sectional interest pervaded the entire discussion.[18]

Lost amidst the charges and countercharges was an opportunity for substantive debate on what the peacetime navy's approximate size and peacetime commercial role should be. Although the navy had protected commerce for decades the dramatic growth of the American economic activity abroad dictated a serious reevaluation of the navy's commercial role. Individuals such as Henry A. Wise of Virginia, William C. Preston of South Carolina, Caleb Cushing of Massachusetts, Charles Ingersoll of Pennsylvania, and Richard Bayard of Delaware attempted to emphasize that issue, but their arguments were overwhelmed by more parochial considerations. Most critics of naval expansion who mentioned the issue simply rejected out of hand the idea that a larger and more active navy was required to defend the nation's maritime commerce. Opponents argued that the navy had enough money, ships, and men to supply adequate protection, provided that existing resources were used efficiently. Even former Secretary of the Navy Levi Woodbury, an architect of Jackson's commercial diplomacy in the Far East, questioned the need for increased expenditures.[19]

Although they constituted a distinct minority in their section, a number of southerners reflected their section's increased concern by supporting naval expansion and emphasizing the importance of the navy to the economic prosperity of the South and the Mississippi Valley. The lack of adequate naval protection in the Gulf, noted Henry Wise of Virginia, most seriously endangered the "cotton and tobacco of the South and West." Endorsing the need for a large navy yard on the Gulf, Louisiana Senator Alexander Barrow emphasized that naval expansion here was "not a local question; the whole valley of the Mississippi is interested—so are the Northern and Middle sections of the country." After all, a blow struck at New Orleans would be felt by the "whole commercial range of the Union." Disdaining all the "buggermugger about a declining treasury," South Carolina Senator William Preston endorsed Upshur's plan of building "up a navy commensurate with the increase of commerce. It is our glory and our strength, and it is our duty to protect it."[20]

Eventually the 2nd session of the 27th Congress acted more favorably on the navy program than national economic conditions and the tone of the debate indicated it might. Congress authorized preparation of a new navy code of rules and regulations and approved the reorganization of the Navy Department. The measure increased the staff of the Department and replaced the Board of Navy Commissioners with five bureaus, each to be administered by a navy captain responsible to the Secretary. Congress approved Upshur's request for a large increase in appropriations and authorized the expenditure of more than $6,588,894, including $2,000,000 for the increase and repair of warships. Combined with the special appropriations of $250,000 and an existing surplus of $742,000 from 1841, the total was the largest ever made for the navy in peacetime prior to 1842. In fact, the navy spent $8,397,000 in fiscal 1842, or approximately 33 percent of total federal expenditures for the year.[21] Congress also provided funds for the Depot of Charts and Instruments and authorized creation of a Naval Observatory, but Upshur's other recommendations fared worse. A bill to create the additional ranks of Admiral, Vice Admiral, and Rear Admiral never reached the House floor. The bill to increase the Marine Corps by 246 officers and 2,365 enlisted men did not pass either house. The idea of establishing a naval school drew such sharp criticism that it was not presented to Congress in legislative form. Although Upshur was disappointed with congressional treatment of his program, the Navy Department had actually done very well in a time of financial stringency, sectional tension, and partisan resentment.

In his annual report of December, 1842, Upshur renewed his campaign by requesting approval for those naval proposals which the previous session of Congress had defeated or tabled. Internal reform, modernization, and expansion were again the themes of Upshur's program. In regard to naval construction, Upshur now recognized the futility of seeking approval for additional frigates so he concentrated on authorization for smaller warships and additional funds to maintain a more active duty for existing ships. Specifically, he sought to place more ships in commission and have them spend more time at sea than they had previously. The constant activity would enhance the training, discipline, and experience of both sailors and officers while constantly displaying the American flag along the far-flung "tracks of our commerce."[22]

As he had in 1841, Upshur attempted to refute naval critics by emphasizing the direct economic benefits rendered by the navy and stressing the need for increased protection to American commerce. During the Opium War in China, a two-ship squadron had done "all that could have been expected," but it was "owing more to good fortune than to our strength, that our commerce has suffered no major interruption" there. On the African coast the United States had no squadron to discharge its treaty obligations with Great Britain in suppressing the slave trade. In addition, a "rapidly increasing" American commerce there was unprotected, with the result that several American vessels "have been captured by the natives, and their crews barbarously murdered." In the Pacific a squadron of five or six vessels could not "protect our commerce and people, along a coast of three thousand miles in extent, and throughout an ocean four thousand miles wide." Even in the Mediterranean, where conditions remained peaceful, the intervention of the navy had been required in Morocco to maintain respect for the American flag by securing redress for an outrage against the American consul.[23]

Although Morocco, West Africa, the East Indies, and the Pacific seemed far removed from the United States, Upshur argued that "there is a local and particular interest in nine-tenths of our country, which demands a respectable naval establishment." The "various agricultural and manufacturing classes scattered throughout the country, and connected with and dependent upon this trade, have an indirect interest not less apparent" than the commercial centers of the seaboard. In addition to the whaling and economic interests of the Pacific, the economic prosperity of the Great Lakes and the invaluable trade of the Gulf were vitally involved. Upshur estimated that "not less than two-thirds of the entire commerce of our country, exclusive of the whale fisheries, passes through the Gulf of Mexico." Furthermore, virtually all of this trade was forced by the predominant winds and currents of the region to go through the Gulf of Florida, a "narrow strait" which could be blockaded by two "active, steam-frigates." The fact that the "greatest portion of our commerce" could be "annihilated" by an enemy having command of that area made the subject "of a deep and daily increasing interest." "Is, or is not, their commerce worth the cost of a naval power adequate to protect it?"[24]

Upshur emphasized that naval expansion would stimulate, not drain, the economy. For example, establishment of a navy yard in the lower Mississippi Valley would create a ready market for western iron, hemp, and other commodities: "Every branch of western industry would feel, directly or indirectly, the influence of such an establishment. . . . " More important, the "wealth of a nation did not consist in the quantity of gold . . . in its treasury. . . . It is rich only in proportion as its people are rich. . . . Nine-tenths of the appropriations to the navy are paid back to our own people for materials, labor, and subsistence. It is thus *put into circulation*, paying debts, supplying wants, and sustaining credit." Naval appropriations, then, helped stimulate the economy rather than impose a "dead tax upon the treasury." "Every dollar thus employed increases the *tax-paying ability* of the people to twice that amount; and this tax-paying ability is the true wealth of the nation." In addition to creating demand for American copper, iron, hemp, coal, and food, naval appropriations provided "employment to industry, encouragement to enterprise, and patronage to genius."[25]

For an era in which a federal deficit was abhorred and limited federal expenditures extolled as articles in the republican creed, Upshur's arguments were thoughtful and farsighted but they had little direct impact on existing attitudes in Congress. Upshur's report again received wide publicity and considerable praise, but Congress remained unmoved. Given the signing of the Webster-Ashburton Treaty in 1842 and the continuing depressed economy, there seemed less reason than a year before to increase naval expenditures. Even such friends of the navy as John Quincy Adams rejected the need for increasing the size of the naval force overseas in a time of fiscal stringency. Nor was Upshur's vision of the peacetime navy accepted. The Secretary, said Representative Samuel Gordon of New York, should "get some of these large ideas of a grand and magnificent navy out of his head, and come down to what a democratic navy should be."[26]

In the end Upshur was fortunate to avoid substantial cuts in the navy budget by the 3rd session of the 27th Congress. Asserting that "nine-tenths of the evils under which our navy was suffering, resulted from the high salaries paid to its officers," James A. Meriwether of Georgia proposed a 20 percent reduction in those salaries. Although defeated in the House by a narrow 82 to 74 margin, Meriwether's motion set the tone for the debate by unleashing calls for retrenchment.[27] The naval appropriation bill eventually provided approximately the same level of financing as in 1842, but further increases were out of the question.

In spite of his failure to convert a majority in Congress to his blueprint for a modern navy, Upshur made considerable progress toward his goals with the resources at hand. The appropriations for 1842 and 1843 combined with an existing balance from 1841 permitted Upshur substantial latitude in building new ships, remodeling existing ones, and initiating various technological experiments. He was able to have four frigates completed and six sloops of war begun. In addition, the iron hulled warship *Michigan* was finished, the ironclad *Stevens Battery* begun, and the steamer *Princeton* constructed. The *Princeton* was particularly noteworthy because it was the first screw driven warship in the world and carried two large modern guns in addition to its twenty-four conventional cannons. As a result of new construction and the recommissioning of existing warships, the number of vessels in service increased dramatically during Upshur's brief tenure. In December, 1841, Upshur reported a total of nineteen vessels on duty in the Mediterranean, the Atlantic, the Caribbean, the Pacific, and the East Indies (not including the ships attached to the United States Exploring Expedition). Just two years later the annual report of Upshur's successor listed thirty-eight vessels on active duty overseas.[28]

The abolition of the Board of Navy Commissioners in the Department removed a serious obstacle to technological progress and permitted Upshur and reform-minded officers to experiment with iron hulls, steam power, and explosive shells and to create an engineering corps in the navy. In addition, Upshur's appointment of Lieutenant Matthew F. Maury as head of the navy Depot of Charts and Instruments in 1842 and Maury's subsequent appointment as Superintendent of the Naval Observatory in 1844 proved to be of immense significance to the navy's growing commercial role. A stagecoach accident in 1839 had left Maury lame and ruined the young officer's dreams of a career at sea. Instead, the Virginian devoted his considerable energy and talents to the subjects of naval reform, scientific inquiry, and maritime commercial expansion. In addition to his well-known writings on naval reform, Maury was an avid student of navigation, hydrography, and meteorology and was interested in assisting the growth of American commerce overseas. Of particular concern to Maury was the need for the South to recognize and develop its own commercial potential as a center of trade rather than forfeit that position to the cities of the northeast. In 1839, Maury had written an article for the *Southern Literary Messenger* in which he urged the South to use the natural advantages and shorter distance to Europe offered by the great circle routes across the Atlantic in order to capture a share of trans-Atlantic trade.[29] These varied interests combined to make Maury a perfect choice for the position because he understood how scientific activity could be used by the navy to enhance its stature and facilitate the nation's commercial growth.

In the Depot of Charts and Instruments Maury immediately addressed the lack of accurate ocean charts for American naval vessels. Since the navy did not have its own charts for many areas, American commanders often had to rely on foreign charts for sailing instructions. The absence of charts also slowed American merchant ships and added to the difficulties faced by American whalers in remote regions. Maury and several assistants began by cataloguing the information of currents and winds contained in the log books from hundreds of individual naval voyages. By 1843 he had devised a plan to collect additional information by having naval officers record detailed observations daily during their voyages. He intended to use this information to produce a chart which would supply navy officers and civilian mariners with specific information on prevailing winds and currents for any given day and any given place during their cruises. Sea captains would then be advised of the average winds and currents their ships were likely to encounter in a certain season in a specific place and thereby permit them to alter their course to increase the speed and safety of each voyage. Although he met initial resistance from various sources and the charts were difficult and time consuming to produce, they proved to be of immense benefit to navy captains, merchant seamen, and whalers.[30]

Ironically, Secretary Upshur ignored an event of great potential value to the navy's peacetime stature when he refused to capitalize on the return of the United States Exploring Expedition in June, 1842. After it finally departed in August, 1838, the so-called Wilkes Expedition achieved prodigious results under difficult conditions during the next four years. In the South Pacific the expedition conducted extensive surveys of the islands, reefs, and harbors in the Tuamotu, Society, and Fiji Island groups. In the Fijis alone, the explorers charted 154 islands and 50 reefs. At each point Wilkes compiled information on the commercial potential of the various islands and harbors. At the same time, he attempted to enhance respect for the United States and protect American commercial activity in the vast region. In Samoa and the Fijis he negotiated commercial regulations with local authorities and appointed consular officials. Whenever he learned of infringements on American trade or attacks on American whalers or seamen, he attempted to investigate and punish those responsible. In the Fijis in 1840, when natives attacked an American surveying party and killed two of his men, Wilkes attacked two nearby villages, killed dozens of natives, burned the villages, and demanded complete surrender from local authorities. The expedition also visited New Zealand and Australia and sailed extensively in the Antarctic Ocean where Wilkes claimed several positive sightings of the Antarctic Continent between December, 1839 and March, 1840.

From the South Pacific, the expedition sailed to the Sandwich Islands where Wilkes collected more geographic and commercial information, took more surveys, and investigated the state of American commerce in the islands. Then the expedition explored the coast of North America from the Oregon Country to San Francisco Bay in 1841. During this time, Wilkes surveyed Puget Sound, the Oregon Coast, the lower reaches of the Columbia and Willamette rivers, northern California, and San Francisco Bay. Wilkes also dispatched shore parties to explore the interior of the Oregon Country and northern California. Finally, the expedition sailed back across the Pacific and returned home via the East Indies, the Indian Ocean, and the Cape of Good Hope. Along the way more surveys were made and a commercial treaty signed with the ruler of the Sulu Island group. At each point on the four-year voyage, civilian scientists joined the naval explorers in the collection and classification of a huge amount of scientific data and natural specimens for later study and display in the United States.[31]

When he returned to the United States, however, Wilkes and his crew were not received as national heroes. Instead, they met indifference and even hostility except for the praise they received from some newspapers. In Washington a resolution of commendation failed in the House, and the Senate defeated a resolution to have Wilkes and his officers appear. At the Navy Department Wilkes experienced a cool reception and was virtually ignored at a White House reception. Several reasons explain such a peculiar greeting for men who had achieved so much in an era of intense national pride. Controversy surrounding the preparation of the expedition created extensive criticism and resentment toward Wilkes and his officers before they ever departed. Wilkes' appointment as commander was galling to a number of officers who had more seniority than Wilkes and believed that he was unqualified for the position. The voyage itself was plagued by dissension and morale problems. Although able, Wilkes imposed a form of discipline which many of his crew found high handed and excessive. In addition, a number of his crew even disputed his sighting of Antarctica. After returning, Wilkes filed charges against several members of his crew who in turn filed charges against him. In the subsequent court-martial proceedings, the court found Wilkes guilty of seventeen instances of illegal punishment and sentenced him to a public reprimand. Moreover, the Exploring Expedition was the project of a Democratic administration and Wilkes returned to an intensely partisan atmosphere in which a Whig Congress battled an outcast Whig President.[32]

Divided as they were, neither the administration nor the Whig majority in Congress embraced Wilkes, and he found his only real strong advocate in Democrat Benjamin Tappan. The Ohio Senator was an amateur conchologist who had taken a personal interest in the expedition and was persuaded by Wilkes to take his side against the administration. As Chairman of the relatively unimportant Joint Committee on the Library of Congress, Tappan became instrumental in the authorization of funds to preserve the expedition's specimens and to publish its extensive findings. Finally, the naval officers who originally had been so critical of the Wilkes appointment and the way in which the expedition was prepared had not put their bitterness aside, and some, like Matthew F. Maury, were in positions of considerable influence in the Department. The result, then, was a lost opportunity for Upshur and the navy to use the extraordinary achievements of the Exploring Expedition to demonstrate the tangible commercial value of the peacetime navy.

Although largely unappreciated and unacknowledged at the time, the Exploring Expedition set an important example which some of Wilkes' sharpest critics later followed as they pressed for other naval exploring projects. In spite of the jealousies, bickering, and partisanship which surrounded the enterprise, the value of the Exploring Expedition soon became apparent. Wilkes' exploration of the Pacific Northwest coast demonstrated the immense importance of San Francisco Bay and Puget Sound to the United States while showing that the mouth of the Columbia River was unsatisfactory as a great potential harbor. The geographic and commercial information collected by the expedition at each stop also proved to be of practical value to the whalers and sea captains who sailed the Pacific. According to *Hunt's Merchants' Magazine* in 1845, the usefulness of this information more than repaid the cost of the expedition. In short, it was this much maligned exploring venture which would serve as a model in many ways for the Department's extensive exploring activities in the 1850's.[33]

On the operational level, Secretary Upshur asserted the navy's commercial role through the instructions he prepared for his commanders. Detailed and meticulous, Upshur's instructions emphasized that the primary peacetime role of the navy was the active protection of American commerce and citizens abroad. Although he admonished American officers to act with care and to observe the rights of other nations, Upshur emphasized that they should move decisively to protect lawful commerce, to redress individual wrongs, and to prevent future transgressions. Unlike previous Secretaries, Upshur urged constant activity for his officers to insure the widest possible protection and ordered the commanders of the Brazil and Mediterranean Squadrons in 1842 to exchange ships on a regular basis. "Our flag will better show the strength," he instructed Commodore Charles Morris of the Brazil Squadron, "by being displayed at as many places as possible." Where specific problems or difficulties existed, Upshur did not hesitate to specify the manner in which squadron commanders were to utilize their ships. In 1842, for example, he ordered Commodore Morris to dispatch one small vessel to St. Augustus Bay on Madagascar to protect American whalers there and then to send another small warship six months after the first. The caliber of Upshur's instructions is indicated by the fact that paragraphs and even whole letters were used intact again and again for years. Particularly noteworthy were the detailed orders he prepared for Commodore Matthew Perry as commander of the African Squadron in 1843. On the sensitive question of slave trade Upshur prepared instructions which passed the searching scrutiny of abolitionist John Quincy Adams and were used without alteration for more than a decade.[34]

Conditions on the navy's distant stations remained relatively stable during the Tyler Administration. As a result, individual commanders were not confronted with serious challenges or attacks on American commercial interests overseas nor did they have opportunities to extend American commercial interests through their own initiative and action. When incidents did occur, they were minor, the most noteworthy being the so-called *Sancala* Affair, in which the American government ultimately displayed moderation in asserting its rights. During the conflict between the Argentine and Uruguay, Commodore Daniel Turner of the

Brazil Squadron ordered Captain P. F. Voorhees of the frigate *Congress* to Montevideo with instructions to protect American commerce but to maintain a "strict and unqualified neutrality" while an Argentine blockade remained in effect. Since joining the navy in 1809 Voorhees had progressed steadily, been promoted to Captain in 1838, and received command of the *Congress* in 1842. But his strong convictions and willingness to act precipitously did not serve him or this mission well. On September 29, 1844, the Argentine armed schooner *Sancala* carelessly fired on the American merchant ship *Rosalba* while pursuing a fishing boat from Montevideo. After a brief investigation, Voorhees' forces seized the *Sancala* as well as other ships of the Argentine Squadron. Voorhees also released several captured fishing vessels held by the Argentine force and released a number of Montevidean prisoners and American seamen. Although he soon freed the other ships, Voorhees held the *Sancala* and her crew for displaying a false flag.[35]

Argentine officials demanded explanations and apologies, but the matter stood unresolved until Commodore Turner arrived in late October, informed the Argentine Commander that the United States would respect the blockade, and restored the *Sancala* to her commander in November. Although Turner did not disavow Voorhees' actions, Secretary of State John C. Calhoun conferred with the new Secretary of the Navy John Mason, expressed the regret of the U.S. government, and assured Argentine authorities that Voorhees would be disciplined. The subsequent court-martial, held in 1845, found Voorhees guilty of five separate charges in the affair, reprimanded him, and suspended him for three years.

In the Pacific, unexpected developments placed Commodore Lawrence Kearny in a difficult situation when he reached Honolulu on his return voyage to the United States from China in early July, 1843. In February, 1843, Lord George Paulet in command of the British warship *Carysfort* had seized provisional control of the islands from the King, replaced the Hawaiian flag with the British, and appointed a joint commission to rule. Described as a "young man of whose intellectual capacities little can be said" by U.S. Commercial Agent William Hooper, Paulet had acted to forestall a French takeover although he acted ostensibly to protect the claims of British citizens.[36] When Kearny arrived in Honolulu on July 5, he acted with restraint and avoided a confrontation with Paulet. After investigating and receiving information from Hooper, Kearny registered a formal protest with the King on July 11 and sent a copy of the document to Paulet. In his protest, he declared that the King and Lord Paulet will be held "answerable for any and every act by which a citizen of the United States . . . shall be restrained in his just and undisputed rights and privileges, or may suffer inconvenience or losses. . . . " Although Kearny was anxious to return to the United States, he agreed to remain in the islands in response to a petition on July 18th from a group of prominent American residents who pleaded for his protection. Fortunately, the incident soon ended with the arrival of British Rear Admiral Thomas who consulted with the King, refused to accept the provisional cession, and restored the islands to the King on July 31, 1843. Although Kearny had not effected the restoration, he had acted with characteristic good judgment and his restraint might well have avoided a confrontation with the impetuous Lord Paulet. Actually, Kearny's conduct, exemplary as it had been, carried no diplomatic significance because the British government formally disavowed the provisional cession in July, 1843, after the government learned of the action.[37]

Kearny had no way of knowing it, but his actions in Hawaii were consistent with the Tyler Administration's position on Hawaii. In December, 1842, a delegation from the Sandwich Islands had arrived in Washington and requested that the United States provide formal recognition of the independence and full sovereignty of the Hawaiian King, Kamehameha III. After discussing the matter President Tyler and Secretary of State Daniel Webster outlined a response known as the Tyler Doctrine. Because of the commercial and strategic position of the islands at the crossroads of the Pacific, Webster emphasized that the United States "are more interested in the fate of the islands, and of their government, than any other nation can be." At the same time, the administration claimed that the United States did not seek special privileges or exclusive control over the islands and would help sustain their independence, security, and prosperity. In his response to the Hawaiian delegation Webster emphasized that "no power ought either to take possession of the islands as a conquest, or for the purpose of colonization, and that no power ought to seek for any undue control over the existing Government, or any exclusive privileges or preferences in matters of commerce." In the event that any power pursued "any opposite policy" President Tyler promised "a decided remonstrance" by the United States. The Tyler Doctrine represented a well conceived American policy on the Hawaiian Islands. On the one hand, the policy reflected administration recognition of the great religious, commercial, and strategic interest in the islands. On the other hand, the policy demonstrated the administration's understanding that the United States had neither the inclination nor the power to take permanent control of the islands. But in any event, the islands would bear close scrutiny in the future and be designated as a standard point of call for American naval vessels in the Pacific.[38]

In the Far East, conditions after 1843 did not compel the navy to play the kind of role it had performed during the cruises of Commodores George Read and Lawrence Kearny. In December, 1842, President Tyler asked Congress to appoint a special commissioner to China to negotiate a formal commercial agreement after he learned of the Treaty of Nanking. When Congress approved in March, 1843, the administration first asked Edward Everett, the American minister to England, to serve as Commissioner. When he declined, Caleb Cushing from Massachusetts accepted the appointment.

To assist Cushing, the Navy Department dispatched a three-ship squadron under the command of Commodore Foxhall A. Parker. Although Parker was to visit certain ports and perform certain other routine duties, the Secretary informed Parker that the primary objective of his cruise was to assist Cushing and facilitate the diplomatic objectives of the State Department. After arriving at Macao in February, 1844, Cushing established his mission and initiated negotiations with the Chinese. Although Cushing planned to travel to Peking, deliver a letter from the President directly to the Emperor, and negotiate the treaty there, the Chinese demurred. The usual routine of Chinese delay and evasion followed before Cushing persuaded the Chinese to negotiate a formal treaty, but he was not permitted to deliver the President's letter to the Emperor nor to travel to Peking. Signed at the village of Wanghia, near Macao, on July 3, 1844, the treaty extended official commercial privileges to the United States by including fixed tariff duties for American goods and most-favored-nation status to the United States. Americans were to be permitted to trade and reside at the five treaty ports, extraterritorial rights were extended to include civil and criminal cases, and protection was to be extended to shipwrecked American sailors and vessels seeking refuge from storms. In effect, the treaty secured officially and expanded those privileges which Commodore Kearny had persuaded the Chinese to extend in 1842.[39]

While Cushing was occupied at Macao, the brig *Perry* sailed to Whampoa and dispatched a force of sixty men to assist the American factory at Canton. There a mob of Chinese had surrounded the American compound. When Americans tried to remove the Chinese by force, one of the Chinese was killed. Fortunately, American forces dispersed the mob and restored order. After completing his work, Cushing sailed for the United States in the *Perry* in late August, 1844. After cruising Chinese waters for several months without major incident, the other two ships of the squadron also departed for the United States by the end of 1844, thereby leaving the United States without a naval presence in Chinese waters for more than one year.

On the Africa station in 1843 attention centered on the troublesome and sensitive problem of policing the slave trade in cooperation with Great Britain under the terms of the Webster-Ashburton Treaty. However, inadequate naval protection had helped create a hostile environment for American trade along the west African coast where natives subjected legitimate American trade to constant danger and periodic attacks. In 1841, at the village of Little Berebee on the Ivory coast, the American schooner, *Mary Carver*, carrying a cargo valued at $12,000 had been captured and her crew murdered. Although Upshur had issued instructions in August, 1842, for Commander William Ramsey to obtain reparation, it was Commodore Matthew C. Perry who finally took action in December, 1843. Appointed to the Africa Squadron in March, 1843, Perry commanded four warships. In addition to his detailed instructions on the slave trade, Perry was ordered to provide "all the aid and support" which lawful American trade required: "it is the chief purpose, as well as the chief duty, of our naval power to see that these [commercial] rights are not improperly abridged, or invaded."[40]

By December, 1843, Perry had already touched at a number of points along the coast and taken steps to provide security for American commerce and black American colonists in Liberia. On December 13, 1843, Perry's entire squadron anchored off Little Berebee. Two hundred sailors and marines then landed and pitched a tent on the beach so that the American contingent would not have to enter the hostile village to hold a conference with the local ruler, King Ben Krako. At the meeting, King Krako, a man of great size and strength, was accompanied by several subordinates and an interpreter. In regard to the *Mary Carver* outrage, the King provided an explanation which Perry found preposterous, and a general melee ensued. The Americans killed the King and several natives in the scuffle and burned the village. The following day, Perry proceeded to Grand Berebee and held a conference with several other local chiefs, all of whom disclaimed any part in the *Mary Carver* attack and praised the killing of King Krako. Here local authorities signed a treaty which specified that natives in the area would not plunder trading ships or molest missionaries.[41]

In the Gulf of Mexico and on the west coast of North America, the Tyler Administration's interest in Texas, deteriorating relations with Mexico, and the intrigues of England and France in Mexico and California combined to create a pressing need for a stronger naval presence. As Secretary of the Navy, Upshur also played a significant role in the formulation and execution of the administration's foreign policy toward Mexico. As a long-time friend of the President and one of his few trustworthy political allies, Upshur held foreign policy views similar to Tyler's. Both men were strongly pro-southern in orientation, both sought the annexation of Texas, and both strongly suspected the abolitionist and territorial designs of Great Britain in North America. They assumed that England was maneuvering to keep Texas independent, to encourage the abolition of slavery there, and to induce Mexico to cede at least a portion of California to England.[42]

Within two months of joining the Tyler Administration, Upshur reflected his anxiety over California in the sailing instructions he prepared for Commodore Thomas ap Catesby Jones, the new commander of the Pacific Squadron. Noted for his determination and aggressiveness, Jones was a veteran of thirty-seven years in the navy and one of the officers Upshur had consulted during the fall of 1841 in formulating his plans for naval reform. From Upshur's point of view the fellow Virginian was an ideal man to place in an unsettled area of vital interest to the nation. Significantly, Jones would command seven ships on the Pacific station, the strongest force yet stationed there. In his instructions the Secretary reminded Jones that the "primary objects" of maintaining a naval force on the Pacific coast were the protection of commerce and the improvement of discipline among the officers and men of the squadron. In the event of any "outrage on our flag, or interruption of our commerce, or oppression of citizens of the United States," Jones was to afford "every aid, protection and security consistent with the law of nations. . . . " Noting the unsettled situation on the west coast, Upshur emphasized the need for constant naval activity, the importance of respecting the rights of other nations, and the necessity of maintaining strict neutrality in the event of war between two other nations. On the California coast increasing American commerce and the weakness of local authority "renders it proper . . . that occasional countenance and protection should be afforded to American enterprise in that quarter." At least one small warship should cruise the coast and the Gulf of California constantly to extend such protection and to collect pertinent geographic information "on the bays and harbors . . . [and] their conveniences as places of security, [and] their facilities for trade. . . . " In implementing his orders, Jones was to avoid exciting the jealousies or hostilities of other "powers having possessions or claims in that quarter."[43]

Upshur met privately with Jones several times before the Commodore sailed in January, 1842, on the frigate *United States*. Although the substance of their conversations is not known, the two men undoubtedly discussed California. When he departed Jones presumably understood that Anglo-American relations remained tense and that the British harbored designs on California. The Commodore also knew of his own government's desire to obtain part of upper California including San Francisco Bay, and he understood the deteriorating state of relations between the United States and Mexico. Not only had Mexico refused to settle the outstanding claims of American citizens, it had also refused to acknowledge Texas independence and threatened to renew hostilities. In addition, the bankrupt state of the Mexican treasury seemed to invite foreign intrigue and possibly the sale of upper California to England.[44]

Although relations with England improved during 1842, those with Mexico worsened as Mexico refused to conclude a claims settlement and renewed war on Texas. In response, Upshur strengthened the navy in the gulf by dispatching additional vessels and ordering commanders there to make sure that American commerce continued uninterrupted. Lieutenant Oscar Bullus, commander of the schooner *Boxer*, was ordered in March to cruise the coast from Pensacola to Yucatan "with a view to the protection of American interests. . . . " In June, 1842, Upshur ordered the new steam frigate *Mississippi* to the gulf and warned Captain William D. Salter to be prepared for war. The expected arrival of Mexican steamers from England presaged an attack on Galveston and would jeopardize American lives and property there. Although he was to observe his nation's neutrality and to observe a legal Mexican blockade, Salter should not respect "mere paper blockades" and "you will not yourself respect any such [blockade] should you be called in to protect the rights of our people trading with ports not guarded by an actual force. . . . " In September, 1842, after Mexican forces occupied San Antonio, a frigate and several schooners were dispatched to further strengthen American forces in the gulf.[45]

In the meantime Commodore Jones had arrived at Callao, Peru in May, 1842, and rendezvoused with other ships in his squadron. During the summer, he cruised between Callao and Valparaiso while receiving unconfirmed, but disturbing, rumors. He heard that the United States and Mexico were on the brink of war and that Mexico had sold, or was about to sell, California to Great Britain. Then on September 4, 1842, the entire British naval force at Callao sailed suddenly, allegedly under sealed orders from England. According to current rumors, the British fleet was headed for Panama where it would embark British troops from the West Indies and then occupy California. Jones reacted immediately and set sail for California. En route Jones prepared a long report to

Secretary Upshur explaining his actions on the basis of his initial instructions and the best possible information he had available. Jones dispatched the sloop *Dale* to Panama to forward the report to the Navy Department. While at sea, Jones prepared his men for the coming action by drilling them in gunnery and small arms fire. As he neared Monterey on October 18, 1842, the Commodore issued a general order stating that the American force must take California from the Mexican enemy, and then be prepared to hold it. Warning his men not to destroy property or harm the civilian population, he spoke of the need to reconcile the local citizens to American occupation.[46]

After he arrived off of Monterey, Jones attempted to determine whether in fact war existed between the United States and Mexico. Although unable to confirm a state of war, Jones collected information and observed activities on shore which led him to believe that war existed. Accordingly, on October 19th, he ordered an American force ashore to demand the surrender of California, and the following morning the Mexican authorities capitulated. American marines then took possession of the town, occupied the fort, raised the American flag, and fired the appropriate cannon salutes. Also seized were several Mexican government ships as prizes. Within a day of the occupation, however, various newspapers and private letters indicated that, as late as August 22nd, no war existed and rumors of a pending Mexican cession of California were incorrect. Jones now promptly reversed himself by striking the American flags which flew over the fort and the town, raising Mexican flags again, firing a salute from his warships, and retreating with his troops to the American vessels in the harbor.[47]

When news of the seizure reached Washington in January, 1843, the Tyler Administration apologized immediately to the Mexican minister and offered to compensate Mexico for any damages incurred. To congressional inquiries, the President forwarded a number of documents, but not Upshur's instructions to Jones on the ground that their publication would harm the national interest. To help mollify congressional critics who believed that the administration was intent on provoking war with Mexico to facilitate the annexation of Texas, Upshur permitted John Quincy Adams to read Jones' sailing instructions. Although Adams thought the orders were overly aggressive, he conceded that the Commodore had acted without authority.[48]

Significantly, Secretary Upshur argued he could not take action against Jones until all the facts in the case were known. Although he recalled Jones in March as commander of the Pacific Squadron, Upshur did not convene a board of inquiry. Moreover, when Jones finally did return to the United States, he was immediately given command of the ship-of-the-line *Ohio* and was later reassigned to command the Pacific Squadron in 1848. In fact, the mild treatment accorded Jones by the Navy Department accurately mirrored the administration's continuing anxiety over California. Upshur's response also reflected his own views about the forceful manner in which the navy should be employed to protect American commerce and rights on the west coast. Although he had to acknowledge that Jones had made a mistake in this instance, Upshur sympathized with the Commodore's reasoning and believed it imperative not to make an example of Jones to other enterprising naval officers who might be placed in similar situations overseas in the future.[49]

Although Upshur took care to avoid a recurrence of the Monterey incident in his sailing instructions to Jones' replacement, the Secretary emphasized the necessity of aggressively defending the nation's interest along the Pacific coast. Upshur now acknowledged that France or England might conceivably establish a settlement in California through an agreement with Mexico. The United States "could not witness such an occurrence without great concern, and they would not fail to take prompt measures upon the subject," but Commodore Dallas himself should "not attempt to prevent, by the interposition of force, settlements by other nations, which, for ought you can know to the contrary, may be authorized by the Mexican Government." Rather, Dallas was instructed to use "any lawful means" without further consultation with the Navy Department to secure a "Naval Depot upon some good harbour" along the west coast or in the Sandwich Islands.[50]

In the disputed Oregon Country, Upshur instructed Dallas to use his squadron aggressively to protect American commercial interests. Should England or any other nation attempt to take possession of the mouth of the Columbia River, the Commodore was instructed to make a "temperate yet firm representation" demanding that "no restriction whatever, shall be placed upon American citizens engaged in lawful pursuits. . . . " If that moderate approach failed, Dallas was to "distinctly announce your purpose to *enforce* the rights of your countrymen at every hazard." If any nation attempted to interrupt American commercial vessels there, "you will extend to them the most prompt and effectual protection in any mode which the circumstances of the case may require. In a word, you will assert for your country and countrymen, the perfect freedom of the Columbia River. . . . " Although he had been momentarily embarrassed by the Monterey incident, Upshur had every intention of utilizing the navy fully to assert American national interests and commercial rights on the west coast.[51]

In the spring of 1843 Upshur's contributions to the navy were cut short by the death of Acting Secretary of State Hugh S. Legaré and the appointment of Upshur as his replacement. In the remaining months before his death in the *Princeton* explosion in February, 1844, Upshur concentrated on the annexation of Texas. To replace him, Tyler selected David Henshaw, a Massachusetts Democrat, who served less than seven months before he was replaced in February, 1844, by Thomas Walker Gilmer and then John Mason, both Tyler supporters from Virginia. Although each man was competent, they lacked the superior ability, drive, and vision of Upshur and the momentum gained in the department was quickly lost.

Abel Usher had served less than two years and many of his recommendations were either defeated or ignored, but his tenure as Secretary of the Navy had a far-reaching impact on the peacetime navy. His internal reforms in the Department and the elimination of the Board of Navy Commissioners made further reforms much easier. His program of naval construction provided the basis for a more active navy around the world. His commitment to technological progress and experimentation prevented the navy from falling farther behind the navies of Europe. His attention to detail in the drafting of standing orders to his commanders helped to redefine the operational meaning of the protection of commerce and give that peacetime naval duty a much broader and more aggressive connotation. Finally, his strong vision of the navy as an active arm of American foreign policy and commercial expansion outlined a model for like-minded naval officers, government officials, and politicians to endorse and develop. In short, Upshur had done much to provide the vision and the naval resources which served as the foundation for increased commercial support by the navy during the 1850's.

5.

"A New Commercial Era"

Great as has been our progress in the past, there is a prophetic voice which tells us that we have but begun to enter upon that bright and glorious "empire of the seas" which is yet to be ours.

DeBow's Review,
"The Commercial Age," September, 1849

Between 1844 and the early 1850's different, and often conflicting, forces shaped American naval development. In the short term the navy languished, suffering from a lack of firm leadership, political support, and external demands on its services. As a result these years were not marked by a dramatic growth of the navy's peacetime commercial role. Naval activity on the overseas stations continued, but dramatic and substantial commercial achievements did not occur. At the same time, far-reaching developments were underway which would increase the need for an active peacetime navy and enhance its commercial role after 1850.

During the mid– and late–1840's the navy lacked either a President who used it as Jackson had or the type of pressures which demanded naval initiative as events in China had in the early 1840's. In the United States the drive for naval reform and expansion quickly lost momentum once Upshur's term as Secretary ended. Public indifference permitted traditional anti-navy attitudes to reemerge in Congress. Although more politicians, editors, and businessmen realized the need for an efficient modern navy, strong supporters of the peacetime navy remained a small minority. Neither the Whigs nor the Democrats in Congress placed the navy high on their lists of political priorities and many remained hostile. Nor did the administrations of James K. Polk, Zachary Taylor, or Millard Fillmore press for naval reform and expansion. Polk was a Tennessee Democrat who held traditional agrarian attitudes toward the navy and did not believe that a large navy was essential to implement his aggressive foreign policy. During the Oregon Crisis he did not press for immediate naval expansion, and, during the Mexican War, the administration used a piecemeal approach to address the need for a much larger navy. Presidents Taylor and Fillmore held more sympathetic attitudes toward the navy, but both were weak Presidents who did not seriously address the navy's problems or use its potential. Both of these Whig Presidents remained preoccupied with domestic political problems while pursuing a foreign policy that eschewed further expansion, avoided international confrontation, and sought to preserve American neutrality.

Overseas, the situation on the navy's several distant stations remained relatively quiet, and naval commanders were not forced to play critical diplomatic or commercial roles. In the Far East, the Mediterranean, South America, and Africa, sensitive political situations arose and individual incidents occurred, but these problems tended to be minor and did not have a significant impact on naval development. Nor were most naval officers instructed to play an aggressive commercial or diplomatic role in these years.

In spite of this situation American expansionism in the 1840's promised further expansion of the peacetime commercial role of the navy. The acquisition of Oregon and California created a long Pacific coastline, new strategic concerns, and additional economic interests, all of which had to be protected by the navy. In the Caribbean the movement to acquire Cuba, the need to establish an isthmian passage, and the desire to break British hegemony in Central America produced greater interest in the entire region. Along with the expansionism of the 1840's went a rising "gospel of commerce" which advocated aggressive American economic activity overseas as a means of guaranteeing the nation's prosperity while simultaneously spreading democracy, Christianity, and civilization to people around the globe. However, this territorial and commercial expansionism did not have a direct and immediate impact on the navy. It was not until the early 1850's that the nation's acquisition of new territory, determination to extend its political influence in the Western Hemisphere, and drive to expand its foreign trade in the Pacific produced a host of pressures for more naval support. And even then, these forces did not create a strong political movement to expand and modernize the navy. Instead, the nation's outward economic and diplomatic thrust gave rise to pressure on the Navy Department, Congress, and the President from special interests groups and lobbyists for specific naval projects.

Although the nation's territorial acquisitions of the 1840's were confined to North America, Manifest Destiny held long-term naval implications because it envisioned a commercial as well as a continental empire. In addition to the hunger for new land, a strong sense of providential mission, a presumption of racial and political superiority, and a desire to gain strategic security in North America, American expansionism manifested a drive to create a North American base for a worldwide commercial empire. Several factors combined in the early 1840's to produce this new version of expansionist ideology known as Manifest

Destiny. First, recent achievements had instilled a great sense of pride and confidence in the republic, and Americans looked impatiently to the day when all of North America would be theirs. Second, the rapid spread of the frontier and the dramatic population increases of the 1820's and the 1830's persuaded many Americans that they needed additional living space for future generations. Third, Anglo-American hostility and the reassertion of British power seemed to pose a renewed threat to the security and freedom of the republic. In spite of the Webster-Ashburton Treaty in 1842, many Democrats believed that England intended to take possession of Oregon and California as well as assert control over Texas, Central America, and the Caribbean. Fourth, the lingering economic depression convinced many politicians that territorial expansion was needed to open additional foreign markets for American agricultural surpluses. In the agricultural states of the West, slack demand and plummeting prices met the abundant harvests of the early 1840's. In 1842 and 1843 prices for cotton, wheat, wool, corn, beef, and hogs all reached new lows and the volume of agricultural exports suffered alarming declines. As they diagnosed their economic plight, western politicians concluded that their problems could not be solved permanently by a high tariff, a home market, or a change in government fiscal policy. Instead, the only real cure for low prices, overproduction, and intense competition was access to new overseas markets. Although American farmers depended heavily on European and Caribbean markets for their commodities, most politicians believed that the greatest guarantee of future prosperity lay in the Pacific with the fabled markets of China, Japan, India, and the East Indies.[1]

These factors combined with expansionist impulses and ideology to produce a rampant expansionism marked by arrogance, belligerence, and impatience. In addition to reaffirming the traditional concepts of geographic predestination, political superiority, and providential mission, Manifest Destiny reemphasized the vision of the United States as a great commercial and maritime as well as a territorial and continental empire. The immediate task was to reach the Pacific by adding all of Oregon, upper California, and the Southwest to the Union. These acquisitions and the others which were expected to follow in North America would provide enough land to guarantee economic prosperity and political liberty to future generations. At the same time, this American continental empire would serve as the base for an overseas commercial empire. As they studied the globe, expansionists concluded that the United States occupied a strategic central position between Asia and Europe. With Oregon connected to the Mississippi Valley and to the eastern seaboard via transcontinental railroad and isthmian canal, the United States would command the trade of Asia, the Pacific, South America, and the Caribbean in addition to serving as the avenue through which European commerce to Asia and the Pacific had to pass.[2]

Helping to feed the commercial dreams of the expansionists was an expansive American commercial ideology. Americans had always been noted for their enterprising nature, but the nation's commercial aggressiveness became especially intense in the 1840's and 1850's. Whigs and Democrats disagreed sharply on the impact which tariff duties had on foreign trade, but both parties concurred on the need for new markets and overseas commercial growth to absorb the nation's burgeoning surpluses. Newspapers and journals of all political persuasions carried a heavy diet of commercial statistics, economic information, and geographic material on opportunities overseas. The burgeoning commercial spirit of the era was embodied in *Hunt's Merchants' Magazine*. Founded in 1839 in New York by publisher, Freeman H. Hunt, the bipartisan *Merchants' Magazine* represented the New York business community and paid close attention to the economic implications of political issues. Embodied in the wealth of material in the magazine was a compelling commercial ideology, or "gospel of commerce." A steady stream of articles emphasized that American commerce would improve the republic in countless ways while spreading democracy, Christianity, and civilization to the far corners of the earth. In the introduction to his first edition, Hunt spoke of "Commerce" as a "science . . . calculated to elevate the mind, and enlarge the understanding. . . ." Commerce was the most honorable pursuit a man of talent and enterprise can engage in. "Commerce is now the lever of Archimedes; and the fulcrum . . . wanted to move the world, is found in the intelligence, enterprise, and wealth of the merchants and bankers, who now determine the questions of peace or war, and decide the destinies of nations."[3]

Hunt welcomed the prospect of a world in which national destinies were determined by enlightened men of commerce. Frequent articles on commerce and the progress of civilization, the advantages and benefits of commerce, commerce as a liberal pursuit, and commerce and the commercial character extolled the benefits of commercial activities. If properly practiced, went the arguments, commerce ennobled the merchant and produced innumerable benefits for society and mankind. Writers who examined the history of commerce inevitably concluded that the most progressive and civilized societies were also the most active commercially, while the most regressive, closed and autocratic were the least commercial. From this gospel, aggressive merchants, businessmen, ship captains, and adventurers could take heart. Not only were their wealth and power being enhanced by commercial expansion, but also the values of democracy, Christianity, and civilization were being spread to lesser peoples around the world. And all of this was being achieved without military occupation or political repression.[4] Initially, their great faith in the power of commerce rendered many proponents of the "gospel of commerce" indifferent to the need for a stronger navy to support commercial expansion. Only when specific American economic interests overseas were challenged did these men demand naval action.

In addition to the commercial gospel carried in Hunt's magazine and other publications was a tremendous volume of information on commercial opportunities available overseas. Articles on parts of the Pacific, Africa, India, and the Middle East proliferated as the 1840's passed. Increasingly, the focal point of such interest was the Pacific. Here the opening of China, the Americanization of Hawaii, the great success of American whalers, the achievements of Wilkes' Exploring Expedition, and various first-hand accounts combined to intensify

American interest. Given the rising surplus of agricultural products, the far-reaching enterprise of the American people, and improvements in transportation, the wealth of the Pacific seemed ripe for an American harvest.

Overseas economic activity had always been vital to the commercial centers of the Atlantic seaboard, but the 1840's and 1850's also witnessed increasing support in the South and Midwest for commercial expansion and new markets. Between 1837 and 1859 southerners organized a series of commercial conventions in an effort to achieve a southern economic self-sufficiency and to stimulate commercial activity in the slave states. Men like Lieutenant Matthew F. Maury and later James D. B. DeBow spearheaded an abortive drive to have the commerce of the Caribbean and South America controlled by the South. Between 1846 and the Civil War *DeBow's Review* represented the focal point of this movement as it preached its own gospel of sectional politics, territorial expansion, and commercial growth.[5]

In the Midwest numerous politicians joined such leaders as Thomas Hart Benton and Stephen Douglas and looked to Oregon and California as the key which would permit their region to become the center of a rich worldwide commercial empire once a transcontinental railroad to the west coast was completed. Although a sharp appetite existed in the region for the virgin soil of Oregon, Illinois Democrat James Semple expressed a popular sentiment when he declared that with Oregon "we are about to connect ourselves with the Pacific Ocean, to open our way to a new and indefinite commerce, and bring ourselves into connection with Asia, Polynesia, and Southern America, by the most direct, natural, and easy route." To midwestern politicians, then, Oregon and California represented stepping stones to the Pacific, not the end of the drive to the west coast. Indicative was the opinion of one Illinois legislator in 1849. When he became convinced that Quincy, Illinois, was the logical starting point for the transcontinental railroad, Richard Yates predicted that those railroad cars would carry "to our doors the commerce of India and China, and of the islands of the sea. . . . And as for Quincy, this being the terminus . . . it would make her a mighty city,—a city which would rival Carthage in her pride of power,—the great commercial emporium of the Mississippi Valley, into whose commission houses would pour the commerce of the world."[6]

Ironically, the Democratic Party with its traditionally strong agrarian attitudes provided the policies which hastened American development of an American commercial empire abroad. The Whig Party had long been concerned about foreign trade, the whaling industry, fishing rights, and commercial contacts in the Pacific, but the Whigs had never linked these economic concerns to the type of expansive foreign policy espoused by the Democrats in the 1840's and the Whig commitment to high tariff duties seemed sure to inhibit the growth of American foreign trade. As early as 1839 the *Democratic Review* endorsed a proposed congressional appropriation to survey a canal route across Central America. In 1840 the journal emphasized the critical importance of free trade and commercial expansion to the spread of civilization and liberal political principles. Three years later the *Democratic Review* expressed "vital concern" over the temporary British seizure of the Hawaiian Islands and emphasized that the "vital consequence of their independence to the interests of the United States in the Pacific cannot be overestimated."[7]

With the growing influence of the western wing of the party in the 1840's came a corresponding concern about the need for new territory, the threat of the British in North America, and the necessity of developing new outlets for the region's agricultural surpluses. Although government fiscal policy and the currency policy continued to be important, these issues did not preoccupy party leaders as they had under Jackson and Van Buren. Instead, territorial expansion, federal land policy, federally financed internal improvements, and reduced tariff rates topped the priority lists of western Democrats. Many westerners believed that the acquisition of new territory and a liberal land policy would stimulate economic growth; internal improvements would ease the flow of crops to distant markets; and a low tariff would stimulate trade with England, Europe, and the Caribbean. Accordingly, western Democrats redefined their Jacksonian orthodoxy and supported federally financed internal improvement projects as well as the concept of a transcontinental railroad from the Great Lakes to the west coast when that idea was first proposed by Asa Whitney in 1845.

The election of 1844 made implementation of these policies possible by producing Democratic majorities in both houses of Congress and a narrow victory by James K. Polk. Known as "Young Hickory," the former Tennessee Governor was a traditional agrarian Jacksonian Democrat who had been nominated as a compromise choice in 1844 largely because of his long record of party loyalty. Narrow-minded, determined, and intensely partisan, Polk resolved on a four-point agenda for action from which he did not deviate. He sought to reestablish an Independent Treasury, reduce the tariff, settle the Oregon question, and acquire upper California. To the disappointment of western Democrats he refused to support a program of federally financed internal improvements and vetoed the so-called Rivers and Harbors Bill of 1846 in the face of intense pressure from western supporters. Nevertheless, Polk's commitment to a low tariff and westward expansion promised to stimulate the nation's commercial development and answer the western demand for new soil and new markets.

In December, 1845, Secretary of the Treasury Robert J. Walker launched the administration's campaign for a modified system of free trade. Born in Pennsylvania in 1801, Walker became a lawyer and early supporter of Andrew Jackson before he moved to Mississippi in 1826. He served in the Senate from 1835 to 1845 and distinguished himself as a loyal Jacksonian and fervent expansionist. A man of great energy and intense ambition, Walker hoped to establish a free trade system which would propel his own career to great heights and produce a new era of unlimited commercial prosperity for the United States. In his annual report, Walker reiterated the traditional Jacksonian arguments against a protective tariff as unconstitutional and iniquitous. Protective duties forced the farmer and the planter to pay higher prices for manufactured products at home and excluded their commodities from foreign markets. In the place of protection, Walker argued for a minimal revenue tariff which would give a tremendous impetus to overseas trade. "Let our commerce be as free as our political institutions. Let us, with revenue duties only open our ports to all the world; and nation after nation will soon follow our example." The American home market was "wholly inadequate" to the needs of a nation which had vast fertile soil, could raise a greater variety of crops than any other nation, and could itself feed and clothe nearly all of the world. If fully cultivated, Ohio, Indiana, and Illinois alone could supply food for the entire home market. The same was true of Kentucky for hemp, Mississippi for cotton, and Louisiana for sugar. The growing west, then, had to have access to an expanded foreign market to avoid long term economic depression. Such an expanding foreign market, according to Walker, could only be provided through low duties. After a long and tough struggle in Congress, the so-called Walker Tariff passed by a narrow margin in July, 1846, thereby giving the administration a critical part of its plan to guarantee economic prosperity and commercial expansion.[8]

With foreign policy, the administration also pursued commercial objectives in its drive for new territory. On the Oregon question, Polk was prepared to compromise as long as the United States obtained Puget Sound and free passage through the Straits of Juan de Fuca. After the British rebuffed his initial offer to compromise at 49°, the President reasserted the United States' claim to 54° 40°. Through the crisis winter of 1845–1846, Polk held his ground, but his stand was dictated by political considerations and not by his desire to have all of Oregon. With outspoken Democrats from the Old Northwest insisting that the annexation of Texas and the acquisition of all of Oregon were indivisible issues, Polk would split his party if he offered to concede part of Oregon to England. If compromise did come, then, it would have to be initiated by England. When an offer to compromise at 49° finally came from England in the spring of 1846, Polk referred it to the Senate for consideration. The Senate advised acceptance and later ratified the treaty which resulted. In each case, irate western Democrats opposed the settlement and accused the President of deceit and betrayal.[9]

Despite western cries that Polk had sacrificed the national interest, the Oregon Settlement created a critical commercial foothold on the Pacific for the United States. In addition to the mouth of the Columbia, the United States now had sole possession of Puget Sound and partial control of the Straits. Although many expansionists had long envisioned the Columbia as the gateway to the Pacific and Asia, it became clear by the early 1840's that the mouth of the river did not offer a good harbor. Various reports confirmed the extreme difficulty of crossing the shifting bar at the mouth of the Columbia. The United States Exploring Expedition lost the *Peacock* on the bar, and Wilkes later reported that "Mere description can give little idea of the terrors of the bar of the Columbia: all who have seen it have spoken of the wildness of the scene, and the incessant roar of the waters, representing it as one of the most fearful sights that can possibly meet the eye of the sailor." Once inside the bar Astoria was a small harbor from which "it would be difficult to accommodate any extensive trade." At the same time, Wilkes extolled the beauty, value, and safety of Puget Sound and San Francisco Bay as ocean harbors. Others who knew the geography of the Pacific Northwest expressed similar views. In 1845 Boston merchant William Sturgis delivered a widely publicized lecture in Boston on Oregon. In his address, Sturgis emphasized that "the mouth of the Columbia is at all times dangerous to enter, and for a considerable part of the year almost inaccessible," while the Straits of Juan de Fuca being "easy of access, safe, and navigable at all seasons and in any weather" promised to be "the great channel through which will pass most of the products of the whole region. . . . " These facts were well understood by the Polk Administration and provided the basis for a compromise which protected the nation's commercial and maritime interests in the Pacific Northwest.[10]

Upper California represented another territorial objective which was defined largely by commercial interests. When American diplomats and politicians thought of California, they thought primarily in terms of San Francisco Bay and, later, other harbors farther south. Unable to acquire upper California from Mexico, Polk set a belligerent course. Once fighting occurred in April, 1846, the President sought enough of a war to require Mexican War indemnity to the United States in the form of San Francisco Bay and part of California. However, prosecution of the war proved more troublesome than the President had anticipated. At home, dissidents plagued the administration. In Mexico the enemy fought ineffectively, but the government was not stable enough to negotiate a peace settlement. "Mexico is an ugly enemy," observed Daniel Webster, "She will not fight—and will not treat." As a result, the conflict dragged on for almost two years. By the end of 1847 a vocal movement confronted Polk and urged the seizure of all of Mexico. Proponents in Congress, the press, and the Cabinet argued that the United States should realize its ultimate destiny in North America by absorbing the entire country in the face of continued Mexican intransigence. The President, however, remained largely unmoved by the All Mexico movement and adhered to his original war goals. As a result, the huge territorial acquisitions of the Mexican War were shaped largely by commercial objectives on the Pacific coast.[11]

Unlike Andrew Jackson, Polk did not request an expanded navy to implement his diplomacy. As an agrarian Democrat the President opposed the concept of a large peacetime naval establishment because it violated his basic political principles concerning the need for strict economy in government expenditures and a small professional military. In 1845 he acknowledged the need for a "well-organized, efficient navy" to protect the nation's growing commerce and to defend the nation's coastline. For example, he noted that enemy occupation of Belize, south of New Orleans, would "embarrass, if not stagnate, the whole export trade of the Mississippi and affect the value of the agricultural products of the entire valley of that mighty river and its tributaries." Accordingly, the United States should continue its long-standing policy of providing appropriations for the "gradual increase" of naval supplies and forces. Although he indicated the need for additional warships to augment the existing navy, Polk did not propose a program of major expansion because he believed that continued gradual expansion could occur within the department's existing budget.[12]

Nor did the President rely heavily on the navy to implement his aggressive foreign policy. In the Gulf of Mexico, the administration increased the number of American warships and concentrated them near the Texas and Mexican coasts. Once Texas was annexed the navy was ordered to guard against any Mexican retaliation and to insure that American commerce in the area was not disrupted. In the months prior to the Mexican War, American naval forces in the area under the command of Commodore David Conner performed these responsibilities in an effective and restrained manner. When war with Mexico finally did come in May, 1846, provocation by American naval forces was not among the alleged causes of the conflict. On the west coast, the Navy Department dispatched additional warships and placed American commanders on the alert. In "secret and confidential" orders dated June 24, 1845, Secretary of the Navy George Bancroft instructed Commodore John D. Sloat to avoid war with Mexico, unless he ascertained beyond a doubt that Mexico had declared war against the United States, then "you will at once possess yourself of the port of San Francisco, and blockade or occupy such other ports as your force may permit. . . . " If peace should continue Sloat was to send an exploring party to Oregon to reassure residents there, to reconnoiter the Columbia and Willamette valleys, and to collect information on Puget Sound and the Straits. Sloat, however, remained at Mazatlan in his flagship the *Savannah* because he feared war and this town offered the closest communication link to Washington, D.C. At the same time, he ordered other ships in the squadron to visit Hawaii, cruise the coast of upper California, and sail to the mouth of the Columbia River, where the schooner *Shark* sank off the bar in September, 1846.[13]

During the Oregon Crisis of 1845–1846, the President assumed a belligerent posture toward England but made no preparations for actual war. His message to Congress in December, 1845, carried antagonistic statements toward England and France, but also stated specifically that "no additional appropriations are required" for the navy. The fact that Polk understood the folly of war with England and probably always intended to compromise on Oregon does not account completely for his indifference toward needed naval expansion. Secretary of the Navy Bancroft had noted the need for more steam warships in his annual report of December, 1845.[14] Then in March and April, 1846, supporters of naval expansion published reports from the Navy Department which detailed the weaknesses of the navy. In a war, they argued, the lack of steam warships would prevent the American navy from directly combatting the navy of England or from effectively protecting American commerce through convoys. The only option left would be the raiding of foreign commerce by single warships and privateers. Nor would the U.S. Navy be able to defend the Atlantic or Gulf coasts against the British Navy with its string of bases stretching from Canada to the Caribbean. Although these reports overstated the case, their publication stimulated immediate support for naval expansion. In Congress, however, separate bills in the House and Senate aroused sharp opposition and neither ever came to a vote. In the Senate, the proposal to build ten steam warships quickly bogged down in the debate over Oregon. As such, the bill received little support or consideration on its own merits. Although the President acknowledged publicly the need for additional war steamers in March, 1846, the administration did not attempt to rally Democratic support for the naval expansion bills.[15]

Once the Mexican War began, the navy played an important military role on the Pacific coast and in the Gulf of Mexico. Naval vessels prevented Mexican gunboats and privateers from disrupting American commerce. American naval power was instrumental in the conquest of California as American forces captured Monterey, San Francisco, Los Angeles, San Diego, and the ports of Baja. In the Gulf, the navy captured a number of Mexican seaports and provided essential support for the two American armies invading Mexico. In addition to its transporting of American troops and supplies, naval power made the landing at Vera Cruz possible and provided important support for General Winfield Scott's march on Mexico City. In short, American naval dominance on both of the enemy's coasts seriously injured Mexico's war effort.[16] This contribution was achieved in spite of minimal support from the administration in Washington. Officers complained frequently of inadequate supplies, poor facilities at Pensacola, and long delays in the arrival of supplies. The navy also needed more warships and many of those provided proved unsuitable for effective use along the Mexican coast. Throughout the war, the administration refused to assign high priority to the navy, and Congress provided for the navy's needs in piecemeal manner. In May, 1846, Congress authorized the department to purchase or charter vessels for the military effort. As a result, the navy acquired various small, shallow draft vessels including six steamers, four brigs, three schooners, and three storeships, but these ships proved ill-suited to wartime service in the Gulf. In March, 1847, Congress also authorized the construction of four steam warships and approved funds to build additional convertible steamships, but a comprehensive program of wartime expansion and construction was not undertaken.[17]

The 1847 legislation resulted from a late hour compromise in the 2nd Session of the 29th Congress in which Georgia Whig Thomas B. King inserted the mail subsidy into the bill authorizing construction of the new warships. In addition to being a lawyer and planter, King was also a commercial entrepreneur and railroad promoter who had been born and raised in Massachusetts. As a congressman in the 1840's, he maintained close ties to the New York commercial community, included shipping and railroad promoter W. H. Aspinwall among his friends, and had been an advocate of steamships which could be converted into warships since the early 1840's when he first chaired the House Committee on Naval Affairs. For his efforts to establish and subsidize the steamship lines, King received the warm praise of the Whig press and a New York banquet in his honor given by the merchant community. Actually, the 1847 legislation represented only part of a larger federal government effort to create and subsidize lines to LeHavre, Liverpool, and Bremen. In the Western Hemisphere, Congress appropriated funds for a steamship line from New York to Chagrés and for a line in the Pacific between Panama and Oregon. Eventually, Congress provided $14.5 million in subsidies before terminating the program in the late 1850's.[18]

Unfortunately, the steamship subsidy plan did not serve the navy's short-term needs or long-term interests. Used by England in the 1830's and first proposed in Congress by King's Naval Affairs Committee in 1841, the proposal combined federal subsidies to establish private steamship lines with the construction of naval steamships. Private American steamship lines would receive federal subsidies to carry mail between the United States, England, Europe, and points in the Western Hemisphere. The federal funds would be used to build and maintain new steamships which would be so constructed to permit their conversion into efficient warships for the navy in the event of war. In addition to strengthening the nation's naval defenses, argued proponents, the subsidies would underwrite overseas commercial activity by establishing steamship lines to compete with similar European and English enterprises. Secretary of the Navy Upshur and President Tyler endorsed the idea, and Congress approved legislation in 1845 authorizing the Postmaster General to contract for the transport of mails to foreign countries. Upon demand by the government as full payment for the cost, ships used in the service were to be transferred to the navy for conversion into warships. The initial act proved ineffective and renewed efforts resulted in the 1847 measure. In addition to the construction of four steamers for the navy, the act provided $385,000 annually for ten years to the E. C. Collins Line to support a line of five steamships. These ships were to be built to navy specifications as first-class warships and were to make two round trips per year between New York and Liverpool. Naval officers were to supervise the construction of the steamships and to "command" the civilian crews of the ships on their Atlantic runs.[19]

Although the use of federal funds to serve both civilian and military objectives proved irresistible to Congress, the program hurt naval development. The convertible steamship program created official sanction for the misleading concept that civilian steamships could readily be converted to fighting warships in time of war. Although merchant ships could perform some auxiliary functions during wartime, they could not substitute for regular warships. Conversion had always been difficult in the Age of Sail, but it became virtually impossible in the emerging Age of Steam. Given the complexity of new technology and the increasing demands imposed by iron armor and explosive ordnance, effective steam warships had to be designed and fitted for that purpose.[20]

In addition, the convertible steamship program proved particularly harmful to peacetime naval development. Obviously, steamships carrying mail across the Atlantic could not be used by the navy in peacetime to cruise the oceans of the world in protection of the nation's commerce. More important, however, than the use of a few steamships was the political ammunition which the program gave to opponents of naval expansion. They could now argue that the navy did not require additional steam warships because these vessels would be available in wartime when they were needed but not in peacetime when they were not needed. In fact, this argument was accepted not only by naval opponents but by some of its strongest supporters such as Representative King who made exactly that argument in his House Report on the subject in 1846.[21]

By the end of the Mexican War, the United States seemed poised on the verge of a new era. Despite the ominous specter of the slavery question, the republic seemed to be entering an epoch of unprecedented international power, political influence, and economic growth. The acquisition of Oregon and upper California had added magnificent harbors, valuable natural resources, and 1,600 miles of coastline on the Pacific. The nation's geographic position promised to guarantee full status as a world power and extensive participation in the trade of the Pacific, South America, and the Far East. Once the nation established a transportation link between the two coasts and the Mississippi Valley, the United States would stand at the center of the world's commerce. In fact, the new commercial era seemed already underway as American trade jumped sharply in 1847 and 1848 from the doldrums of the early and mid–1840's. And more territorial additions seemed sure to come as expansionists focused their attention on Cuba, Mexico, Canada, and various parts of Central America.

In his December, 1848, message to Congress, President Polk observed that the United States "stands higher in the respect of the world" and occupies "a more commanding position among nations than at any former period." In addition, Polk claimed that the "whole country was never more prosperous than at the present period, and never more rapidly advancing in wealth and population." Acquisition of the Pacific coast would now permit the nation to "command the rich commerce of China, of Asia, of the islands of the Pacific, of western Mexico, of Central America, the South American States, and of the Russian possessions" on the Pacific. According to Polk, the acquisitions of Texas, Oregon, and California with its rich mineral resources were "of greater consequence and will add more to the strength and wealth of the nation than any which have preceded them since the adoption of the Constitution."[22]

It was Secretary of the Treasury Robert J. Walker, however, who most imaginatively summarized the administration's commercial dreams. In 1847 and 1848 Walker excited widespread enthusiasm through the unlikely medium of his annual treasury reports. In what were essentially free trade treatises, Walker predicted that a policy of unrestricted commerce combined with the nation's geographic position, immense productive capacity, and the application of steam power to oceanic commerce promised to revolutionize in our favor the commerce of the world. "This is a new commercial era," asserted Walker, in which the American republic would achieve "her destiny . . . as the centre and emporium of the commerce of the world." The region which most excited Walker was the Pacific and particularly China, "containing nearly one-third of the population of the globe."[23] Although protectionists grumbled about the heresy of free trade, Walker's arguments were widely and enthusiastically hailed in the press. Numerous papers labelled Walker's reports as among the "ablest" in American history, lauded the Secretary's "intellectual greatness and statesmanlike sagacity," and concurred with his "beautiful and eloquent" description of "the manifest destiny of our great republic."[24]

Although many disputed his ideas about the tariff and free trade, Walker's view of the nation's commercial destiny was shared by most Americans, whether Whig or Democrat. The political rhetoric of the day included a heavy content of confident assertions about the nation's unlimited commercial destiny in the world. Looking back on the achievements of the Polk Administration, Stephen Douglas of Illinois admitted that one could only "be startled and dazzled as if beholding at one panoramic view the mighty work of ages." As "the favored nation of the world," the United States awaited an extraordinary future. "With our broad expanse of country, our fertile soil, and our universal enterprise, who can predict the destiny and greatness of our people."[25] In New Orleans in 1849, James D. B. DeBow extolled the great benefits of commerce to all of mankind and confidently asserted an unlimited destiny for the United States. "Great as has been our progress in the past, there is a prophetic voice which tells us that we have begun to enter upon that bright and glorious 'empire of the seas' which is yet to be ours."[26]

From London, American Minister Abbot Lawrence expressed a similar sentiment in 1850 when he surveyed the strategic and economic position of the United States and asked rhetorically, "who can say what may not be the destiny of United America?" Although Whigs tended to be less enthusiastic and more restrained in their assessments, no one expressed the commercial dreams of the nation better than New York Senator William H. Seward. Speaking in the Senate in 1850, Seward noted that the "world contains no seat of empire so magnificent as this, which . . . offers supplies on the Atlantic shores to the overcrowded nations of Europe, while on the Pacific coast it intercepts the commerce of the Indies. The nation thus situated . . . must command the empire of the seas, which alone is real empire."[27]

In fact, the extreme confidence of these visionaries proved well founded. During the 1850's U.S. commerce grew at a staggering pace. Between 1849 and 1860 total American foreign trade increased by 144 percent from a value of $281,557,371 to a value of $687,192,176. Exports rose by 138 percent from $140 million in 1849 to $333 million in 1860 and imports by 150 percent from $141 million to $353 million. During the same period, the registered tonnage of the United States increased from 1,258,756 to 2,379,396 or 89 percent, and the tonnage entered or cleared in United States ports from 5,412,045 to 12,087,200 or 123 percent. In fact, the great part of this growth occurred in traditional American markets with England, Europe, and in the Caribbean. But this fact did not diminish the expectations or the enthusiasm of most politicians that the ultimate commercial destiny of the nation lay in the far reaches of the Pacific Basin.[28]

The increase in American trade, the new Pacific coastline, the need to safeguard the flow of gold from California, the necessity of protecting the isthmian route, and the nation's burgeoning Pacific interests demanded a western naval base, an increased naval presence in the Pacific, and new principles in the formulation of American peacetime naval policy. But these changes came at a slow pace. The Polk Administration left the navy in a weaker comparative position in 1849 than it had been in 1845. Although the navy had more men, a larger budget, and more ships in 1849 than it had four years earlier, it was less capable of dealing with its accelerating peacetime responsibilities. Most of the ships chartered or purchased to fight the Mexican War proved unusable in peacetime and were sold or scuttled. Nor had the navy kept pace with European technological advances. With the exception of several steam warships, the navy's vessels were now old and outdated. In addition, the convertible steamer program further weakened the peacetime navy by diverting government resources to the steamship lines. The mail subsidies also created the unfortunate illusion that the program benefited the national interest by permitting American companies to compete with those in England and Europe.

The need for a modern peacetime navy was further intensified after 1848 by the changing nature of American expansionism. Prior to 1848, the nation's acquisitions had been continental and produced primarily by population pressure, diplomacy, or land based military action. After the Mexican War, the expansionist movement remained strong, but no appropriate, contiguous territory was available. Canada, because of British power, and Mexico, because of a population deemed "unsuitable," were not viable acquisitions. Cuba remained attractive, but Spain would not consider selling the island. In the Caribbean, Central America, and the Pacific, potential acquisitions also posed serious problems, not the least of which was British power.

The prospect of new possessions such as Cuba, Yucatan, or Mexico also posed a racial problem for the United States because these areas contained relatively large populations of what were viewed as inferior colored peoples. Predominant American beliefs about the racial inferiority of nonwhite peoples precluded their admission into the American Temple of Freedom and their assimilation into American society as citizens. In 1848, when some had proposed the annexation of all of Mexico, critics such as Representative Edward Cabell of Florida had asked whether the nation should "by an act of Congress, convert the black, white, red, mongrel, miserable population of Mexico . . . into free and enlightened American citizens, entitled to all the privileges which we enjoy?" To this proposition, most Whigs and Democrats, expansionists and anti-expansionists, answered no.[29]

At the same time, most expansionists also opposed the alternative of creating a European style empire of colonial possessions and subject populations. Beyond the obvious violence to the republic's basic political precepts, such an arrangement promised to increase federal power and corrupt the American political system. Has the world ever known a republic, asked Horace Greeley of the *New York Tribune*, "which extended its boundaries by the subjugation of diverse and hostile races without undermining thereby its own liberties?" In fact, American

foreign policy had long been committed to the dismemberment of existing colonial empires not the creation of a new one. Given these obstacles and the
additional problem posed by the sectional crisis of the 1850's, the only logical
outlet for American expansionism was the concept of an extensive maritime
commercial empire envisioned by men like Robert Walker and William H.
Seward. Increasingly after 1850, Americans channeled their considerable expansionist energies into overseas economic activity in pursuit of the "empire of
the seas" of which Seward had spoken.[30]

American merchants, diplomats, missionaries, and adventurers began to pour
into the Pacific as Americans at home looked eagerly to their future destiny
there. Indicative of American interest and expectations was a proposal in May,
1848, from Thomas B. King's House Naval Affairs Committee to establish a
steamship line along the northern great circle route from San Francisco or Monterey to Shanghai and Canton as well as a separate line from Hawaii to California.
King's detailed report emphasized that only "Certainty and rapidity of intercourse
are now wanted" to bring China and the United States together and to "build
up a commerce more extensive than has probably ever heretofore existed between
two nations." When connected to New York and New Orleans by a transcontinental railroad and an isthmian canal, the California to China steamship line
would cut thousands of miles from the present route, save thousands of dollars
in shipping cost, and thereby allow the United States to dominate the trade of
China. "The completion of this system of communication," asserted King,
would undoubtedly "cause the balance of trade with all nations to turn in our
favor, and make New York, what London now is, the great settling house of
the world." The measure directed the Secretary of the Navy to use three or four
large war steamships to establish a mail and passenger line from San Francisco
or Monterey to Shanghai and Canton as well as to employ one large war steamer
to create a line from Hawaii to California. In addition, the Secretary was authorized to "establish such depots of coal as may be found necessary to supply
the steamers. . . . " Although Congress never approved the proposal, it generated
considerable public enthusiasm and support in the press. Prominent supporters
included William H. Seward, Aaron Palmer, and Commander James Glynn, and
later Secretary of the Navy John P. Kennedy, who endorsed the measure in a
February, 1853 report to Congress and recommended the establishment of coal
deposits on islands in the Pacific to supply naval steamers in the Pacific.[31]

The first administration which had the task of confronting the ramifications
of the nation's new "ocean-bound" status was the Whig administration of Zachary Taylor. Taylor had never voted in a Presidential election and had no political
experience, but his stature as a war hero and his lack of clearly defined positions
on the political issues of the day made "Old Rough and Ready" the most electable
candidate for the strife-ridden Whig Party. Once inaugurated in 1849, Taylor
proved ill-equipped to provide strong leadership or to deal effectively with the
question of what status slavery would have in the newly acquired federal territories. The new President faced Democratic majorities in both houses during the

31st Congress and headed a party which was itself seriously divided over the slavery issue. As a Louisiana slaveholder, Taylor was not only suspect to many northern Whigs, but also alienated southern Whigs by supporting the admission of California as a free state, endorsing the organization of New Mexico and Utah as free territories, and stating that he would sign the Wilmot Proviso if it passed Congress. With neither the President nor the Congress able to handle the slavery question, it dominated national politics during Taylor's brief administration before culminating in the great crisis of 1850.

In such an atmosphere, foreign policy, commercial diplomacy, and peacetime naval policy occupied secondary roles in national affairs. In neither his Inaugural Address nor his one annual message to Congress did Taylor address the diplomatic, commercial, or strategic implications of the nation's new position on the Pacific. In foreign policy Taylor and Secretary of State John M. Clayton of Delaware steered a cautious and pacific course. Neutrality and nonintervention now replaced bellicose diplomacy and aggressive expansionism. And a primary concern for American commercial interests overseas supplanted the drive for more territory. In the Hawaiian Islands, for example, the United States signed a commercial treaty in 1849 and reaffirmed the Tyler Doctrine after French troops landed and took control of government buildings in Honolulu. But the threat of a permanent French takeover did not produce a naval reaction or a sharp diplomatic protest from the United States.[32] In response to the revolutions in Europe, the Taylor Administration expressed sympathy for the ideals of the revolutionaries but pursued a steady course of neutrality.

In the Caribbean, the administration issued a neutrality proclamation in response to attempts to overthrow Spanish control of Cuba, warned Americans against participation in illegal filibustering efforts, and promised to arrest and punish offenders. American naval officers were instructed to prevent American-based filibustering expeditions from leaving the American coast. Although these activities achieved only limited success, they helped frustrate the filibustering efforts of General Narciso Lopez. At the same time, the administration used the navy in 1850 in a show of force to persuade Spanish authorities to free those American filibusterers who were captured by Spanish naval forces.[33] In Central America, the administration rebuffed the efforts of aggressive diplomatic agents. Both Elijah Hise and Ephraim George Squier signed treaties with Nicaragua guaranteeing the United States exclusive rights to build a canal across the country. However, Secretary of State Clayton refused to submit these treaties to the Senate and decided instead to negotiate directly with England for joint control of any canal. The resulting Clayton-Bulwer Treaty provided for joint Anglo-American control of the proposed canal and committed both nations not to occupy, fortify, or colonize any part of Central America. Signifying a strong American strategic and commercial interest in the region, the Clayton-Bulwer Treaty represented the Whig administration's commitment to resolve Anglo-American differences in the area through negotiation rather than confrontation or the annexation of "weak sister republics."[34]

In his approach to naval policy, Secretary of the Navy William B. Preston of Virginia reflected the President's general caution. Chosen for political reasons, Preston lacked experience in naval affairs and devoted more effort to the political interests of the President and the Whig Party than he did to the navy during his sixteen month term. He did, however, prove to be a competent administrator who proposed a number of naval reforms to Congress in 1849. He also criticized the construction of convertible mail steamers because he realized that they would never be useful as warships. In his annual report of 1849, Preston acknowledged the need for a naval base on the west coast and for more warships in the Pacific. If the trade of the Pacific were to become an "American commerce and an American trade" as it ought to, an American steam navy was required in the Pacific. Having made those recommendations, Preston failed to pursue them vigorously with Congress. As a result Congress did not authorize the construction of additional steamers, and the budget of the Navy Department actually declined by approximately 19 percent between 1849 and 1850.[35]

When President Taylor died suddenly in July, 1850, he was succeeded by a longtime supporter of the navy, Millard Fillmore of New York, but party divisions plagued Fillmore as various factions maneuvered for control of the Whig Party. In the State Department, Fillmore replaced Clayton with Daniel Webster and then, when he died in 1852, with Edward Everett of Massachusetts. In Central America, Fillmore accepted the controversial Clayton-Bulwer Treaty and attempted to avoid confrontation with England while endorsing proposals to build a canal across Nicaragua and a railroad across some route in the region. Fillmore also attempted to combat American-based filibustering projects against Cuba by using federal officials and the navy to prevent these expeditions from leaving the United States. In spite of these efforts, strong local support in the South served to neutralize government efforts, and leaders of these ventures continued to use the southern states as their base of operations.[36]

In the Pacific, Hawaii remained a troublespot as a permanent French seizure of the islands seemed imminent and the United States tried to decide the extent of its official commitment in the region. After diplomatic efforts to have the French guarantee the independence of the native regime failed, the Fillmore Administration was informed that the Hawaiian King preferred to have a joint protectorate over the islands established by France, England, and the United States, but if that alternative was not possible then he preferred to place Hawaii under American control. Secretary of State Webster responded by reaffirming the American desire to have the islands remain independent, but he emphasized that the United States would protect Hawaii from foreign control. Since the islands were "ten times nearer to the United States" than Europe and "Five-sixths of all their commercial intercourse is with the United States," Webster declared that his government "can never consent to see those islands taken possession of by either of the great commercial powers of Europe, nor can it consent that demands, manifestly unjust and derogatory and inconsistent with a bona fide independence, shall be enforced against that Government." Accordingly, the U.S. Navy would be kept "in such a state of strength and preparation as shall be requisite for the preservation of . . . the safety of the Government of the Hawaiian Islands." Although this commitment placed the Whig administration on a potentially dangerous course, the United States was not compelled to make good on its guarantee.[37]

The Fillmore Administration demonstrated more support and interest in the navy than Taylor's had.[38] Both of Fillmore's Naval Secretaries proved to be capable and committed to a stronger and more efficient navy. William Graham of North Carolina served from July, 1850 to June, 1852, and John Pendleton Kennedy of Maryland served the remaining months of Fillmore's Presidency. As usual during the period, each man was selected primarily for political reasons, but both worked hard to address the navy's many problems. Their reports to Congress in 1850, 1851, and 1852 proposed a series of needed internal reforms, argued the need for naval expansion, emphasized the need for a permanent naval base on the west coast, and endorsed a number of important exploring and diplomatic missions by the navy.[39]

Soon after he took office, Graham requested Lieutenant Matthew F. Maury's assistance in preparing the annual department report for 1850. Maury responded with a detailed analysis of the navy's condition, an assessment of the political prospects for additional support, and a proposed agenda for reform. As Head of the Naval Observatory and a longtime resident of Washington, D.C., Maury well understood that public opinion regarded "all war establishments . . . as necessary evils" in a republic and only the need for "self defense" compelled maintenance of a Navy. The most suitable Navy, then, was one "with powers of expansion to meet all the emergencies of war, while in peace it is not more than sufficient . . . to maintain the police of the seas . . . to command the respect of other nations . . . [and] to assert our rights and to maintain them." In the United States, political attitudes had not even allowed the navy to perform this limited role. By fixing the number and ratio of officers in the navy, Congress in 1843 had ordained that the navy "shall stand still" in an age of rapid change. Just as it was impossible for the nation "to preserve the statu [sic] quo," it was "equally impossible . . . for its 'right arm' . . . to stand still and not wither." Accordingly, the acquisition of the Pacific coast and the recent dramatic increases in foreign trade now rendered substantial reform essential. Both the promotion system and the efficiency of the officer corps needed improvement. On the Pacific coast, a permanent naval establishment needed to be created comparable to the one on the Atlantic coast.[40]

Relying heavily on Maury's expertise and recommendations, Graham's annual report to Congress recommended a reduction in the number of officers by retiring those who were old and inefficient, the advancement of more younger officers quickly on a merit basis, and the creation of the new rank of Rear Admiral for two senior officers. One of the new Real Admirals would command the proposed permanent naval establishment on the Pacific coast where almost 300,000 American citizens were particularly vulnerable to naval blockade because of their dependence on maritime routes for their food supplies. Graham also proposed a modest gradual increase in the size of the navy. Accepting Maury's advice on the political realities of the time, Graham rejected the argument that the size of the American Navy should represent a numerical ratio proportionate to the size of the navies of England and Europe. Instead, in his 1851 report, he recommended authority to build two new warships each year, one of which would be a steam vessel and one a sailing vessel. Willing to accept the importance of steam power, Graham nevertheless feared that rapid technological changes might render new steam warships obsolete and useless to the navy within a short time. He also noted the value of the mail subsidies in establishing new steamship lines and predicted that the new mail steamers would prove to be "a most formidable means" of annoying foreign merchantmen in time of war.[41]

Graham's program had not been approved when he resigned in 1852 to campaign as the Whig nominee for Vice President and was replaced by John P. Kennedy, the moderate Whig politician and literary figure from Maryland. Although he had no record in naval matters, Kennedy proved to be an enthusiastic and resourceful advocate of the navy. He quickly embraced a broad scientific and commercial role for the navy and espoused the type of peacetime role for the navy advocated a decade earlier by Abel Upshur. During his seven-month term, Kennedy pressed for approval of the naval reforms already proposed and urged an ambitious construction program. In his 1852 annual report, the Secretary emphasized that "absolute necessity" dictated the immediate increase of men and ships. The growth of rival nations' navies, the "rapid extension of our domain . . . and the establishment of new lines of commerce on the Pacific" constituted an "irresistible argument" for naval expansion.

In the Pacific, the United States "will both attract and supply an amount of commercial enterprise in the rapid growth and activity of which the world has yet had no parallel. The discovery of America did not give such an impulse to this spirit as we now witness in the energy and occupations of these recent settlements." In the Atlantic, "equally strong" motives existed for naval expansion because the development of large European steam navies required "the habitual and familiar presence of our flag in every region of commerce, sustained by such an amount of force, and of such a quality, as may give some significant token of the resources we command at home." Accordingly, Kennedy repeated Graham's proposed personnel reforms, asked that the enlisted force be doubled from 7,500 to 15,000, and urged that the Marine Corps be increased. The nation also needed to build three first-class steam frigates, three steam sloops-of-war, and several smaller steamers adapted to coastal navigation. Kennedy also recommended that one of the mail steamers be converted to naval use and two unfinished frigates, the *Santee* and the *Sabine*, be completed. The United States must also create a permanent naval base on the Pacific coast and should establish "one or more factories" to build the machinery necessary to equip the navy's steam warships.[42] Although Congress remained unmoved during his short term, Kennedy's naval recommendations were largely renewed by the incoming Pierce

Administration and passed by Congress in an act in April, 1854, which authorized construction of six steam frigates as well as the completion of the *Santee* and the *Sabine*.

Unfortunately for the navy, neither Graham nor Kennedy proved nearly as critical of the convertible mail steamer policy as might have been expected. The politically weak Fillmore Administration was not about to attack the program, given the political clout of the steamship companies and the popularity of the subsidies among many Whigs. In 1852 a major debate did arise when the E. C. Collins Company requested an increase in subsidy from $385,000 to $858,000 per year. In the debate, most Whigs and some Democrats from the upper Atlantic seaboard supported the subsidy plan while most Democrats and a few Whigs from the interior attacked the subsidies. In spite of the spectacular speed records set by the Collins steamers, opponents argued that these public funds might be better spent on the critical transportation needs in the interior than on boat races with the British Cunard line in the Atlantic.

In the debate it became clear that the value of the mail steamers to the navy was limited at best. Reports from naval officers such as Commodore Matthew C. Perry and Commander R. B. Cunningham provided information which cast great doubt on the possibility of converting these steamers to armed warships. Whatever their sailing capacities were, these ships were simply not designed to safely carry munitions, accommodate heavy armament, or withstand enemy bombardment. In 1849, Secretary Preston attacked the mail steamer subsidies as "fraught with incalculable mischief to the navy. . . . " Graham was more equivocal based on the cautious assessment of Maury. While the mail steamers were probably not convertible to first class-warships, their speed would permit them to be employed "with great advantage under the light armaments against the commerce of an adversary."[43]

Even that limited role, however, was questioned by skeptics. Unprotected by a strong American fleet, single steamers would be vulnerable to attack and capture by enemy navy steamers acting in concert. After a long and heated debate, Congress approved the additional subsidy with the stipulation that the subsidies could be terminated upon six months' notice by Congress. Inconclusive as this debate might have been in 1852, it did indicate that the days of the mail subsidy were numbered. Useful as the mail steamers were as a source of national pride, they were expensive to the nation, operated at a considerable loss, and were, at best, of dubious naval value.

Despite the efforts of Graham and Kennedy, the strength of the navy continued to languish during the Fillmore Administration. As a result, one study estimates that by 1853 "the United States possessed not a vessel that could have given battle with prospect of victory against any first class warship of the major European Powers." At the same time, both Graham and Kennedy proved resourceful advocates of the naval commercial enterprises. They encouraged Maury's work at the Naval Observatory, and, with his encouragement, they helped launch several overseas exploring expeditions of great commercial significance. Once again the nation's political leaders in Congress had failed to recognize the pressing need for naval reform and naval expansion, while individual initiative and external pressures continued to force the navy to serve as a vital arm of the nation's burgeoning maritime empire.

6.
Commercial Initiatives in Latin America

> It [the Caribbean Sea] receives the drainage of the two greatest river basins in the world—it is the natural outlet for the produce of the hemisphere and I have therefore seen in it the Cornu Copia of the world and this "universal Yankee Nation" occupying upon its shores the very summit level of commerce.
>
> Lieutenant Matthew F. Maury to Lieutenant William Herndon,
> April 20, 1850

After 1848 American expansionists looked expectantly to the south and to the west. The vast Pacific and the Orient now beckoned eager Americans. Although the precise nature of American expansion in the Pacific remained undefined, few Americans doubted that they would soon dominate the commerce and political destiny of this vast region as they created a far-flung commercial empire in the Pacific. To the south, the nation's destiny seemed more certain and more immediate. The Caribbean had long been and remained an important part of the nation's foreign trade, but its relative commercial importance had declined by the 1850's. Healthy increases in imports and exports in the region were overshadowed during the decade by more rapid commercial expansion elsewhere. At the same time, the Caribbean and Central America's proximity and vital strategic importance to the United States now rendered the region a likely target of expansionist opportunity. In the United States, expansionists assumed that the republic's next acquisitions would come in the Caribbean and Central America. Expansionist pressure and enthusiasm ran particularly high in the slave states as southerners contemplated the acquisition of Cuba and other territories. In addition, expansionists hoped to expel the British from Central America and Americans from all sections anticipated the establishment of an isthmian canal.

In South America, American expansionists envisioned commercial wealth but not territorial possessions. The entire continent provided less than 10 percent of the nation's foreign trade in the 1850's in spite of its relative proximity to the United States. But the limited magnitude of this commerce did not deter the confidence of numerous expansionists, promoters and merchants. They assumed that the acquisition of California and Oregon would unlock the rich potential of the Pacific coast of South America, while the opening of the Amazon and La Plata basins would have a similar effect on the commercial wealth of those regions.

The ambitious dreams of these expansionists, however, were postponed by the Taylor and Fillmore administrations. These two Whig Presidents eschewed the aggressive expansionism of their Democratic predecessor in favor of a much less assertive foreign policy. In the Caribbean and Central America, Taylor and Fillmore charted a course of neutrality and nonintervention as they attempted to foster the nation's commercial interests not the territorial goals of the expansionists. Neither Whig President renewed Polk's efforts to purchase Cuba, and both attempted to stifle American-based filibustering expeditions to overthrow the Spanish in Cuba. With other powers in the region, the United States now avoided confrontation in favor of a policy of diplomatic conciliation. The Whigs did not press Mexico for further territorial concessions or attempt to provoke a new diplomatic crisis. In Central America, these administrations attempted to define and preserve the nation's transit rights through diplomatic agreements such as the Clayton-Bulwer Treaty with England.

Although their policies brought sharp attacks from Democratic expansionists, the Whigs tried diligently to protect American trade and enhance American commercial interests throughout the region. The Fillmore Administration proved particularly sympathetic to American commercial interests in the Pacific and the Far East as well as Latin America by launching a series of naval exploring expeditions. Significantly, two of these naval expeditions held great potential significance for the future of American trade with the Caribbean and South America.

During the 1850's the navy conducted exploring expeditions to the far corners of the globe.[1] U.S. naval officers participated in efforts to find the Northwest Passage and to locate the missing English explorer, Sir John Franklin, in 1850–1851 and 1853–1855. In addition, a small naval party under the command of Lieutenant William Lynch reconnoitered the west coast of Africa in 1852 to collect preliminary information for a full-scale exploration of the West African interior. Although supporters hoped to locate a suitable spot for a new colony of black Americans in Africa and to encourage American trade in the area, the full-scale expedition never materialized. Of greatest significance, however, were four naval projects launched between 1851 and 1853 to achieve commercial and diplomatic objectives in the Pacific and South America. During the Fillmore Administration, expeditions were dispatched to establish diplomatic and commercial relations with Japan, to chart and explore the northeastern Pacific, to explore the Amazon River basin, and to chart and reconnoiter the tributaries of the Rio de la Plata. Although each of these projects received the support of various scientists and included scientific objectives, the primary purpose of each expedition was either diplomatic, commercial, or both. As such, these naval expeditions collectively represented a significant expression of the nation's maritime Manifest Destiny and an important attempt to have the navy advance the nation's commercial diplomacy in the Pacific and Latin America.

These naval enterprises were the first of their kind since the Wilkes Expedition had returned to the United States in 1842. In spite of the substantial and lasting achievements of that expedition, neither Congress nor two Presidential administrations showed any interest in dispatching similar projects during the 1840's. Several factors account for this reluctance. Controversy and disputes had plagued the so-called United States Exploring Expedition from beginning to end. The residue of bitterness and bad feeling left by the expedition made it easy for Congress and Presidents Tyler and Polk to avoid similar projects. The naval exploring missions which were undertaken later in the decade were much smaller in scale, almost entirely scientific in nature, largely the result of individual initiative by two officers, and not comparable to the Wilkes Expedition or the exploring projects which would follow. In 1848 Lieutenant William Lynch led a small party in the exploration of the Dead Sea and the River Jordan. From 1849 to 1852 Lieutenant J. M. Gilliss led another small party to Chile where extensive astronomical observations were taken. The reports of both Lynch and Gilliss reflected the scientific orientation of their expeditions.[2]

In contrast, the four expeditions launched by the Fillmore Administration fostered the nation's overseas commercial expansion by performing several functions. In South America, the Amazon and La Plata expeditions were instructed to gather extensive geographical, meteorological, and commercial information. Once compiled, this material would provide the basis for further exploration, for commercial agreements, and for private commercial initiatives by American entrepreneurs. These ventures also conducted surveys and prepared charts of the rivers which were explored, thus collecting information which might later prove invaluable to merchants and ship captains who sought to establish trade routes and penetrate these river basins. Finally, each expedition had a diplomatic role. The La Plata expedition was specifically intended to facilitate existing negotiations for a commercial treaty with Paraguay. Although the Amazon expedition did not have explicit diplomatic goals, it clearly was viewed as a project which might be used to facilitate the diplomatic objective of opening the Amazon to external commerce and settlement.

The two expeditions to South America were particularly well suited to the attitudes of the Fillmore Administration. As commercial and scientific projects, they were peaceful in nature and were not intended to provoke a diplomatic confrontation. Both expeditions could also be mounted with existing resources and required few men, ships, or funds. In fact, the two expeditions used only one ship between them. Given their limited size, these projects did not require congressional approval for additional funds and could be launched with little fanfare on the authority of the Secretary of the Navy with the approval of the President. As such, individual initiative in the Navy Department played a major role in the formulation and implementation of these projects.

Under Fillmore, Secretaries William Graham and John P. Kennedy both proved receptive to proposed naval expeditions to the North Atlantic, West Africa, South America, and the Far East. During his brief tenure, Kennedy played a particularly important role in getting the two expeditions to the Pacific as well as the La Plata project underway. When he assumed office in the summer of 1852, Kennedy enthusiastically embraced these proposals because he believed that the navy's rightful peacetime responsibilities should include such positive commercial and scientific projects. And as a proponent of an overseas American commercial empire, Kennedy understood the relationship of naval exploring expeditions to the realization of that vision. In his instructions to the commanders of two of the expeditions, Kennedy emphasized the navy's responsibility to help extend the "empire of commerce and of science." Kennedy also made every effort to insure that the expeditions had either sailed or had received final instructions before the Whigs left office in March, 1853.[3]

But more important than the support of Graham and Kennedy was the role of Lieutenant Matthew F. Maury, who as Superintendent of the Naval Observatory continued to provide a critical source of initiative and direction for naval exploration. By the early 1850's Maury had published a number of his wind and current charts, was well along on his whaling charts, and was completing the research which would result in the publication of his multi-edition volume, *The Physical Geography of the Sea*, in 1855. After a slow beginning, his wind and current charts had a dramatic impact on American commerce. In 1848, a Baltimore captain first demonstrated the practical value of the charts on the route to Rio de Janeiro. Using Maury's sailing directions, the bark *W.H.D.C. Wright* cut thirty-five days from the usual round trip time. Although many experienced sea captains abandoned their own routes reluctantly, the charts were in wide use by the early 1850's. Secretary Graham reported in his December, 1851, annual report that the charts had "materially shortened the passage along the highways by which our commerce passes into and through the southern hemisphere, [to] bring ports of those distant parts of the world some ten days and some several weeks nearer to us than before." Maury's sailing directions proved especially valuable on the New York to San Francisco run in the years following the discovery of gold in California. By 1851 ships using the charts averaged a passage of 144 days while those which did not averaged a passage of 187 days. For clipper ships, Maury's sailing directions helped reduce the passage from New York to San Francisco to a run of 90 to 100 days.[4]

Maury's work with the geography of the oceans placed him in close contact with various sea captains, whalers, and influential merchants, the most important of which was R. B. Forbes of Boston. They provided him with the logs and observations he needed to prepare his charts which they, in turn, used to make their voyages shorter, safer, and more economical. At the same time, Maury understood the need for additional oceanographic information and was in an ideal position to convey his ideas and recommendations for specific projects to the civilian Secretaries of the Navy. Under Fillmore, both Graham and Kennedy relied heavily on his advice. In addition, his suggestions carried the support of many scientists, the maritime community, southern commercial interests, and various other special interest groups. At the Naval Observatory, Maury also attracted and trained a number of young naval officers in his research techniques and schooled them in the importance of hydrographic research. As a result, he produced a group of naval protegés which included John M. Brooke, Thomas J. Page, William Herndon, and Lardner Gibbon, each of whom would play a significant role in one of the naval exploring expeditions of the decade.[5]

Although committed to scientific research and the expansion of knowledge for its own sake, Maury was also an eminently practical man who believed that a strong connection existed between scientific knowledge, commercial expansion, and human progress. For the United States, he envisioned the development of a complex commercial empire marked by free trade, global communication, and commercial progress. Once a practical isthmian transit route was established, the United States would dominate trade between Europe and Asia through the Gulf of Mexico which would stand as "the center of the world and the focus of the world's commerce." Maury also argued that these developments promised a bright future for undeveloped river basins such as the Amazon, the Orinoco, and the Amur. Once these and other remote regions had been explored, their rivers charted, and their potential opened to trade, a natural process of economic growth and human progress would be unleashed. Like many of his contemporaries, Maury argued that there was "no colonizer, civilizer, nor Christianizer, like commerce." In the Amazon, for example, "Encourage commerce . . . and you encourage its settlement, and its cultivation, and the development of its resources," wrote Maury in 1852. "And in doing this you keep bright also that precious chain with golden links, which bind nations together in peace and friendship." According to Maury, then, explorations which promised to stimulate the flow of commerce merited support and encouragement.[6]

Along with the initiative of Maury and the interest of Graham and Kennedy, publicity and support from various individuals and groups outside of the federal government helped create public interest and focus political pressure on specific expeditions. In South America, tremendous commercial opportunity beckoned in the Amazon and the La Plata.[7] Enthusiasts predicted that the wealth of these regions would far surpass the trade of Asia. Some southerners also argued that the Amazon offered an ideal region for the spread of slavery and southern institutions. And the feasibility of the La Plata expedition was enhanced by the acknowledged willingness of the President of Paraguay to receive and accommodate an American expedition. In addition, the indefatigable efforts of promoter Edward A. Hopkins proved critical to the realization of the La Plata proposal. This naval veteran, adventurer, and entrepreneur had spent considerable time in

Paraguay by the time he began to agitate for the commercial opening of the La Plata region in the late 1840's. For several years, Hopkins collected material, wrote various articles on his favorite subject for periodicals and newspapers, attempted to stimulate the interest of American investors, and lobbied for a naval expedition to explore the region and chart its extensive river system.[8]

The fact that Hopkins enlisted the support of the newly formed American Geographical and Statistical Society in 1852 enhanced his cause considerably. The Society's petition to the Secretary of the Navy in support of the project marked the first of several such ventures the Society would endorse and assist before the Civil War. Founded in 1851 to advance geographical science and promote the business interests of "a great maritime and commercial city," the Society was composed of wealthy, well-educated, influential New Yorkers who strongly supported the commercial expansion of the United States. Members included diplomats, bankers, promoters, scientists, government officials, and clergymen. Collectively, these men believed that geographic research and scientific exploration were essential to commercial expansion, the progress of civilization, and the spread of Christianity. Explorers to remote regions like the river basin La Plata carried the commerce, Christianity, and civilization which was thought to characterize American destiny. Given their interest and influence, the members of the Society represented an important source of support for naval exploration.[9]

The idea of descending the Amazon from its Peruvian headwaters to its mouth at Para was conceived by Maury in the late 1840's. He hoped to collect valuable scientific, commercial, and geographical information on the unexplored region which could then be used to help persuade Brazil to open the Amazon to free navigation and external commerce. "The free navigation of the Amazon is the greatest commercial boon that the people of the South and West—indeed, the people of the United States can crave." Maury's interest in the Amazon resulted from his scientific curiosity about the region, his desire to open the area to commercial development, and his belief that the Amazon offered an excellent "safety-valve" for colonization by southerners and their slaves. He also argued that the South could regain its commercial initiative by establishing a lucrative direct trade with the Amazon and South America through the natural trade routes of the Caribbean. Maury believed that an exploring expedition would document the rich commercial potential of the Amazon and help substantiate his theory that the Amazon Valley was "but a commercial appendage of the Mississippi" closely connected to it by prevailing currents and winds. From the mouth of the Amazon, ocean currents flowed into the Gulf, past the mouth of the Mississippi River, through the Florida Channel and into the Gulf Stream. From the Atlantic coast of the United States, favorable winds generally blew south through the Lesser Antilles past the mouth of the Amazon. According to Maury, a tree cut at the headwaters of the Missouri River and another cut at the headwaters of the Amazon would meet in the "Straits of Florida" if each was allowed to float freely. The Amazon and Mississippi River basins, then, comprised two parts of a vast undeveloped commercial empire which could be dominated by southern ports such as New Orleans and Norfolk. "These twin basins are destined by Nature to be the greatest commercial receptacles in the world," wrote Maury in 1852, "No age, clime, nor quarter of the globe, affords any parallel or any conditions of the least resemblance to these which we find in this sea or gulf."[10]

Maury also believed that the thinly populated Amazon Valley might eventually support a population of 2.4 million. To achieve such a destiny, the discipline, intelligence, and skill of the superior civilized white race would be needed. He agreed with his friend and fellow scientist, Arnold Henry Guyot, that "Tropical nature cannot be conquered and subdued, save by civilized man. . . . It is, then, from the northern continents that those of the south await their deliverance; it is by the help of the civilized men of the temperate continents that . . . the man of the tropical lands [shall] enter into the movement of universal progress and improvement. . . . " In the Amazon, Americans from the United States were clearly destined to perform this duty. In a climate he believed to be congenial to cotton, rice, tobacco, and sugar cultivation, Maury expected southerners to settle, transplant their institutions, move their slaves, and become a virtual colony of the Mississippi Valley.[11]

By April, 1850, Maury had persuaded Secretary of the Navy William B. Preston to support a small expedition of one or two officers who would cross the Andes and descend the Amazon. With Preston's permission, Maury selected his brother-in-law, Lieutenant William L. Herndon, and instructed him to select a Passed Midshipman to accompany him and to wait at Valparaiso for further instructions. The thirty-seven-year-old Herndon had joined the navy in 1828, been promoted to Lieutenant in 1841, fought in the Mexican War, and served at the Naval Observatory. He proved to be an excellent choice because he was resourceful and shared Maury's hopes for the Amazon Valley. But the project was delayed by a series of unforeseen developments. After Taylor's Cabinet approved the measure, a squabble occurred between Preston and Secretary of State John Clayton. Then President Taylor died in July, 1850, and his entire Cabinet resigned. Maury next had to persuade Preston's successor to support the expedition which he did within weeks after Graham took over as secretary. Permission for the descent also had to be secured from a reluctant Brazilian government, which took additional time. Finally, the necessary documents and instructions were forwarded to Herndon and his assistant, Lieutenant Lardner Gibbon, in March, 1851.

Dated February 15, 1851, Herndon's official instructions from Secretary of the Navy Graham stressed that the "geographical situation and the commercial position of the Amazon indicated the future importance, to this country, of the free navigation of that river" and Herndon was to help the "government to form a proper estimate as to the degree of importance, present and prospective. . . . "Accordingly, the explorers were to collect as much information as possible on the "navigability" of the Amazon and its tributaries, on the inhabitants of the region, its trade and products, its climate, soil, and production, as well as on the "character and extent of its undeveloped commercial resources, whether of the field, the forest, the river, or the mine." Although the explorers were authorized to make "such geographical and scientific observations . . . as may be consistent with the main object of the expedition," they were reminded explicitly that such observations were "merely incidental, and that no part of the main objects of the expedition is to be interfered with by them."[12]

In addition to his official instructions, Herndon also carried a copy of detailed secret orders from Maury. Written in April, 1850, this extraordinary document revealed the extent of Maury's dreams for the Amazon. To him, this " 'universal Yankee Nation' " was destined to dominate the commerce of the entire Caribbean which he viewed as "the Cornu Copia of the world" because it drained the "two greatest river basins in the world" and stood midway between Europe and Asia via "ship Canal and Isthmus highways." As an essential part of this rich commercial region, the Amazon had to be settled and developed. The only question for Maury was by whom. "Shall it be peopled with an imbecile and an indolent people," he asked "or by a go ahead race that has energy and enterprise . . . ? The latter by all means." The purpose of Herndon's mission was to "prepare the way for that chain of events . . . which is to end in the establishment of the Amazonian Republic. . . . " Once Brazil permitted Americans to navigate the river, American settlers from the free and slave states would follow inevitably "with their goods and chattels to settle and to revolutionize and republicanize and Anglo Saxonize that Valley. . . . " The Amazon would serve both as a "safety valve" for excess southern slaves as well as a rich source of cotton for England. If the United States was the first to secure "the right to navigate the Amazon," Herndon's findings would facilitate American commercial ventures there and make the Amazon "for all commercial purposes . . . a sort of an American colony."[13]

Maury quoted extensively in these instructions from Arnold Henry Guyot to prove that the development of the Amazon could only be directed by the superior races from the northern hemisphere. Like other tropical regions in the world, the Amazon was peopled with feeble and inferior races who were incapable of conquering and subduing the tropical wilderness. It remained for the "privileged races" to impart to the "inferior races the blessings and comforts of civilization. . . . In this way, alone, will the inferior races be able to come forth from the state of torpor and debasement into which they are plunged, and . . . commence . . . the elaboration of the material wealth of the tropical regions, for the benefit of the whole world."[14]

The potential value of Herndon's expedition, then, was far-reaching, and Maury outlined an incredibly detailed series of geographic, scientific, and economic questions to be asked and recorded. In addition to the navigability of the Amazon and its tributaries, Herndon was to determine if any inhabitants would be interested in buying stock in an American steamship company and to take their names and promises. He was ordered to determine the value of gold and silver mines of the Andes, and the potential for growing cotton, tobacco, rice, sugar, hemp, indigo, coffee, cocoa, and numerous other crops. In short, he was to collect as much political, commercial, statistical, and meteorological information as possible about this region which "has hereafter to play such an important part in the affairs of mankind and the world." To do this, Herndon was urged to "pump every traveler, trader, and gentleman you meet with on the Amazon until he is dry." At the same time, Maury explicitly warned Herndon twice in his orders not to define or talk about the real purpose of his mission.[15]

After more than a year of delays the expedition finally got underway. On May 21, 1851, Herndon, Gibbon, Master's Mate Henry Richards, and a small party left Lima. A month later at Tarma, Peru, Herndon decided to split the party. Although he acknowledged this was a "bold, almost rash determination . . . that seemed . . . midsummer madness" for such a tiny expedition, the "extent of the territory to be covered" eventually overrode all other objections. Herndon would travel through the valley of Acombamba, the plain of Junin, and the mining district of Cerro Pasco to the headwaters of the Huallaga River. From there he would descend to the upper reaches of the Amazon and then down to its mouth at Para. Gibbon would take Richards and proceed south into Bolivia, explore the Bolivian tributaries of the Amazon, and then descend on the Amazon to Para. At the beginning of July, 1851, Herndon and Gibbon set off on their separate paths.[16]

By August 1st Herndon had reached the Huallaga River, and five weeks later he had arrived at Nuata on the Amazon. Here he explored and reported favorably on the commerce of the Peruvian frontier area and the prospect for establishing a steamship line between Loreto and Chasuta, a distance of 800 miles entirely in Peruvian territory.[17] By early December, Herndon had reached the Brazilian frontier at Tabatinga, and by early April, 1852, he arrived at Para at the mouth of the Amazon. After a month's wait, he boarded the *U.S.S. Dolphin* in May and arrived back in the United States in July, 1852.

In the meantime, Gibbon had reached Cuzco, Peru, on August 19, 1851. He explored the area for several weeks before proceeding to Bolivia and reaching La Paz on November 21st. From here he travelled to Cochabamba, where in December he met and had an audience with the President of Bolivia, Captain General Manuel Isidoro Belzu. During the conversation, Passed Midshipman Gibbon suggested an agreement between the United States and Bolivia to give U.S. citizens the right to navigate the rivers of Bolivia. Praising the United States, the President politely ignored Gibbon's audacious suggestion and the conversation moved to other subjects. After remaining at Cochabamba for five months, Gibbon departed in May, 1852, and proceeded to the Amazon via the Trinidad, Exaltacion, the Mamore, and the Madeira River. With Richards, Gibbon reached the Amazon River in October, 1852. Here he and Richards recuperated before descending the Amazon to Para and reaching the United States in March, 1853.[18]

Both journeys were long, arduous, and difficult, and required great determination and ingenuity on the part of the explorers. Each was filled with interesting

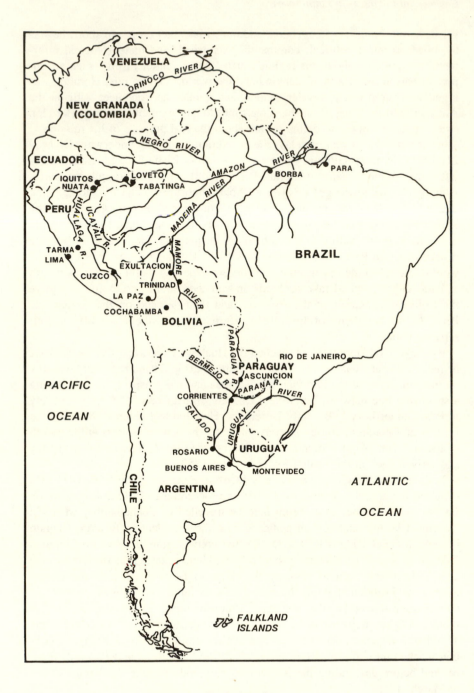

South America

experiences and dangerous incidents. Both explorers could have lost their lives on a number of occasions. As such, the separate accounts of the two journeys make fascinating reading. By January, 1853, Herndon had finished his detailed report. It was submitted to the President and Congress in February and was published in the Executive Documents of both the House and Senate later in 1853. Gibbon's report was finished in January, 1854, submitted to the President and Congress, and published later in 1854 as Part II of Herndon's report. Of the two reports, Herndon's was the more popular by virtue of the fact that it was printed a year before Gibbon's, was written in a more lively style, and was more expansionistic in tone.[19]

Although Gibbon filled his report with pertinent information on the economic and commercial potential of the areas he travelled, it was Herndon's report which most clearly mirrored Maury's instructions and dreams for the Amazon Valley. The two kinsmen clearly shared a similar vision of the Amazon. Herndon's journey and report provided the mass of first-hand observations and information needed to substantiate the validity of Maury's visions. The composite picture of the Amazon which emerges from the report is that of a valley of unparalleled natural wealth and commercial potential. The soil, rainfall. and growing season promised agricultural abundance; the mineral resources of the Andes offered untold wealth in gold and silver; and the natural resources of the Amazon forests awaited only the energy of a civilized race. The recent treaty between Peru and Brazil to appropriate funds for steamboat navigation on the Amazon was a step "toward progress; but it is the progress of a denizen of their own forests—the sloth." Only the opening of the Amazon "to the commerce of the world" would provide for real progress "commensurate with the importance of the act. . . . " In short, the "greatest boon in the wide world of commerce is in the free navigation of the Amazon, its confluents and neighboring streams."[20]

Like Maury, the reports emphasized that the people of the United States were the foreigners most interested in the free navigation of the Amazon. Prevailing winds and currents dictated that "a chip flung into the sea at the mouth of the Amazon will float close by Cape Hatteras." Likewise, ships sailing from the Amazon "for whatever part of the world" were forced to pass the mouth of the Mississippi and the coast of the United States. As a result, the United States was "now Brazil's best customer and most natural ally." Because Brazil was not strong enough to undertake development of the Amazon alone, she should open the Amazon and invite the citizens of the United States with their commercial and maritime genius to help Brazilians "to subdue the wilderness, and show the natives how to work." Then would wealth, power, and civilization be brought to the Amazon. "Then would the mighty river . . . no longer roll its sullen waters through miles of unbroken solitude . . . but, furrowed by a thousand keels, and bearing upon its waters the mighty wealth that civilization and science would call from . . . those dark forests, the Amazon would 'rejoice as a strong man to run a race. . . . ' " In turn, Brazil pointing to its wealth, prosperity, and happiness could say, "Thus much have we done for the advancement of civilization and the happiness of the human race."[21]

Herndon's report was widely noted, praised, and quoted in the U.S. press. In addition, Maury himself had been active in support of his Amazon dreams. In 1852, while Herndon and Gibbon were on their expedition, Maury wrote seven articles for the Washington *National Intelligencer*. Entitled "The Amazon and Atlantic Hopes of South America" and written under the thinly disguised pseudonym "Inca," these articles detailed the natural, commercial, mineral, and agricultural wealth of the Amazon and argued for the free navigation of the Amazon River. In 1853 Maury wrote other articles for *DeBow's Review* in which he reiterated his plea for the free development of the Amazon. In Washington, he lobbied with politicians in the Cabinet and Congress to win support. Maury also succeeded in 1854 in having a Memorial on the Amazon endorsed by the Memphis Convention and introduced in Congress.[22] In spite of public interest in the Amazon and Maury's hard work, little progress was made diplomatically. Authorized to negotiate for the free navigation of the Amazon, U.S. diplomats were unable to persuade Brazil that this was desirable. In South America, both Peru and Bolivia sought the right to navigate the length of the Amazon and passed a decree attempting to force the opening of the Amazon. In Brazil opposition and suspicion gradually declined, but it would not be until 1867 that foreign ships were permitted to navigate the waters of the Amazon.[23]

The expedition to explore the La Plata Basin began on February 8, 1853, when the *Water Witch*, a paddle wheel steamer under the command of Lieutenant Thomas J. Page, sailed from Norfolk with a crew of about sixty men. The decision to dispatch such a venture resulted from several factors. The Fillmore Administration and particularly Secretary of the Navy Kennedy were eager for the government to support another commercial and scientific naval expedition. The political situation in Paraguay and the Argentine seemed propitious, and the idea of an expedition to the La Plata had generated considerable public support in the United States.[24]

Most important in producing the La Plata expedition were the activities of Edward A. Hopkins. At age seventeen, Hopkins enlisted in the navy, and during his five years of service he twice visited South America on cruises with the Brazil Squadron. After a stormy naval career, Hopkins resigned in June, 1845, and immediately received an appointment from the Polk Administration as special agent to Paraguay. In Paraguay, he repeatedly violated his instructions from the State Department, acted in an extremely rash and indiscreet manner, and managed to offend the rulers of both Paraguay and Buenos Aires. In less than a year, he was recalled by Secretary of State James Buchanan. For the next six years, he travelled extensively in Paraguay and attempted to focus commercial interest on the region during his visits to the United States. By 1849 he emerged as an aggressive and indefatigable promoter of commercial opportunity in Paraguay.[25] He wrote promotional articles trumpeting the commercial future for *Hunt's Mer-*

chants' Magazine, *DeBow's Review*, the *National Intelligencer*, and the *Whig Review*. In these articles and in letters to government officials, he advocated free navigation of the La Plata and its tributaries, urged the appointment of well-qualified diplomatic representatives to South America, and advocated an expedition for a hydrographical survey of the region. At the same time, he continued to promote his own interests by attempting to secure an exclusive charter for a steamship company in Paraguay and by offering to organize a manufacturing company and establish an agricultural school.[26]

In January, 1852, he spoke before the recently organized American Geographical and Statistical Society in New York in support of commercial development in Paraguay. In his "Memoir" of Paraguay, Hopkins depicted the great agricultural and commercial potential of Paraguay, argued that the free navigation of the La Plata and its tributaries would double the exports of Paraguay in six months, and emphasized that this burgeoning trade would inevitably gravitate to the United States. According to Hopkins, those provinces of Brazil, Paraguay, and Bolivia drained by the La Plata's tributaries were "much more profitably situated for commercial intercourse than the Chinese empire. . . . " In the name of progress, civilization, and humanity Hopkins urged the United States to embrace this fresh, unlimited opportunity by introducing settlers, steam, and trade into the region. The result would be a "new *Terra firma* of prosperity and peace" as well as the extension of "the *area of freedom*." Several months later, the *Society* responded with a petition to Secretary of the Navy Graham. The petition requested that Graham use his power to conduct "an immediate survey of the river Plata, its affluents and confluents." The information collected would permit merchants and navigators to enter those rivers "for the purpose of trade, for the advancement of civilization, and the promotion of the interests of humanity." "Your Department then, is solicited to take the first step in bringing about a commercial intercourse between the countries of the region and the United States. . . . "[27]

In Washington, this petition as well as increasing public interest in Paraguay met a responsive hearing from Secretary of the Navy Kennedy, who was already in the process of implementing several other expeditions. The La Plata expedition seemed entirely appropriate to him. In addition, the political situation in South America seemed ideal and offered an opportunity for the United States to counteract the influence of Great Britain and France in the region. The government of Paraguay had long favored commercial ties to the United States and had been willing to permit an American steamer to ascend its main rivers. The problem of accessibility to Paraguay was removed in February, 1852, when Justo Urquiza became Provisional Director of the Argentine Confederation and opened the Rio Parana and the Rio Uruguay to international navigation. As Kennedy noted in his annual report in December, 1852, a "vast territory of boundless resources . . . reaching twenty-four parallels of latitude" was now open to the enterprise of those nations which "will be equally prompt to pursue it." Having waited for such an opportunity, Kennedy reported that he would soon dispatch an American vessel to explore the region and serve as "the first messenger of commerce. . . ."[28]

Chosen to command the expedition was forty-five-year-old Lieutenant Thomas J. Page, a Virginian and protegé of Maury. Page had joined the navy in 1827, worked on the coastal survey under Ferdinand R. Hassler in the 1830's, and served in the Mediterranean, Brazil, and East India squadrons. The Virginian had been stationed at the Naval Observatory and had a strong interest in scientific exploration. He had been an early advocate of the North Pacific Exploring Expedition, but had been passed over for command of that project in favor of a senior officer and offered the La Plata expedition instead. Unfortunately, he was not well qualified for this responsibility because he lacked good judgment and tact and proved to be an erratic commander.

In January Page met with Kennedy in Washington before leaving in the *Water Witch* for Norfolk. Kennedy's official instructions, dated January 29, 1853, emphasized the commercial objects of the expedition. Page was to explore the Plata, Paraguay, Parana, and appropriate tributaries to investigate the navigability of the rivers as well as the nature and extent of agriculture and commerce in the adjoining areas in order to determine "the probable extent to which commercial intercourse may be desirable. . . ." The expedition was also to collect natural history specimens and scientific information "to extend the bounds of science" as long as their activities were "not incompatible with the great purpose" of the project. Kennedy emphasized the need for caution and discretion in order to have as favorable an impression on the natives as possible. In the event that American persons or property were injured, Page was to resort to force only "in the last extremity." "The expedition is not for conquest but discovery. Its objects are all peaceful, they are to extend the empire of commerce, and of science. . . ."[29] Along with his official orders, Page received an unofficial memorandum from Maury concerning possible subjects for examination. Maury was particularly interested in determining whether the Amazon and the La Plata River systems were connected by water. Accordingly, he asked Page to collect a variety of information and objects which might help answer this question.[30]

From the outset, the expedition encountered problems. Extensive repairs were required at Norfolk and again upon arrival at Buenos Aires. Along the way, Page was asked, refused, and then was ordered by Commander John Pope to exchange one of the expedition's chronometers with one from the *Vandalia*. Once in Buenos Aires, the *Water Witch* was asked to tow the *Jamestown* of the Brazil Squadron over the bar so she could sail to Rio and then in the absence of the *Jamestown* to remain in the harbor during a tense political situation to protect U.S. citizens there in case fighting erupted. Although violence did not occur, the U.S. chargé d'affaires asked Page to convey General Justo José de Urquiza and his entourage from Buenos Aires to the province of Entre Rios. After sailing to Montevideo for coal in August, the *Water Witch* finally arrived in Asunción, the base of her exploring activities, in October, 1853. After an interview with Paraguay's President Don Carlos Antonio Lopez, Page received permission to ascend the Paraguay River to the border of Brazil. For the next twenty-six months, Page and his crew charted and explored the Parana, the Paraguay, the Uruguay, the Bermejo, and the Salado Rivers in the *Water Witch* and a smaller steamer, the *Pilcomayo*. In addition, Page and smaller parties travelled overland to explore and collect information about several areas unreachable by water.[31]

Unfortunately, Page proved an ineffective diplomat whose conduct contributed to the deterioration of relations between the United States and Paraguay not to a new era of commercial development. After his interview with President Lopez who gave him permission to ascend the Paraguay River, Page angered the Paraguayan leader by sailing beyond the Brazilian border against the President's orders. More serious was Page's involvement in a dispute between Lopez and Edward Hopkins. By 1854 Hopkins had returned to Paraguay with Lopez's blessing as American consul and head of the U.S. and Paraguay Navigation Company. Chartered in Rhode Island with the backing of several capitalists, the company was to build and navigate ships on the rivers of South America and engage in other legitimate business. The company thrived in early 1854 from its base at Asunción until the intemperate Hopkins began to quarrel with Lopez. In August the President accused Hopkins of various legal infractions, closed his operations, and withdrew his authority as American consul.

When Hopkins requested his assistance, Page was drawn into the dispute in spite of his low opinion of the American promoter. Earlier, Page had met and quarreled with Hopkins in 1853 at Montevideo. In spite of his caution and his understanding that both Hopkins and Lopez were to blame for the dispute, Page agreed to evacuate Hopkins and the Americans at Asunción to Corrientes in late September, 1854. The intervention of an American naval officer angered Lopez, and he immediately closed the rivers of Paraguay to foreign warships. Shortly after this incident, Page received instructions from the United States to exchange ratifications of a revised commercial treaty signed in 1852 with Paraguay. Unable to enter Paraguayan waters, Page failed to execute this diplomatic mission and the treaty remained unratified.[32]

The expulsion of the *Water Witch* from Paraguayan waters also led directly to a more serious incident. On February 1, 1855, Paraguayan guns opened fire on the *Water Witch* as it passed the fort of Itapirú on the Parana River, which formed the border between Paraguay and the Argentine province of Corrientes. Lieutenant William N. Jeffers, who had been sent to explore the border area, returned fire and then sailed back to Corrientes. One American was killed and several wounded in the incident. Once he learned of the incident, Page returned to Buenos Aires and spent several weeks in February and March travelling between there and Montevideo in a futile effort to persuade Commodore William Salter of the Brazil Squadron to send naval reinforcements and destroy the fort at Itapirú. Salter refused and, in spite of Page's objection, was sustained by the Navy Department.[33]

Unable to avenge the outrage against the *Water Witch*, Page resumed the work of the expedition by surveying more than 900 miles of the Salado River during the summer and fall. Then with his work nearly complete, Page returned to the United States. After reaching Washington in May, 1856, Page began to plan for a second voyage to the La Plata. His expedition had produced valuable charts of the rivers he had surveyed, a mass of scientific observations and specimens, and encouraging information about the commercial potential of La Plata and its tributaries. The fact that Page was not a trained scientific observer and his expedition lacked a team of scientists rendered his information less valuable than it might have been. However, Page's charts, his report to the Navy Department, and his official report, published in 1859, enthusiastically confirmed the hopes of those Americans who believed that South America, not Asia, offered the greatest commercial potential to the United States. He reported that his expedition had surveyed 3,600 miles of rivers and explored 4,400 miles by land, a vast area which touched parts of the Argentine Confederation, Brazil, Bolivia, and Paraguay. Based on his expedition, Page predicted an era of unprecedented population growth for the region which would be surpassed only by the population growth of North America. The potential for commercial wealth was also extraordinary because the region was "even richer in all natural, mineral, pastoral, and agricultural resources than the great basins of the Oronoco and Amazon. . . . " Noting the awareness and interest of several European nations in the commercial wealth of the region, Page urged immediate action by the United States. Commercial agreements and ties needed to be developed promptly before "alliances are made elsewhere."[34]

Neither the Amazon nor the La Plata naval expeditions led directly to free navigation or unrestricted commercial development in these two South American river basins, but the enterprises made an important contribution to the continuing commercial expansion of the United States. The mass of valuable scientific, geographic, and commercial information produced by the expeditions verified the claims of enthusiasts such as Maury and Hopkins. In so doing, these expeditions helped to further stimulate the expansionist imagination of a nation in the process of creating a vast overseas commercial empire.

7.
Democratic Disarray in the Caribbean

It is very desirable that these people should be taught that the United States will not tolerate these outrages, and that they have the power and the determination to check them.
Secretary of the Navy James Dobbin to Commander George Hollins,
June 10, 1854

When Franklin Pierce became President in March, 1853, many Democrats hoped for a vigorous expansionist foreign policy. As a Democrat committed to sectional compromise, Pierce hoped to avoid further agitation of the slavery question, unite the nation behind the compromise measures of 1850, and pursue an aggressive foreign policy. In the eyes of expansionists, the previous two Whig Presidents had followed a timid, unimaginative, and weak foreign policy. In the Clayton-Bulwer Treaty of 1850 with Great Britain, the United States had renounced claim to exclusive control of any future isthmian canal and acquiesced in British occupation of the Mosquito coast. And neither President Zachary Taylor nor Millard Fillmore had pressed for the acquisition of Cuba or other territorial possessions in the Western Hemisphere. If the nation had not suffered any serious diplomatic setbacks, expansionists argued that negotiation and compromise had replaced bold initiative and decisive action.

By the early 1850's a resurgent expansionism, centered in the Young America movement, depicted the United States as a young giant in "exulting manhood" ready to challenge the old, worn-out powers of Europe. Although many Americans of an earlier age would have abhorred the comparison, the expansionists of the 1850's embraced the image of the nation as an imperial "new Rome." By 1852 Young America had become synonomous with a faction of aggressive, young Democrats who adopted the phrase as a battle cry to oust established party leaders, elevate one of their own, Stephen Douglas, to the Presidency, and translate their expansive dreams into national policy. Led by such men as George Sanders, Stephen Douglas, Robert J. Walker, Robert F. Stockton, and Pierre Soulé, the movement included supporters from all parts of the country but was strongest in the West. Proponents wanted the American republic to eschew its tradition of neutrality and nonintervention overseas and claim a major role in world affairs. Dynamic commercial growth abroad, continued territorial expansion, active American support for the struggling revolutionary movements in Europe, and U.S. dominance in the Caribbean and Central America became the main goals of the movement. "Great, powerful, and rich as are the United States," declared one Young American, "they must become greater, more powerful, more rich." In the Caribbean, these expansionists sought the acquisition of Cuba and other possessions, the annexation of more Mexican territory, and the construction of an isthmian canal.[1]

Using the *Democratic Review* as their political mouthpiece, the Young America Democrats waged a strident campaign in 1852 but failed to take control of the party when New Hampshire's Franklin Pierce received the nomination. Although Pierce was not one of their own, the Young Americans had denied the nomination to the worst of the "old fogys" and ended up with a platform which praised the Mexican War and anticipated the "full expansion of the energies and capacity of this great and progressive people."[2] After Pierce's election, these Democrats could not prevent "old fogy" William L. Marcy from becoming Secretary of State, but a number of avowed expansionists received important appointments. Jefferson Davis and Caleb Cushing were appointed to the Cabinet. In the diplomatic corps, Pierre Soulé was appointed minister to Spain, John Y. Mason to France, August Belmont to Belgium, and James Gadsden to Mexico. As minister to England, James Buchanan's age and vacillating instincts rendered him no friend of Young America, but he was a strong advocate of acquiring Cuba.

In his Inaugural Address President Pierce reiterated his support for the Compromise of 1850 and boldly affirmed that his administration "will not be controlled by any timid forebodings of evil from expansion. Indeed . . . our attitude as a nation and our position on the globe render the acquisition of certain possessions not within our jurisdiction eminently important for our protection, if not in the future essential for the preservation of the rights of commerce and the peace of the world." The new President also emphasized that new possessions would result from "no grasping spirit" but rather from a "just and pacific" foreign policy. Reaffirming the importance of overseas commerce to the United States, Pierce assured his fellow citizens that "upon every sea and on every soil where our enterprise may rightfully seek the protection of our flag, American citizenship is an inviolable panoply for the security of American rights."[3] Such expansive sentiments clearly presaged an enhanced peacetime role for the navy even though Pierce did not outline his expectations here.

During his first year in office Pierce attempted to implement an expansive foreign policy in several ways. The administration authorized South Carolinian James Gadsden to negotiate with Mexico for enough territory to build a railroad through the Gila River region and to acquire parts of Tamaulipas, Nueva Leon, Coahuila, Sonora, and all of lower California for a price of up to $50 million. In England, James Buchanan was instructed to affirm U.S. interest in Central America and to express concern over the extension of British sovereignty to the Bay Islands near Honduras and increasing British influence in Nicaragua. In South America, U.S. representatives to several countries were ordered to press for cooperative action to convince Brazil to open the Amazon to free navigation and commerce. In the Pacific, the administration recognized the possibility of a Hawaiian annexation proposal and had begun to prepare for that eventuality.[4]

But these initiatives were secondary to Cuba which stood as the centerpiece of Pierce's foreign policy. Pierre Soulé, the minister of Spain, was instructed initially not to negotiate for the purchase of Cuba because the administration hoped that Cuba would free itself of Spanish rule without diplomatic action. The administration hoped for a Texas-style revolution in Cuba and knew that extensive preparations were underway for a filibustering expedition to be commanded by Mexican War veteran and former Governor of Mississippi, John A. Quitman. In July, 1853, Quitman visited Washington, talked with a number of influential friends including Attorney General Caleb Cushing and Secretary of War Jefferson Davis, and apparently received assurances that the administration would not interfere or obstruct the expedition. In the meantime Quitman had received a considerable amount of financial and public support in cities such as New Orleans and New York. In August he signed a formal agreement with Cuban revolutionary leaders in New York by which he became the civil and military leader of the expedition with dictatorial powers to raise troops, purchase equipment, issue bonds, and spend money for the purpose of establishing an independent Cuba. Quitman's stature, his influential supporters in the United States and Cuba, and the extent of his preparations presaged success in the minds of many observers and they waited confidently in 1853 for the overthrow of Spanish rule in Cuba. Once that happened, it would be a relatively simple step to annex Cuba to the United States.[5]

In the summer of 1853, an event occurred in the Mediterranean which seemed to symbolize the new administration's vigorous approach to foreign policy and naval power. On June 21st Martin Koszta was kidnapped in Smyrna, placed aboard the Austrian brig-of-war *Hussar* in the harbor, and held there in chains. An Austrian by birth, Koszta had fought for the Hungarian revolutionaries in 1848–1849, been forced to flee the country, and then resided for a time in the United States. Although not a naturalized American citizen, Koszta had signified his intention of becoming a U.S. citizen when he returned to the eastern Mediterranean. Koszta's seizure created an uproar among foreigners in Smyrna, and a delegation of them demanded his release. American consul Edward S. Offley was sympathetic to Koszta's plight but probably could have done little had it not been for the fortuitous arrival of the American sloop-of-war, *St. Louis*, the day after the incident. After meeting with Offley, Commander Duncan N. Ingraham visited the *Hussar* where he was told that the Austrian captain had gone ashore. The two Americans then visited the Austrian consul and naval commander on shore and received permission to board the *Hussar* and visit with the prisoner.[6]

On June 24th Offley wrote to the American legation at Constantinople for instructions and was informed by the secretary of the legation, John Porter Brown, that American protection should be extended to Koszta and that continued efforts should be made to secure his release. Brown also wrote to the Austrian consul demanding Koszta's release. To this, the Austrian responded that Koszta's arrest was completely legal under existing treaties. To Commander Ingraham, Brown sent copies of his letter to Offley, his official dispatches, and his recommendation that Ingraham recapture Koszta promptly and let the governments negotiate later. Support for precipitous action was added by the presence of New York Congressman Caleb Lyon, a rabid proponent of naval expansion and Young America ideas. Lyon met with Offley and Ingraham in Smyrna and then at the height of the crisis he wrote a note to Ingraham on July 2nd in which he approved "Taking the exile Koszta per force. . . . Do not let this chance slip to acquit yourself nobly and do honor to our country. . . . The eyes of nations are upon the little *St. Louis* and her Commander. . . . For God's sake, and for the sake of humanity, stand for the right!''[7]

Ingraham had visited the *Hussar* the same morning and issued an ultimatum to her commander: Koszta was to be released or he would be taken by force if an answer was not received by 4 o'clock that afternoon. The *St. Louis* and the two Austrian warships present then cleared their decks for battle. At the same time, Consul Offley managed to persuade Austrian officials to place Koszta in custody of the French consul pending a settlement of the dispute. Koszta was then delivered in chains to the French consulate where his irons were removed, and he remained until October, 1853, when an agreement permitted his return to the United States.

In fact, Commander Ingraham had acted in a daring, heroic, and probably foolhardy, fashion. His eighteen-gun sloop faced an Austrian brig, sloop, and three small steamers totalling twenty-six guns. Armed conflict might well have resulted in the defeat of the *St. Louis* and the continued detention of Koszta. In this instance, however, American determination and bravado had carried the day, brought the surrender of the prisoner, and the vindication of the American flag. For his action, Ingraham was praised by the administration, lauded by the American and European press, and rewarded with a medal authorized by a joint resolution of Congress in 1854.[8]

In Washington, the Austrian Chargé Chevalier J. G. Hülsemann demanded the return of Koszta, official American disavowal of Ingraham's actions, and satisfaction for this insult to Austria. Secretary of State William Marcy reviewed the whole affair carefully and drafted a reply which rejected Austrian demands and reasserted American rights in strong terms. In fact, the Pierce Administration used this Hülsemann letter much as Secretary of State Daniel Webster had exploited an earlier Hülsemann protest over American treatment of Louis Kossuth, that is, to bid defiance at a European monarchy. In December, 1853, President Pierce reported tersely that Koszta's seizure and detention at Smyrna had been illegal because he was "clothed with the nationality of the United States...." Accordingly, the conduct of American officials in the case "has been fully approved by me" and "compliance with the several demands of the Emperor of Austria has been declined."[9]

Along with Pierce's assertive foreign policy went a program of naval expansion, reform, and rejuvenation. In the decade since Abel Ushur had been Secretary of the Navy, no administration had undertaken a coherent and systematic program of naval reform and expansion. With seven different men serving as Secretary, even those who wanted to strengthen the navy had not served long enough to make a lasting difference. At the outset, it appeared that James C. Dobbin would fit into that same category as Secretary. The forty-nine-year-old North Carolinian had served one term in the House of Representatives, as Speaker of the North Carolina House of Delegates, and as a key Pierce supporter in the 1852 Democratic Convention. Inexperienced in naval affairs, Dobbin nevertheless was prepared to devote a great amount of time, energy, and thought to the navy's problems.[10]

Once in office, Dobbin quickly recognized the navy's woeful condition. If challenged the navy could not have actively protected the nation's far-flung commerce, fought effectively against the fleets of either England or France, or adequately defended the nation's coastline. Even if it remained unchallenged, the navy was not capable of serving as an effective arm of Pierce's expansive foreign policies. In 1853 the navy totalled some seventy ships of all types and classes and included about 2,100 guns. Probably forty of these vessels could have been prepared for service in a period of several months, but many of these were old and obsolete in one way or another. In contrast, England boasted a fleet of about 650 ships and 17,000 guns in 1854 while France had 328 ships and 7,100 guns. The U.S. Navy also lagged behind Russia and Holland in total ships and guns. Moreover, the navies of Europe included an increasing number of modern, screw driven steamers with up-to-date armament and gunnery. Although the United States had wisely avoided gauging the adequacy of its own navy by comparison with the number of ships and guns in the various European navies, the American Navy had not even kept pace with the nation's own peacetime needs. Since 1844 the nation had added to its long coastline, more than doubled its imports and exports, and nearly doubled its registered merchant tonnage. However, the size of the navy in 1853 was approximately what it had been a decade earlier, and it had only a few steam warships. Nor had the navy kept pace with developments in armament, gunnery, and steam power. The service was also limited to 7,500 men, not enough to man a fifty-ship fleet, and shackled by a rigid seniority system, antequated rules and regulations, and serious problems in the enlisted ranks.

In his annual report of December, 1853, Secretary Dobbin addressed the problem by arguing that the "maintenance of our proper and elevated rank among the great Powers of the world; the just protection of our widespread and growing commerce; the defense of our thousands of miles of coast along the Atlantic and Pacific oceans, the lakes and the Gulf of Mexico; the recent improvements in the art of naval architecture adopted by other nations" all demonstrated "the necessity of an increase of the Navy." Such a program would best preserve the interests and peaceful intentions of the nation. "It is true, indeed, our policy is peace. No lust of dominion, no spirit of aggression, marks out *our* course. Our national mission is, by the moral force of example, to illustrate the blessings of liberty and peace, civilization and religion." At the same time, Dobbin emphasized that a "new empire" in the Pacific had "as if by magic, sprung into existence. San Francisco promises . . . to become another New York, and our prosperous trade in the Pacific, amid the wonders of commerce, to bear the same relation to China and Japan which that of the Atlantic coast bears to the continent of Europe and Great Britain." Although the American navy did not need to compete with those of Europe on some kind of ratio, the navy did need to "*at least be large enough to command our own seas and coast.*" Without adequate naval protection, the nation's existing coastal fortifications were but "a shield without a sword."[11]

Dobbin recommended the construction of at least six first-class, screw driven steam frigates because recent developments had demonstrated the superiority of screw driven steamers and the vulnerability of paddle driven steamers. He also recommended that the size of the service be increased from 7,500 to 10,000 men, that existing naval yards be improved, that the existing code of rules and regulations be revised, that the seniority system be modified, that a naval retirement board be created, and that general conditions and pay for both officers and enlisted men be improved.

Given the expansive climate of opinion in 1853 and a general recognition of the need for naval rejuvenation, the call for expansion and reform did not generate intense opposition or criticism. Congress increased naval appropriations, approved several of Dobbin's reform proposals, and passed a bill to build six first-class steam frigates and to complete two previously authorized sail frigates. Although the measure eventually passed without a division in the Senate and by a huge bipartisan margin in the House, a brief spirited discussion in the House underlined the latent hostility which still existed to a large peacetime navy.

On March 28, 1854, Virginia Democrat Thomas Bocock, the Chairman of the House Naval Affairs Committee, explained the steamer construction bill and reiterated the compelling arguments which Dobbin had presented the previous December. While the navy had not grown in the past decade, tremendous increases in the size of the nation's territory and commerce had occurred. In addition, the navy needed to be modernized in accord with important recent technological developments. Bocock also emphasized that the nations of Europe were on the verge of a "furious war," which would involve all of Europe and have serious consequences for the United States. Only a strong navy would permit the United States to command the "immunity and rights of neutrality," while taking full advantage of the commercial opportunities which would develop in Asia. "England will be too busily engaged with her powerful foe to have any spare time to protect her eastern trade," predicted Bocock, "and that fertile stream will pour almost undivided into our lap; China, Japan, and all the bright Orient, will load our vessels and enrich our merchants." A European war of any duration would also involve Spain, increase the likelihood of revolution in Cuba, and present a "golden opportunity" for the United States to annex Cuba in good faith. If that did not occur, several outstanding grievances might compel the United States "to take redress into our own hands." Bocock also emphasized the extent and gravity of the English threat to American commerce around the world. In the Western Hemisphere, he was particularly concerned about the British protectorate over the Mosquito coast and the eventual need for the United States to expel the British from Central America. It was, in short, time for the United States to assume a more manful foreign policy and seize its "manifest destiny." "It is *manifest destiny* which will ever make a strong, vigorous, and healthful race overrun and crush out a weak and effete one. Our people *will go* South among the Mexicans and Spaniards, and *will* carry with them the love of our civilization and of our liberty. . . . *This is manifest destiny*. It will go on. . . . We must then take the bolder alternative, and prepare to sustain ourselves manfully."[12]

Two days later Bocock's call for naval expansion to sustain an aggressive foreign policy brought a sharp rebuff from Thomas Hart Benton. The seventy-two-year-old Benton was now serving a single term in the House after three decades in the Senate. Never a champion of the navy, Benton was an old-style state rights, agrarian, Jacksonian Democrat from Missouri, who had nevertheless been willing to vote for naval appropriations when necessitated by such national crises as the French claims controversy of the 1830's. He had also been a sharp opponent of Great Britain, an aggressive expansionist through most of his career, and an early proponent of the American empire in the Pacific. Now, in 1854, he conceded his willingness to support a navy for national defense and for the "protection of commerce" in a narrow sense, but he denounced naval expansion "for conquest" or merely to contest "for the supremacy of the seas." Benton emphasized that the United States did not need a large navy because it was "a continent, not an island; our policy is peace, not aggression; it is defense, not conquest." If the republic intended to remain at peace and did not contemplate a "system of aggression, of foreign conquest," naval expansion and competition was but a ridiculous "contest of ship carpenters."[13]

Although Benton had exaggerated his case against a peacetime navy, he well understood that naval expansion was viewed by some politicians as an integral part of their visions of imperial grandeur. Benton's apprehensions were almost immediately substantiated by the comments of New York's Caleb Lyon, recently returned from his trip to Smyrna where he had urged aggressive action by Commander Ingraham in the Koszta affair. In a few entertaining remarks, Lyon urged a "prompt increase of the Navy" to defend *"American rights, American interests, and American honor"* around the world. The nations of Europe were near war, China was in constant turmoil, the countries of South America were in a state of insurrection, and Central America was being dismembered. According to Lyon, the "files of the State Department are groaning with complaints" from aggrieved Americans abroad. A case in point was the unresolved *Black Warrior* incident. In February of that year, Spanish authorities in Cuba had confiscated the cargo of the American steamer for a technical violation of port regulations. Instead, "Cuba should have been taken in, sir, and satisfaction demanded afterwards." [Laughter and great applause] In a world in which the United States could expect continued intense rivalry with England, the only answer was an effective navy. " 'The Nation Who Wisely Wields Thy Trident, O! Neptune, Alone is Arbiter of the Empire of the World.' " To Benton's criticism, Lyon reacted by moving to amend the measure to authorize the construction of twelve first-class steam frigates and reminded his amused colleagues that in ancient days scheming politicians had also laughed at Noah and his Ark. "They laughed at him; they said it was too big—that the expense of building it was too great; but when the deluge came, it preserved him, while they were engulfed and destroyed." [Laughter] Lyon concluded by reminding the venerable Benton that his generation had passed from the scene: "we live in young America. [Laughter] We live in a progressive age; and the . . . spirit of manifest destiny— is in our brain; it is in our heart; it throbs in our nerves. We cannot get rid of it."[14]

Although Lyon's hyperbole amused his listeners, a number of supporters of the steamer construction bill hastened to distinguish their position from that of Young America. In succession, several politicians endorsed the bill but emphasized that they did not endorse a policy of conquest and aggression. In the midst of the discussion, Bocock attempted to clarify the intent of the bill by emphasizing that the navy was not intended "for offensive operation" but "merely to defend our commerce. That is exactly what I want—nothing more."[15]

Although Congress easily approved the naval steamer bill in April, 1854, the controversy over the Kansas-Nebraska Bill soon overshadowed the issues of naval expansion and foreign policy. The measure aroused sharp bipartisan opposition from the free states because it repealed the Missouri Compromise and opened federal territory north of 36°30′ to slavery. The proposal passed Congress in May and received the President's signature on May 30, 1854, but it turned out to be a hollow victory because of the far-reaching impact it had on public opinion, sectional tension, party politics, and the future of the Pierce Administration. An immediate victim of the controversy was the President's Cuba policy. With southern expansionists becoming increasingly impatient for action, Secretary of State Marcy had instructed Pierre Soulé to offer Spain up to $130 million for Cuba. If that failed, then Soulé was to direct his efforts "to the next most desirable object, which is to detach that Island from the Spanish dominion and from all dependence on any European power."[16]

The Kansas-Nebraska uproar, however, forced a change in the administration's aggressive Cuba policy by the end of May. "The Nebraska question has sadly shattered our party in all the free states," reported Marcy to John Mason, "and deprived it of that strength which was needed and could have been much more profitably used for the acquisition of Cuba."[17] Under sharp attack, Pierce realized that he would further weaken his administration by substantiating anti-slavery charges that he was a tool of the slave power determined to have Cuba at any cost. On May 31, 1854, Pierce responded with a proclamation declaring that the federal government would prosecute violations of the existing neutrality laws. This action had two immediate results. First, it undermined a Democratic attempt in the Senate Foreign Relations Committee to repeal the neutrality laws. Second, it hurt preparations for John Quitman's filibustering expedition to Cuba. In New Orleans a grand jury issued no indictments of illegal activity, but a federal judge there did force Quitman and two associates to post a $3,000 bond to guarantee their observance of the neutrality laws.

In Spain, Soulé's lack of credibility precluded any serious negotiation with Spain for Cuba, but the State Department instructed him in August to meet with Buchanan and Mason and discuss possible strategy for the acquisition of Cuba. With the Crimean War underway and the Spanish government confronted by revolution, the time seemed right for Spain to cede Cuba. The subsequent meeting in October, 1854, in Belgium between the three diplomats produced a report to the administration known as the Ostend Manifesto which emphasized the importance of Cuba to the United States, recommended the purchase of the island from Spain, and implied that the United States would be justified in "wresting it from Spain" if she refused to cede it peacefully.[18]

In Washington, the report received a hostile reception from the beleaguered administration. The Democrats had suffered heavy defeats in the fall elections and Pierce well understood that an attempt to take Cuba forcibly would further weaken the Democratic party in the North. Unfortunately for the President, the contents of the report were known and the document was published by the end of November, thereby producing a storm of criticism which effectively ended Pierce's dreams of acquiring Cuba. According to historian David Potter the Kansas-Nebraska Act and the Ostend Manifesto stand as the "two great calamities of Franklin Pierce's Presidency." In foreign policy, the Cuba issue had now been translated irrevocably from a traditional national goal to a sectional demand of the slave power. Moreover, the overall strength of the Pierce Administration and its expansionist policies had been mortally wounded.[19]

During the summer of 1854 the actual weakness of the President's Caribbean policy was momentarily disguised by a naval incident in Central America. After the discovery of gold in California, Nicaragua became increasingly important to the United States. From the eastern United States, the easiest route to California for thousands of eager immigrants was by ship to Greytown at the mouth of the San Juan River, up the stream into Lake Nicaragua, across the lake, overland to Lake Managua, across this body of water, then overland twelve miles to the

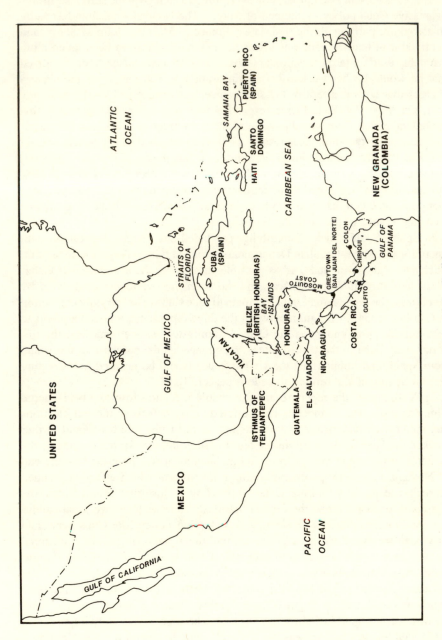

Central America and the Caribbean

Pacific, and on to San Francisco via steamer. The route also offered one of the two logical sites for an isthmian canal whenever the project was undertaken. In response to the demand for passage to California, Cornelius Vanderbilt formed the Accessory Transit Company, secured a monopoly grant from Nicaragua, and established a thriving business which averaged 2,000 passengers per month from 1851 to 1856.

The British countered American interests in the area by maintaining a colony in Belize, affirming its claims to the Bay Islands and retaining its protectorate of the Mosquito coast between Cape Honduras and the San Juan River. A potential clash had been averted in 1850 by the Clayton-Bulwer Treaty which prohibited American and British colonization in Central America, precluded exclusive control by either nation of an isthmian canal across Central America, and provided for cooperation in the construction of such a canal. But this agreement was sharply criticized in the United States and threatened by the 1852 British proclamation of the Colony of the Bay Islands. After it became a "free city" in 1852, Greytown or San Juan del Norte became the focal point of U.S. determination to maintain its interests in the area. At issue was a dispute between the authority of Greytown officials and the Accessory Transit Company. In the harbor at Greytown at the mouth of the San Juan River stood the island of Punta Arenas where the Company had its quarters and storehouses. In early 1853, the Company also built a hotel there to house transit passengers thereby permitting them to avoid Greytown and the Company to evade various local regulations. In response, Greytown officials demanded that Punta Arenas be vacated and periodically threatened the Company's property there. At the same time, American naval officers had been instructed to protect American property and lives.[20]

The situation worsened in May, 1854, when an American captain of one of the Company's ships shot and killed a native boatman. When black Greytown residents attempted to arrest the captain, the U.S. minister to Nicaragua, Solon Borland of Arkansas, intervened and held the crowd off at gunpoint. This incident led to the attempted arrest of Borland, who was injured by a broken bottle during the confrontation. Borland then returned to the United States and urged strong action. In response, the administration dispatched the sloop-of-war *Cyane* to Greytown. Commander George Hollins, who had already occupied Greytown and Punta Arenas briefly in 1853, was now instructed to demand immediate indemnity for past damages to the property of the Company, a prompt apology for the insult to an American official, and assurances of good behavior in the future. Although these objectives were to be realized without "a resort to violence and destruction of property and loss of life," Hollins was reminded that "It is very desirable that these people should be taught that the United States will not tolerate these outrages, and that they have the power and determination to check them."[21]

After arriving on July 11, 1854, Hollins conferred with Company officials and the American commercial agent, Joseph W. Fabens. That same day, Fabens formally demanded an indemnity of $16,000 for outrages on American property

and citizens, $8,000 in claims to the Company, a formal apology for past out-
rages, and assurances "of future good behavior. . . . " The next morning Commander Hollins issued a proclamation declaring that the American demands were
to be met "forthwith" or that he would bombard the town the next day. The
proclamation was posted but brought no response from local officials. The next
day, Hollins sent a steamer to evacuate any residents who wanted to leave and
then at 9:00 A.M. opened fire on Greytown. After intermittent shelling throughout
the day, a detachment was sent ashore to destroy what remained of the town by
fire. By evening destruction was virtually complete, although none of the town's
300 residents were killed.[22]

This blatant destruction of a defenseless town might have created a crisis in
Anglo-American affairs by signifying that the Pierce Administration now intended to assert the interests and power of the United States in Central America
through the use of military force. In fact, the shelling of Greytown did not
represent a new initiative by the United States. Instead, Hollins' action was an
isolated attempt to defend American property rights and was not part of a larger
effort to extend American influence, challenge British power, or exert American
sovereignty over the "free city" of Greytown. As such, the incident reflected
the confusion in administration policy and did not create a serious crisis with
Great Britain. In June, 1854, the two nations had concluded the Canadian Reciprocity Treaty which resolved tension over fishing rights near Canada and
established custom duties on agricultural imports from Canada. Although the
British protested to American minister James Buchanan, neither country wanted
to reverse the improvement which had begun in Anglo-American relations, and
so the Greytown bombing never became a major issue.

Subsequent developments in Nicaragua further underlined the confusion of
Pierce's Caribbean policy. A civil war in Nicaragua prompted the Constitution-
alist faction to invite American adventurer William Walker and his small army
of Americans to assist their cause. After eluding American authorities in the
spring of 1855, Walker and his force reached Nicaragua and joined the civil
war. Within a short time, Walker gained control of the civilian government with
support of such key figures as Cornelius Vanderbilt who headed the Accessory
Transit Company. In June, 1856, Walker was elected President of Nicaragua in
a tainted election. In the United States, filibustering ventures like Walker's were
viewed by many expansionists as an initial step which would pave the way for
large scale American settlement and the eventual annexation of these areas to
the United States. In fact, Walker was a ruthless and autocratic man who one
follower labelled a "freckled little despot" and was badly misunderstood by
most of his followers in the United States. Although he planned and led several
filibustering expeditions to Mexico and Central America, historians have not
found conclusive proof that Walker sought to annex either Mexico or Nicaragua
to the Union or to create a democratic republic in either country."[23]

From the outset the Pierce Administration was suspicious of Walker and
warned American citizens not to participate in the venture. American naval

officers in the area were also warned not to interfere in the civil war and instructed to take necessary action only to protect American commerce and lives. At the same time, enthusiasm for Walker ran high in the United States, and more than 1,200 Americans had flocked to Nicaragua by the spring of 1856. Although the administration objected to the premature recognition of the Nicaraguan Republic by American chargé d'affaires John H. Wheeler, it formally received the Nicaraguan minister in May, 1856. At the Democratic Convention, Pierce's supporters endorsed Walker's venture, as did the party's official 1856 platform. However, Walker's days as President of Nicaragua were numbered. He foolishly antagonized Vanderbilt by revoking his Company's charter and aroused the military opposition of a Central American alliance which fought to oust his regime. Finally, in May, 1857, Walker avoided defeat only by surrendering to U.S. naval officer Charles Davis. Throughout the whole process, the Pierce Administration had responded with uncertainty to the Walker expedition and as a result had hurt American interests in Central America by substantiating local suspicions that the United States intended to use filibustering missions as a pretext to take control of the region.

Frustrated in Cuba and Central America, Pierce's expansive ambitions also failed to meet expectations in other quarters. For example, Commissioner David Gregg negotiated a treaty in 1854 for the annexation of Hawaii. However, the draft which arrived in Washington in November, 1854, proved unacceptable because it provided for the immediate admission of Hawaii into the Union and specified a grant to the King of $300,000 which the administration thought too large. Other problems also needed to be resolved, but the death of the King and the ascension of his anti-American heir ended chances for annexation.

The sectional crisis also had a serious impact on the administration's naval policy as well as its diplomacy. Secretary Dobbin continued to argue the need for naval reform, expansion and modernization, but with little effect. His appeal for a second squadron in the Pacific was ignored and his calls for additional screw driven, steam warships went unheeded by Congress. Instead congressional support for the navy waned as politicians bickered over the use of domestic hemp, the size and placement of existing naval yards, the role of the Naval Retirement Board, and similar questions. Only in the last hours of the administration did a coalition of southerners add an amendment to the Naval Appropriations Bill which provided for the construction of five shallow draft steamers.

In the Caribbean, American naval initiative languished. A riot at Colon, Panama, in April, 1856, killed fifteen Americans and wounded sixteen others. After an investigation, the American special commissioner filed a report which blamed the local police for helping to plan the riot, concluded that the local government was incapable of maintaining order, and recommended that the United States immediately occupy the isthmus from coast to coast. In September, a detachment of 160 men from the *St. Mary's* and the *Independence* landed and occupied the railroad station at Colon for three days. Although taken to guarantee the transit route, this action proved to be an ineffective gesture. In subsequent negotiations with New Granada, U.S. diplomats proposed that the South American government pay for the loss of American life and property in the riot, recognize Panama City and Colon as self-governing cities, and cede several islands in the Bay of Panama to the United States to use as a naval station. When New Granada summarily rejected these proposals, the Pierce Administration's hopes for a naval base in Panama ended.[24] In Santo Domingo, negotiations to secure a land grant for an American naval base at Samana Bay also failed in 1853 and 1854 as British and French diplomats there effectively undermined the American proposal.[25]

The one exploring expedition in Central America which held potential significance was Lieutenant Isaac G. Strain's mission to the Isthmus of Darien in 1854. However, the venture was never of great interest to the Pierce Administration because it represented part of a joint effort by the United States and several other countries to find a practical canal route across the isthmus. Once underway the expedition experienced great difficulty. After he became lost and several of his party died in the jungle, Strain and several others were fortunate to escape with their lives. When they returned, they brought no proof of a viable canal route as Strain concluded that he had explored a route which was completely impractical for a canal.[26]

Overseas, the navy's responsibilities and the safety of American commerce remained stable in the Mediterranean, the Atlantic, and the Pacific. The Crimean War did not disrupt American commerce significantly or present a challenge to American neutral rights on the high seas. On the African coast, the slave trade continued to be more of a diplomatic and political nuisance than a threat to American commercial interests. On each of its overseas stations, naval vessels continued to execute their customary duties with little difficulty. At the same time, the administration's official instructions to its squadron commanders indicated no systematic attempt to use the navy as part of a diplomatic strategy for further commercial expansion.

Despite the hopes of expansionists, the election of a new Democratic President in 1856 proved a disappointment. As a former Secretary of State and Minister to England, James Buchanan brought more diplomatic experience to the White House than any man since John Quincy Adams. During his term Buchanan maintained an office in the State Department and exercised strong influence in his administration's foreign policy. Although he was a vacillating politician and had never been a proponent of the Young America creed, Buchanan well understood the value of a vigorous foreign policy at a time of domestic crisis. He readily accepted the 1856 Democratic Platform which called for "free seas and progressive free trade throughout the world," endorsed the principles of the Monroe Doctrine as "sacred," expressed sympathy for efforts "to regenerate" Central America, recommended United States control of transit routes in Central America, and avowed "our ascendency in the Gulf of Mexico. . . ."[27]

Hoping to avoid further agitation over the slavery question and resolve the conflict in Kansas, Buchanan intended his main sphere of initiative to be foreign affairs where he hoped to use an assertive policy to reinstill a sense of national unity and pride at home. In the Caribbean, Buchanan wanted to expand American power by using the navy to protect American lives and property and to intervene where unstable political situations existed. On several occasions, he asked for congressional authority to use military forces to protect American interests in the region. In addition, Buchanan hoped to purchase Cuba, acquire additional territory from Mexico, and establish naval coaling stations. He also believed that legitimate colonization from the United States and existing claims against several governments could be used as leverage to acquire possessions in the region. Accordingly, he denounced the ''lawless expeditions'' of filibusterers such as William Walker because they hurt the United States by creating bitterness and tension in Central America.[28]

In attempting to crack down on Walker, however, Buchanan faced the same difficulties his predecessor had. After Walker returned to the United States from Nicaragua in 1857, he began to organize another expedition, eluded federal attempts to block him, and sailed for Nicaragua in November. Near Greytown, he slipped by the unsuspecting Commander Frederick Chatard of the *Saratoga* and landed with a force of about 200 men at Punta Arenas. When informed of this development in Panama, Commodore Hiram Paulding sailed immediately in the *Wabash* and reached Greytown on December 6, 1857. Paulding was an experienced officer nearing his sixty-first birthday and had compiled a distinguished naval record which dated back to 1811. He had been honored for gallantry during the War of 1812, promoted through the ranks to Captain, and assumed command of the Home Squadron in 1855. Two days later, Paulding landed with a force of 300 men and forced Walker to surrender. After being conveyed to Panama, Walker returned to the United States to complain of his illegal capture on foreign territory by U.S. naval forces and to begin planning for yet another filibustering expedition to Nicaragua. In the United States a controversy erupted in early 1858 over the legality of Paulding's conduct. Supporters of Walker criticized Paulding for exceeding his authority and the Neutrality Act of 1818 by landing on foreign soil and forcing Walker's surrender. In response, Paulding's defenders acknowledged that the naval officer may have exceeded the letter of his authority but emphasized that Walker was the one who had violated the neutrality laws. They also noted that Nicaragua formally thanked the U.S. government for Paulding's action.[29]

Apparently reacting to strong southern pressure, the administration pursued an uneven course. The President reported to Congress that Paulding had committed ''a grave error'' but praised him as ''a gallant officer'' who had acted ''from pure and patriotic motives and in the sincere conviction that he was promoting the interest and vindicating the honor of his country.'' At the same time that Paulding's action was rebuked by the President, the Navy Department punished Commander Chatard for permitting Walker to elude his patrol.[30]

To support an aggressive foreign policy, Buchanan and his Secretary of the Navy, Isaac Toucey, requested in December, 1857, that Congress authorize construction of ten small steamers at a cost of $2.3 million. Noting that the five steam sloops-of-war approved earlier that year were too heavy for use in very shallow waters, Toucey asked for additional steamers of "light draught, great speed, and heavy guns." In making his request at a time of economic recession, Toucey emphasized that it was "not the policy of our Government to maintain a great navy in time of peace." The United States should not burden itself with an "overgrown naval establishment" in a mistaken effort to compete "in the magnitude of their naval preparations" with other commercial powers. Instead, the American republic should maintain a navy "unsurpassed in its efficiency and completeness" within "its limited extent."[31]

These rather moderate views reflected the new Secretary's own political attitudes and those of the administration he served. To his position, sixty-four-year-old Toucey brought experience from an undistinguished political career in Connecticut, less than one term in the U.S. Senate, and brief stints as Polk's Attorney General and Acting Secretary of State. As a northern Democrat with southern sympathies, Toucey fit well into Buchanan's Cabinet and viewed the navy's needs from a pro-southern perspective. He argued for the type of very small, light warships which would be of most value in the Caribbean and along the shallow coastline of the South.[32]

After Congress authorized eight additional small steamers in June, 1858, Toucey recommended the purchase of nine steamers and the construction of ten more steam warships in December. "What we more especially need in time of peace," emphasized Toucey, "is a larger number of vessels capable of entering the rivers and harbors of all foreign countries, as well as our own." In the Western Hemisphere, the unstable condition of many areas required warships which would approach these countries "frequently, and at every accessible point." The fact that four or five small steamships could be built and maintained for the cost of a single large warship meant that American commercial interests would be protected more effectively over a larger portion of the globe. While large warships made a more impressive appearance abroad, small fast steamers were every bit as useful and formidable in protecting commerce in peacetime. Moreover, these light warships were much more valuable to the United States in defending its long coastline and adjacent waters. "The waters of the Gulf of Mexico and those contiguous to it . . . are to be guarded, like inland seas, with jealous care, and should be made to swarm with these floating fortifications." Unlike previous advocates of naval expansion, Toucey tailored his recommendations to the administration's Caribbean policy and to Southern political pressures. Although small steamers could be used to protect American trade overseas, these vessels were most useful in the Caribbean and the Gulf. As such, the construction of these small warships drew sharp criticism from northerners who preferred more traditional warships and feared that the new steamers would be used to advance pro-slavery schemes in the Caribbean.[33]

Overseas the Buchanan Administration used and condoned vigorous naval action in defense of American rights and commerce. Secretary Toucey launched several minor exploring ventures in Central America and the Pacific. In the Caribbean, the Fijis, and South America, naval forces intervened on numerous occasions. "At no period, when we were not actually engaged in war," reported the Secretary at one point, "has the Navy been more actively employed than during the past year." In 1858, the Department dispatched a naval force to Cuban waters to resist British naval efforts to police the slave trade by searching merchant vessels flying the American flag. In September, 1860, American naval forces landed during an insurrection in Panama City and jointly occupied the town with British forces until order was restored in early October.[34]

In the Fijis in October, 1858, Commander Arthur Sinclair of the sloop *Vandalia* was attempting to resolve outstanding claims against local rulers when he learned that cannibals had captured an American merchant vessel on the island of Waya and allegedly eaten the two Americans on her crew the previous April. Sinclair chartered a small vessel to negotiate the coral-infested waters and dispatched a force of fifty men under the command of Lieutenant C. H. B. Caldwell who secured the assistance of a local chieftain and sailed to Waya. In response, the offending Lomati tribe acknowledged the murders, bid defiance to the Americans, and challenged them to combat: "we have heard of the Papillangi [foreigners]; we wish to meet them in battle. . . . Come, Papillangi, our fires are lighted, our ovens are hot, has not the evil spirit given you to us? Come. . . ." The next day, October 10th, Sinclair landed his forces, marched them for several difficult hours over rugged terrain, and destroyed the mountain village of the Lomati. In the battle which ensued, the Americans suffered six casualties while killing or wounding thirty of the natives. Although the long-term effect of the incident was unclear, Caldwell received the praise of the commanding officer of the Pacific Squadron and the Secretary of the Navy. In 1859 Toucey noted that the action had "taught the savages a lesson which will be remembered in those barbarous islands."[35]

Buchanan's most significant naval initiative was the expedition to Paraguay in 1858–1859. After Lieutenant Thomas J. Page returned from the La Plata in 1855, he began to plan for a second expedition to complete the work of the first mission. In March, 1857, Congress approved $25,000 to support a second expedition to the region. In addition, Page secured the support of R. B. Forbes who agreed to build a steamer for the venture and then charter it to the navy for $300 per month. Named the *Argentine*, the ninety-eight-foot vessel awaited Page's arrival in the Argentine by March, 1858. In the meantime President Buchanan had declared his resolve to settle the diplomatic dispute with Paraguay and requested congressional approval in December, 1857 to use force if necessary. In Congress, the lobbying efforts of the Paraguayan Navigation Company overcame the reservations of several Senators, and the President was authorized in June, 1858 "to adopt such measures and use such force" as "necessary and advisable" to gain satisfaction for the *Water Witch* incident. Congress also approved $10,000 to cover the expenses involved in settling the dispute.[36]

The administration then assembled a huge squadron by contemporary American naval standards. It consisted of nineteen ships, most of which were small steamers, 2,500 men, and 200 guns, under the command of Commodore William B. Shubrick. Lieutenant Page was to accompany the squadron as commander of the frigate *Salinas*. The disproportionate size of the expedition was clearly not determined by the magnitude of the task at hand. If ten ships had been sufficient to open Japan, it is difficult to understand why twice that number was required to settle a minor diplomatic dispute with a weak, distracted, and land-locked nation in South America. Not all of the American ships could hope to ascend the hundreds of miles of river which lay between Paraguay and the coast. In addition, a blockade, if required, could be imposed by a few warships because Paraguay was only accessible via the Parana River. Although he didn't divulge his real purpose, President Buchanan undoubtedly hoped to divert American attention from its domestic problems and to send a message to the nations of Europe and Latin America that the United States had the power and the will to defend its rights and expand its influence in the Western Hemisphere. In this sense, the naval expedition to Paraguay represented only one act in what the Buchanan Administration expected to be a larger diplomatic drama.[37]

To serve as Commissioner, the administration selected James B. Bowlin, a St. Louis attorney and former minister to Colombia. The State Department instructed Bowlin to demand an apology for the attack on the *Water Witch*, indemnity for the seaman killed in the incident, damages for the losses suffered by Edward Hopkins' company, and ratification of either the 1853 treaty or a new diplomatic agreement. When the squadron departed in October, 1858, Shubrick also carried orders to establish a blockade if negotiations should break down as well as to destroy fortifications that threatened safe passage for the squadron and to use force, if necessary, to occupy the capital. Alarmed by the potential threat of armed intervention by the United States in the region, Argentine leaders worked to facilitate a peaceful agreement before the arrival of the American squadron. Although he did not function as an official mediator, Argentine President Justo José Urquiza conferred with officials from both the United States and Paraguay to arrange a tentative settlement. As a result, agreement came quickly once Bowlin arrived in Asunción in February, 1859. The settlement included a new treaty of amity and commerce which opened Paraguayan ports to American ships, submission of the company's damage claims to arbitration, a letter of explanation and apology for the *Water Witch* incident, $10,000 for representatives of the slain seaman, and a special letter authorizing another American exploring expedition to the Paraguay and Parana Rivers.[38]

Once the dispute was settled the naval squadron dispersed leaving Page to begin his exploring duties with the *Argentine* and the *Alpha*, a second small steamer placed at Page's disposal by Forbes. From March, 1859 until October, 1860, the expedition explored and charted the Paraguay, Parana, Bermejo, and Uruguay Rivers. In December, 1860, Page returned to the United States with a wealth of geographic, scientific, and commercial information. Unfortunately, his reports and charts from the expedition were never completed because Page joined the Confederacy soon after the Civil War began.

In spite of Buchanan's willingness to use the navy to further his diplomacy, the worsening sectional crisis distracted the President, weakened his political strength, and doomed his expansionist foreign policy. As the political situation deteriorated in the United States, the President proved unable to enhance American power in the Caribbean. Spain refused to discuss the sale of Cuba and Congress later rejected Buchanan's request for the funds necessary to make a reasonable offer for Cuba. Buchanan also had little success in persuading Congress to support various diplomatic initiatives. The Senate rejected claims treaties with both New Granada (Columbia) and Costa Rica. Congress declined Buchanan's request that he be authorized to use American forces to guarantee the neutrality and protection of the states in Central America and any isthmian transit route in which the United States held a treaty interest. In addition, Congress denied Buchanan's 1858 request to establish military posts and create a "temporary protectorate over the northern portions of Chihuahua and Sonora. . . ." Similarly, the Senate refused to ratify the 1860 McLane-Ocampo Treaty in which Mexico granted the United States transit rights and the authority to police the route for a $4 million payment.[39]

Congress also frustrated Buchanan's attempt to establish naval stations in Central America. In 1858, Ambrose W. Thompson, the head of the Chiriqui Improvement Company, wrote a long memorandum to Buchanan in an effort to interest the administration in establishing a naval station in the Chiriqui region and securing for the company the right to carry mail from New York to California via the Chiriqui route. By this time the Navy Department had received a report that the Chiriqui coal deposits were of particularly high quality and was anxious to secure access to coal in the area. After several delays Secretary of the Navy Toucey signed an agreement with Thompson and the Chiriqui Improvement Company in May, 1859, by which the United States received an unqualified and toll-free right-of-way to the Company's road from Chiriqui Lagoon to Golfo Duke on the Pacific Ocean. For its coal depots and naval stations, the United States secured title to a maximum of 5,000 acres on both the Chiriqui Lagoon and the harbor at Golfito. In addition, the United States was granted access to the Company's various harbors and waters and the right to whatever coal the navy needed. In return, Thompson and the Company would receive $300,000 provided the Congress approved the contract at its next session. After questions were raised about the validity of the Company's title and the suitability of the coal for naval purposes, Congress provided $10,000 for an expedition to answer these questions. Led by Captain Frederick Engle, the naval expedition completed its work by late 1860 and issued an enthusiastic report in January, 1861, extolling the quality of the coal and the naval value of the Chiriqui facilities. But as Buchanan left office and the nation sank into Civil War, Congress still had not acted on the proposal.[40]

Although Buchanan failed to achieve his major objectives, the United States signed a number of diplomatic and commercial agreements and experienced a marked improvement in relations with Great Britain. A brief Anglo-American war scare in 1858 ended when the British ceased their efforts to search suspected slavers flying the American flag in Caribbean waters. England also retreated from its position in Central America by acknowledging Honduras' ownership of the Bay Islands and recognizing the sovereignty of Nicaragua over part of the Mosquito coast. Ultimately, however, these achievements offered small consolation to a President who had hoped to reunite a divided nation behind a vigorous foreign policy.

Under Pierce and Buchanan, the navy occupied a contradictory position in the Caribbean and Central America. The proximity of the region rendered it vital to the commercial, strategic, and diplomatic interests of the nation. And both administrations hoped to acquire Cuba and other possessions, extend American power, and challenge British hegemony in the region. Given its geographic character and the fact that the United States could marshall a relatively large naval force in the area, the Caribbean might well have served as an ideal arena for the United States to employ its navy in support of a vigorous, imperialistic foreign policy. Instead, the role of the navy in the Caribbean proved to be inconsistent, erratic, and ineffective. Although it continued to execute its customary duties of protecting American lives, property, and neutral rights, the navy was unable to exert significant diplomatic, political, or strategic influence in the region. And while the navy's continued protection of American trade proved useful, these activities had little direct impact on the dramatic growth of American commerce in the Caribbean during the 1850's.

The navy's anomalous position in the Caribbean is largely attributable to the failure of Democratic foreign policy. After 1852 the Caribbean and Central America became the focal point of American diplomacy as Pierce and Buchanan sought to achieve territorial, political, and strategic objectives there. This expansionism generated considerable public enthusiasm from a wide audience in the United States eager to recapture the aggressive momentum of the 1840's. Gauged by the volume and intensity of its popular literature, the expansionism of the 1850's rivalled that of the previous decade. In reality, however, the expansionists failed to realize their ambitious dreams. By the eve of the Civil War Cuba remained in Spanish control, the isthmian canal was still a distant dream, and England continued to be the dominant foreign power in Central America.

Several factors had combined to frustrate the goals of Pierce and Buchanan and to produce considerable disarray in their foreign policy. First, and most important, was the sectional tension which permeated every political issue and engulfed traditional expansionist objectives to the south. By 1854, a large number of northerners viewed the acquisition of Cuba, not as a desirable national goal, but as a part of a southern scheme to increase the power of the so-called Slave Power. Anti-slavery forces also denounced various private filibustering projects as illegal and transparent efforts to build a southern empire in the Caribbean. In a decade increasingly dominated by sectional tension, these and other allegations seriously debilitated the nation's Latin American policies.

Second, many Americans had fundamental misgivings about the character of the Democrats' proposed Caribbean policy. The United States had long followed the diplomatic precepts of neutrality, nonintervention, self-determination, and commercial reciprocity. Now the Pierce and Buchanan administrations seemed intent on a bellicose and imperialistic policy in the Caribbean. Through annexation, colonization, or military action if necessary, the United States would acquire Cuba and other possessions. At the same time, the expansionists argued that diplomatic intimidation and military force might be necessary to establish a canal route, acquire naval stations, exert political pressure, and expel the British from the region. This proposed departure from traditional national policies frightened many Americans. Admittedly, the expansionism of the 1840's had been aggressive, arrogant, and forceful, but the United States was acquiring sparsely populated, tenuously held, contiguous territories. In the Caribbean, some Democrats now proposed the forceful acquisition of overseas possessions inhabited by large colored populations. Given the implications of such imperialism for the American republic in the 1850's, it would have been extremely difficult for the Pierce and Buchanan administrations to build and sustain a concensus for such policies even if the sectional crisis had been considerably less serious than it was.

Third, the United States now confronted major European powers in an area which was removed from North America and of considerable diplomatic and commercial importance to these nations. Spain was not about to cede Cuba to the hated Americans, and in that determination she had the encouragement of both England and France. Similarly, the British were determined to maintain their extensive commercial interests and political influence in the Western Hemisphere and they were not about to allow the United States to build, control, and fortify a canal in Central America. Moreover, the British maintained a strong naval presence supported by a series of bases in the region. As a result, diplomatic victories and territorial expansion would have been far more difficult for the United States here than they were a decade earlier in North America.

Despite frustrations for Democratic policy in the Caribbean, the nation's traditional commercial, political, and strategic interests did not suffer significantly during the 1850's. In fact, the setbacks of the decade occurred largely in the eyes of the expansionists. Although Cuba remained Spanish, few Americans doubted that the island would eventually fall to the United States. And most Americans believed that the United States would one day build and control an isthmian canal. Nor did the British constitute a serious long-term threat in Central America. The British acknowledged their willingness to allow the United States to build a canal as long as equal access for other nations was provided. And by the late 1850's the British government was prepared to relinquish control of its protectorates in Central America. At the same time, American trade prospered in the Caribbean during the decade. In the five-year period from 1856 to 1860, U.S. imports from Cuba and the West Indies almost tripled over what they had been in the period from 1846 to 1850, and U.S. exports to these same areas nearly doubled in the same time span.

The role of the U.S. Navy in the Caribbean closely mirrored Democratic foreign policy there. On the one hand, the navy continued to protect American commerce. With trade routes long established, neutral rights secure, and piracy rare by the 1850's, these duties proved to be relatively routine. When American forces did intervene, the actions tended to be minor and brief. On the other hand, the navy did not serve as a strong arm of an aggressive diplomacy because of the failure of Democratic foreign policy in the region. Neither Pierce nor Buchanan ever attempted to use the navy in a systematic or sustained manner to help realize their imperialistic visions. For the U.S. Navy, that development proved most fortunate because it was woefully unprepared to assume such responsibilities. The great majority of American naval officers had neither the training, inclination, nor experience to play an imperialistic role. In addition, the navy lacked the men, the ships, and the resources for such duties, and what ships the navy did have were technologically inferior to those of the British Navy. In retrospect, it is extremely difficult to understand how the navy could have sustained an imperialistic policy in the Caribbean before the Civil War.

8.

The "Empire of Commerce" in the Pacific

It is idle to suppose, that because the policy of the United States has hitherto been to avoid, by all possible means, any coalition, or even connection with the political acts of other nations, we can always escape from the responsibilities which our growing wealth and power must inevitably fasten upon us.

Commodore Matthew C. Perry, 1856

The confident mid-century expectation that a new era had dawned for the United States in the Pacific produced high hopes and a host of proposals for American activity there, including plans for major naval expeditions to Japan and the North Pacific. The Fillmore Administration strongly supported these two Pacific ventures and did everything possible to insure that they were underway by the time the Whigs left office in March, 1853. As a result, the expedition to Japan sailed in November, 1852, and the expedition to the North Pacific received its final sailing instructions the following February. In the next three years these two naval expeditions would carry out their missions under a Democratic administration which praised their efforts but proved much less supportive of such activities than the Whigs had. In addition to being preoccupied with its diplomatic goals in the Caribbean and Central America, the Pierce Administration watched as the Kansas-Nebraska question provoked a controversy which weakened its expansionist policies. The United States, then, was in no position to capitalize fully on the achievements of these two expeditions. In spite of their great significance for American interests in the Pacific, the implications of the two Pacific expeditions were largely overlooked by the government after Perry's return to the United States in 1855.

As originally conceived the two Pacific expeditions were similar to the Amazon and the La Plata expeditions of the early 1850's. Supporters noted that each venture would require few additional ships, men, or resources. The expedition to Japan was originally planned as part of the duties of the East India Squadron rather than as a separate undertaking. Only after its first Commander was removed in November, 1851, did the project begin to assume the form of a major naval and diplomatic initiative. Unlike the other three projects, the North Pacific Exploring Expedition required additional resources and congressional action, but those needs were provided by a $125,000 appropriation amendment to the Naval Appropriation Act in 1852. With both Pacific expeditions pressure from special interest groups and the initiative of key individuals proved critical. From the maritime and commercial centers of the northeastern United States, a host of promoters, merchants, ship captains, politicians, and whaling captains urged these initiatives. Persistent pressure came from the New England whaling community which complained of the great danger and difficulty involved in operating in the North Pacific and the China merchants who sought a safe and direct oceanic route from the East coast to Asia. At the same time, a particularly instrumental role was played during the late 1840's by Aaron H. Palmer, a New York promoter and commission merchant who extolled the commercial potential of Asia and worked tirelessly on behalf of his dreams. In addition to collecting and publishing a mass of information on the commerce of Asia and the Middle East, Palmer lobbied prominent officials in three different administrations on behalf of diplomatic, commercial, and exploring projects in the Far East.

The origins and development of the Perry Expedition to Japan very much fit the haphazard pattern of federal government action on behalf of American overseas commerce in the antebellum period. What distinguished the expedition to Japan from the other exploring expeditions was its diplomatic character, the size of its naval squadron, and its exceptional leadership. Once appointed to command the East India Squadron in 1852, Commodore Perry's vision, initiative, and influence transformed the mission and his extraordinary talent permitted him to achieve most of his objectives.

As an exotic, remote, and secluded land in Asia, Japan had long held a fascination for Europeans. After initial contact with the Europeans, Japanese rulers began to suppress Christianity and exclude all foreigners in the early seventeenth century. In 1638 authorities banned all intercourse with the outside world. The only contact existed at the small island of Deshima, off Nagasaki, where the Dutch maintained a small settlement and factory under severe restrictions. Once or twice per year a Dutch ship brought the few items which Japan sought from the outside world and carried away a few Japanese items to Europe. During the Napoleonic Wars the Dutch chartered a number of American ships to fly their colors and visit Deshima, but this early and trifling American commerce with Japan ended once the Dutch resumed trade in their own ships in 1813. For the next four decades Americans had virtually no contact with Japan.[1]

In 1815 Captain David Porter became the first American to propose an official expedition to Japan. During the War of 1812 Porter, in command of the frigate

Essex, had ranged widely in the Pacific, attempted unsuccessfully to annex Nukuhiva in the Marquesas Islands, and harassed British whalers in the eastern Pacific before being defeated and having his ship captured by the British in 1814. After his return to the United States, Porter wrote a letter on October 31, 1815, to President Madison and proposed that American ships be sent into the Pacific to "introduce civilization" and secure American commerce. "We, Sir, are a great and rising nation . . . whose shores are washed by the Atlantic and the Pacific. . . . We border on Russia, on Japan, on China. . . . " Specifically, he recommended a scientific and diplomatic expedition to Japan and the Far East. "The time may be favorable," advised Porter, "and it would be a glory beyond that acquired by any other nation for us, a nation of only 40 years standing, to beat down their [Japan's] rooted prejudices, secure to themselves a valuable trade, and make the people known to the world."[2]

After the Madison Administration ignored Porter's visionary proposal, American interest in Japan grew slowly. In 1832, when the Jackson Administration authorized Edmund Roberts to negotiate commercial treaties with several Asian nations, Japan was one of those included. After concluding treaties with Siam and the Sultan of Muscat, Roberts was unable to continue to Japan. In 1835 Roberts was again authorized to treat with Japan during his second mission to Asia, but he died in Asia before he had the opportunity to approach Japan, where he almost certainly would have failed to establish diplomatic contact. An edict in effect since 1825 specified that foreign ships, with the exception of Dutch and Chinese vessels, were to be bombarded when they approached the Japanese coast. In 1837 Olyphant and Company, an Anglo-American firm at Canton, dispatched the *Morrison* to Japan with seven shipwrecked Japanese sailors, three Christian missionaries, and a cargo of goods to trade. Presumably, the return of the Japanese sailors would win Japanese gratitude and help open the door to trade and Christian missionaries. Avoiding Nagasaki, the *Morrison* sailed toward Yedo and anchored at Uraga, but never made official contact and received a shelling from shore batteries before retreating without landing the Japanese sailors. The *Morrison's* supercargo, Charles W. King, wrote a book in 1839 on this incident entitled *The Claims of Japan and Malaysia Upon Christendom* in which he urged an official expedition and a formal treaty to prevent future insults and to open Japan. His demands, however, stimulated neither official support nor public interest.[3]

By the mid–1840's the situation in Japan seemed to have changed. Three years earlier the edict to bombard all foreign ships was modified. In 1845 the Japanese treated a British naval survey vessel respectfully when it entered Japanese waters and permitted the American whaleship, *Manhattan*, to land twenty-two sailors it had rescued and to obtain provisions at Uraga in the Bay of Yedo. Meanwhile in the United States, interest in Asia continued to grow after the Cushing mission to China and in 1845 the Polk Administration dispatched a mission to exchange treaty ratifications with China and to negotiate a treaty with Japan. When the Commissioner to China, Alexander H. Everett, became ill, his naval escort, Commodore James Biddle, decided to continue the mission. After exchanging ratifications with China, Biddle in the 90-gun *Columbia* sailed on to Japan along with the sloop-of-war *Vincennes*. Arriving in the Bay of Yedo in July, 1846, Biddle achieved nothing and committed a number of blunders in the process. He permitted dozens of armed guard boats to surround his ships and Japanese sailors to board and inspect his ships. Without an interpreter, he dealt directly with minor Japanese officials, showed himself freely on board, and entrusted the President's official letter to a minor official at Uraga. The Japanese refused to accept the letter and ordered the American ships to depart with a curt note from a local official. To receive the reply, Biddle left his ship to board one of the Japanese guard boats which he mistook for the official junk. The response he received was not a letter from the Emperor, as Biddle believed it would be, but a letter which was without address, seal, or date. In the process of boarding the Japanese guard boat, the Commodore was rudely pushed or bumped by a Japanese sailor. Although the Japanese offered to punish the offender, the damage was done. Lacking explicit instructions which would have permitted his retaliation, Biddle departed with the assistance of a tow from the Japanese.

The effect of the Biddle mission on subsequent Japanese-American relations has long been the subject of dispute. Contemporary American observers charged that Biddle had hurt the dignity of the United States in Japanese eyes by exposing the weakness of the American "barbarians." However, some observers then and scholars since have challenged that contention and have argued that Biddle's conduct actually helped ease the way for formal relations with the Japanese by giving them a favorable impression of Americans and American intentions. At any rate, the Biddle mission had a direct influence in the short term on such naval officers as Thomas Glynn and Matthew Perry. To these officers the lesson of the Biddle mission was that the only way to deal with the Japanese effectively was to assume a tough posture, demand respect for the American flag, and make it clear that the United States had both the power and the will to protect its national honor.[4]

In 1849 the navy instructed Commander Glynn to sail in the *Preble* to Nagasaki to pick up fifteen whalemen who were being held there by the Japanese. Unlike Biddle, Glynn demanded respect for the American flag and the return of the American seamen. He sailed his ship through a cordon of guard boats and anchored within cannon shot range of the city. In the subsequent negotiations he threatened to bombard the city if the Americans were not released, which they were within two days. When he returned to the United States in 1851 Glynn pressed the Fillmore Administration for a diplomatic mission to open Japan. In the meantime, he had also urged the owners of the Pacific Mail Steamship Company to support the opening of ports in Japan. The strategic placement of the islands, the existence of adequate coal supplies, and the excellence of Japanese harbors rendered a diplomatic agreement with Japan essential to the establishment of a steamship line between the United States and Asia.[5]

By 1850 growing American interest in Japan had created considerable pressure on the federal government for a diplomatic mission to Japan. As an emerging Pacific power, the United States was clearly ready to expand its political influence in the Pacific Basin, increase its economic activity in the area, and establish close ties with the Far East. Although the factors which drove Americans into the Pacific applied to Asia in general, American interest focused increasingly on Japan. No European nation had yet succeeded in opening Japan to the western world. In addition, the Japanese islands were of great strategic importance to the United States and were closer to the American republic than were other parts of Asia. It seemed appropriate, then, for Japan to be the objective of an American diplomatic initiative. In addition, Protestant missionaries sought a new field of activity, and some editors and politicians pressed to introduce republican values and civilization to the "backward" Japanese.

The main pressures, however, were economic and commercial. The opening of China and the Treaty of Wanghia had quickened commercial interest in other parts of Asia including Japan. Although actual American trade with China did not increase dramatically during the 1840's, the American shipping tonnage involved in that trade did. More important, Asia continued to symbolize the magical promise of unlimited commercial wealth for Americans in the Pacific. In 1845 commercial pressure persuaded Representative Zadoe Pratt of New York, the Chairman of the House Select Committee on Statistics, to introduce a resolution proposing "to dispatch suitable diplomatic and commercial agents" to Japan and Korea. The next year a group of New York businessmen involved in overseas commerce submitted a memorial to the Senate. The document outlined the grievances they suffered because the nation lacked a commercial treaty with Japan. Although the Senate Foreign Relations Committee took no action on this petition, interest and pressure continued to build during the late 1840's.[6]

American whaling interests also sought a treaty with Japan. By the late 1840's the great majority of the nation's whaling fleet of over six hundred vessels was operating in the Pacific. The value of the Pacific fleet was estimated at approximately $17 million. The opening of new whaling grounds in the Okhotsk and Kamchatka Seas in the mid–1840's increased the number of vessels operating in the northeastern Pacific. By 1845 there were 263 whalers operating in the North Pacific. Although that number decreased during the late 1840's, it would again surpass 200 ships annually between 1852 and 1855. In the northeastern Pacific whaling captains confronted uncharted seas and difficult navigation. They needed safe ports to replenish their provisions and repair their ships. In bad weather, they needed harbors in which to take refuge. Another irritating problem was the plight of whalemen who were shipwrecked on Japanese shores. The Japanese imprisoned and sometimes mistreated these unfortunate mariners. The shipwrecked Americans retrieved by the Glynn Expedition returned to tell of their cruel mistreatment. Commodore David Geisinger incorporated Commander Glynn's experiences with the Japanese and the narratives of several captives into a report which was presented to the House of Representatives on August 28,

1850. In addition to depicting the cruel treatment accorded the American sailors, the report documented the extreme suspicion and hostility with which the Japanese treated foreigners. Glynn's interviews with Japanese officials were reproduced verbatim and demonstrated how seemingly unreasonable and intransigent the Japanese were and how Glynn had succeeded only by being equally adamant and threatening the use of superior naval force.[7]

Ultimately, public and political interest and desire for diplomatic contact with Japan were shaped and directed by Aaron H. Palmer of New York. As Director of the American and Foreign Agency, which served as commission agents for the sale of steam vessels and machinery, Palmer lobbied constantly during the latter 1840's on behalf of an expedition to Japan. His knowledge, energy, and commitment to the project ultimately made him the one individual most responsible for the project. Beginning in 1839 Palmer collected, organized, and published a mass of material on the political conditions and commercial potential of East Africa, the Middle East, Southeast Asia, China, Japan, and Korea. Embodied in a variety of letters, pamphlets, and reports, this material outlined the great commercial potential of these areas, and urged the establishment of diplomatic relations with countries such as Korea and Japan, and the expansion of formal commercial relations with Asia, the Middle East, and East Africa. In March, 1845, he sent a detailed letter to Representative Charles I. Ingersoll, Chairman of the House Foreign Affairs Committee, on the potential of American trade with the Orient and the need for a special diplomatic mission to open and expand American commerce throughout the region. Eight months later, Palmer sent another long letter to Secretary of State James Buchanan. In addition to the special diplomatic mission to Asia, Palmer urged the establishment of a U.S. naval base in the Indian Archipelago, the appointment of an American Superintendent of Trade in the East, and the dispatching of Consuls and Vice Consuls to a number of ports in the western Pacific. Much of the information in this report found its way into a report by Buchanan to the House in February, 1847 on American commerce with the nontreaty countries.[8]

In a letter to President Polk in January, 1848, Palmer addressed a copy of his *Memoir Geographical, Political, and Commercial* on the present state and future potential of American trade with Siberia, Manchuria, and the islands of the North Pacific. Reiterating the need for a special mission to the Orient, Palmer emphasized the importance of this rich potential commerce to the United States. Once submitted to the Senate, the *Memoir* was revised and expanded by Palmer, and then 2,250 copies were printed by the Senate.[9]

His failure to move the Polk Administration did not deter Palmer, and with a new administration came renewed efforts. In April, 1849, Palmer submitted to Secretary of State John Clayton a detailed geographical, political, and commercial survey of the countries of East Africa, the Middle East, Central and Southeast Asia, China, Korea, and Japan. In September Palmer followed with another letter to Clayton in which he proposed a mission to demand "atonement and indemnification" from the Japanese for their past treatment of shipwrecked

Americans as well as other concessions. The United States should appoint a Commissioner "with the requisite authority and instructions" and dispatch him "with the whole United States squadron in the Chinese seas" to the Bay of Yedo in Japan to demand an audience with the "seagoon [*sic*], or head of the proper department of the imperial government." The Commissioner should then deliver an ultimatum with the following demands: First, "full and ample indemnity and reparation" for the shipwrecked Americans and a guarantee for the future hospitable treatment of such Americans. Second, assistance in refitting and purchasing provisions for those American vessels which were forced by "stress of weather" to enter Japanese ports. Third, the opening of "certain ports" to American commerce and the right of having American consuls reside there and the accrediting of an American Commissioner to the Court of Yedo. Fourth, the privilege of "establishing coaling stations for American trans-Pacific steamers . . . at a port or ports in Japan proper. . . ." American whalers were also to be permitted to catch whales along the coast and in the bays of the Kurile Islands. Fifth, each of the foregoing articles was to be embodied in a treaty similar to the Treaty of Wanghia.

Since the Japanese enjoyed an extensive maritime commerce along the coast, Palmer emphasized that an American naval commander could insist on American terms by threatening to blockade the Bay of Yedo and other vulnerable ports. However, a blockade would not be necessary, argued Palmer, if the presence of the American squadron were combined with "due courtesy, firmness of purpose, and unwavering decision" by the American commissioner. Such a course would bring "Japan within the political pale of the western nations; open up that rich, populous, and productive empire to our commerce, secure the desired privileges for our steamships and whalers . . . and reflect lasting credit on . . . General Taylor's Administration."[10]

In 1850 Palmer added an important convert when Maine Senator Hannibal Hamlin, Chairman of the Senate Committee on Commerce, helped win Senate support for two resolutions. One called on the Secretary of State to report on the mistreatment of American sailors in Japan, and one requested the Secretary to outline trade prospects with Asia. The first resolution produced the so-called Geisinger report on Japanese treatment of American whalemen, and the second resolution resulted in Palmer's employment by the Department of State to produce yet another report and gave him the charge to submit a plan to open relations with Japan directly to the President. In a letter dated January 6, 1851, Palmer respectfully recommended that Fillmore use the existing East India Squadron and the commissioner to China to conclude commercial agreements with Korea, Cochin China, Siam, Burma, and the Indian archipelago as well as with Japan and its dependencies. A series of such missions would justify the appointment of resident ministers and consuls in those countries, enhance American trade in Asia, and provide valuable information of great value in selecting "suitable coaling stations" and establishing steam communication between San Francisco and Asia. Palmer reiterated the value of a mission to Japan and argued that grievances by the Japanese and their arrogant behavior required a strong naval mission of "tact, energy, and firmness of purpose" to "bring the haughty and intractible seogoon [*sic*], his 'councillors of State,' and spiritual 'mikado,' into some satisfactory arrangements, and open that empire to our commerce."[11]

In subsequent months Palmer had several conversations with Secretary of State Daniel Webster and further detailed his suggestions for the proposed mission. In the meantime, Commander Glynn returned to the United States in January, 1851, went to Washington, and lobbied for the expedition during the late winter and spring. In the meantime, after Commodore John H. Aulick was selected to command the East India Squadron in May, he suggested that the return of sixteen shipwrecked Japanese sailors then at San Francisco might be used as a pretext to establish commercial relations with Japan.[12] The idea was approved by the President, and Aulick was instructed by Secretary of State Webster to convey an official letter from the President to the Emperor at Yedo, to return the ship-wrecked Japanese sailors, to reach an agreement to purchase Japanese coal, and to sign a treaty of amity and commerce. Based on the earlier treaties with Siam, Muscat, and China, the agreement should open one port to American trade and guarantee protection for shipwrecked Americans in Japan. Foremost in Webster's mind, however, was coal, not trade. To form the "last link in the chain of oceanic steam navigation" on behalf of both commerce and humanity, Japanese coal was required to sustain a steamship line from California to China. It was, according to the Secretary of State, "a gift of Providence, deposited, by the Creator of all things, in the depths of the Japanese islands for the benefit of the human family."[13]

The squadron assigned to Aulick consisted of the steam frigate *Susquehanna* and two sloops-of-war, the *Plymouth* and the *Saratoga*. Aulick's official orders from Secretary of the Navy Graham made it clear that the mission to Japan was to be supplemental to the regular duties of the East India Squadron. In fact, Aulick was to convey several passengers to Rio de Janeiro on his outward voyage including the Brazilian minister to the United States, the U.S. minister to Brazil, and the U.S. chargé d'affaires to the Argentine Republic. On the voyage, the Commodore quarreled with the Captain of the *Susquehanna*, William Inman, and was charged by Robert Schenck, the American minister to Brazil, with unethical conduct toward the Brazilian minister. Allegedly, Aulick led the Bra-zilian minister to believe that he personally had paid for the Brazilian's expenses on board during the voyage. As a result of this dispute, Secretary of the Navy Graham removed Aulick from his command in November, 1851.[14]

As Aulick's replacement, Graham made the best possible selection in Com-modore Matthew C. Perry. At the time of his appointment, the fifty-eight-year-old Perry had compiled a distinguished record of naval service. His long record of command included outstanding service during the Mexican War and diplomatic experience in the Mediterranean and along the west coast of Africa. Perry well understood the relationship between naval power and diplomacy. In addition, he was one of the navy's most creative and progressive officers. A leading naval reformer in the late 1830's and 1840's, he had helped found the Naval Lyceum, supported the use of steam power in naval vessels, helped pioneer innovations in ordnance, and overseen the construction of the government mail steamers in the late 1840's.

Although Perry much preferred and asked to command the prestigious Mediterranean Squadron, he informed Secretary of the Navy Graham in December, 1851, that he would be willing to command the East India Squadron if the sphere of action and size of the squadron were "so enlarged as to hold out a well grounded hope of its conferring distinction upon its commander." In January the Department ordered Perry to Washington where he conferred with officials there before receiving his orders in March to command the East India Squadron. From the outset, Perry's command contrasted sharply with that of Aulich because of the great care, time, and energy which went into the preparations. Perry also requested and received a much enlarged squadron. Three ships were added immediately and others were to follow. Perry then selected first-rate men as his officers. Commanders Franklin Buchanan, Sidney S. Lee, and Joel Abbot were chosen to command the *Susquehanna*, the *Mississippi*, and the *Macedonian*. Commander Henry A. Adams was selected as Perry's chief of staff with the title Captain of the Fleet, and Lieutenant Silas Bent became his flag lieutenant. Perry knew each of these personally from the Gulf Squadron during the Mexican War.[15]

Throughout 1852, Perry collected as much information and learned as much about Asia and Japan as he could. He met with naval officers who had sailed in the western Pacific and visited New Bedford in April to talk to whaling captains who knew the area. He read extensively on Japan and conferred with German scholar Philipp Franz von Siebold. As a result, Perry was exceptionally well versed in the history, society, manners, religion, and customs of the Japanese by the time he sailed. Perry also took great care in purchasing a variety of presents for the Emperor and other Japanese officials. These gifts were selected to demonstrate the culture and technological advancement of American civilization. In addition to volumes of Audubon's *Birds of America* and *Quadrupeds of America*, Perry included an assortment of champagne, cordials, and perfumes. More important were the gadgets and machine products, including rifles, pistols, carbines, farming implements, a daguerreotype camera, a telegraph, and a quartersize railroad complete with locomotive, tender, coach, and track.

In addition, Perry played a major part in reshaping the expedition and preparing his own instructions. He not only insisted that the squadron be enlarged, but he also convinced the Fillmore Administration to make the mission to Japan his primary duty in contrast to the orders which Aulick had carried. Although Perry received his written orders to command the squadron in March, 1852, these orders were general and Perry did not receive his specific detailed instructions until November, 1852. In this interim period, Perry conferred with new Secretary of the Navy John P. Kennedy and dying Secretary of State Daniel Webster who suggested that Perry be permitted to draft his own diplomatic instructions. When he departed Perry carried detailed instructions from Kennedy, a copy of diplomatic instructions from the State Department (to the Navy Department), and a letter from the President to the Emperor of Japan.[16]

Most specific in regard to Japan were the instructions Perry himself had drafted for the State Department. Signed by Acting Secretary of State C. M. Conrad, this document detailed the background, objectives, and conduct of the mission to Japan. The need to protect American sailors in the seas off Japan, the recent dramatic settlement of California, and the advances in communication which placed the United States and Asia in close proximity all dictated a formal agreement to achieve three main objectives. First, some permanent arrangement for the protection of American seamen and ships wrecked or driven into their ports by bad weather should be effected. Second, American vessels should be permitted to obtain provisions, water, and fuel, and, if necessary, to refit in Japanese ports. Of particular importance was the need "to establish a depot for coal. . . . " Third, American vessels should be allowed to use one or more Japanese ports to sell or barter their cargoes, but these commercial rights need not be exclusive. In addition, the squadron was to explore and survey the coast and islands of Japan and to reinforce American claims against China.

To achieve these objectives, the American naval commander was authorized to use his "whole force" but was reminded that the mission was to be of a "pacific character. . . . " In his conduct, he would need to be "courteous and conciliatory, but at the same time, firm and decided." While submitting "with patience and forbearance to acts of dishonesty," Perry should nonetheless "do nothing that may compromit . . . his own dignity, or that of the country." Instead, he should "impress them with just sense of the power and greatness of this country" and convince them that past forbearance in the face of Japanese insults was the result of a desire for friendship not of timidity. The instructions emphasized that the mission was to be of "a pacific character. . . . " The Commander would resort to force only in "self defense" or "to resent an act of personal violence" offered to himself or one of his officers.[17]

Secretary of the Navy Kennedy included a copy of this letter with his own sailing instructions and urged Perry to use them as his "guide." In his instructions, Kennedy emphasized the importance of the exploration of the Japanese islands and the great value of collecting scientific and geographic information. The Secretary also stressed the importance of secrecy to the success of the mission. All members of the squadron were to abstain from writing to friends, journals, or newspapers on the progress of the mission, and any journals or notes they kept were to be the property of the government until formally released.[18]

The letter from the President to the Emperor repeated much of what Perry's State Department instructions said. The purpose of the mission were "friendship, commerce, a supply of coal and provisions, and protection for our shipwrecked people," stated the President. The letter stressed the importance of coal to American steamships and stated that, if the Emperor did not want to open trade permanently, a five- or ten-year experiment might be tried. Although he emphasized that Perry was "to abstain from every act" which could disrupt Japanese tranquility, the President stressed that the United States was "very much in earnest in this."[19]

After entertaining President Fillmore, Secretary of the Navy Kennedy, and other members of the administration on his flagship, the *Mississippi*, at Annapolis, Perry sailed for Norfolk before departing for Asia on November 24, 1852. His departure was less than auspicious. With the *Princeton* under repair and the storeship *Supply* already underway, the *Mississippi* sailed via the Cape of Good Hope to join the squadron and arrived at Hong Kong in April, 1853 to find the *Saratoga*, *Plymouth*, and *Supply* in port.[20] To Perry's chagrin, the *Susquehanna* had sailed for Shanghai to provide protection to American merchants under the threat of violence created by the Taiping Rebellion. After refueling and visiting Canton, Perry sailed for Shanghai where he found the *Susquehanna* and an anxious merchant community which petitioned the Commodore to remain there with his squadron and organize a landing party to defend the city. Ignoring this pressure and the appeals of American minister Humphrey Marshall, Perry decided to sail as soon as possible but consented to leave the sloop *Plymouth* at Shanghai. During his stay in China Perry added two important men to his number. As a longtime missionary in China who knew the language and cultures of Asia well, Samuel Wells Williams provided valuable service to Perry. And an American journalist, Bayard Taylor, kept detailed notes and journals which Perry later used extensively in preparing his official *Narrative*.

On May 17, 1853, the flagship *Susquehanna*, the *Mississippi*, the *Supply*, and a chartered American barque sailed for the port of Naha on Great Lew Chew (Okinawa) in what later became known as the Ryukyus. From Madeira en route, Perry had written the Navy Department on the importance of establishing "ports of refuge and supply" as a base for the mission to Japan. Lew Chew seemed an ideal choice for such a base because the harbor was good and accessible to Japan and the people were docile, unarmed, and backward. Their only defense was their considerable ability to evade, procrastinate, and ignore foreigners and their demands. Although nominally under the control of a Japanese Daimyo, the islands were semiautonomous, and their proximity to Japan insured that Perry's actions and the size of his squadron would be reported to authorities on the main Japanese islands. In other words, Lew Chew provided an excellent place for a dress rehearsal.[21]

After reaching Naha on May 26, 1853, Perry began his work. He refused to meet with two natives who met the American ships or to receive two local officials who arrived with greetings and presents. Only when the Regent for the ruler of the island visited the *Susquehanna* did Perry receive him, conduct appropriate ceremonies, and inform the Regent that he would visit the royal palace at Shuri on June 6th. The horrified officials of Lew Chew attempted several diversions to prevent the American visit but all failed. On the appointed day, Perry and an impressive entourage landed, refused further attempts to divert them, and proceeded to Shuri. The Commodore rode in an elaborate sedan chair constructed for the occasion to emphasize his exalted station. After visiting the

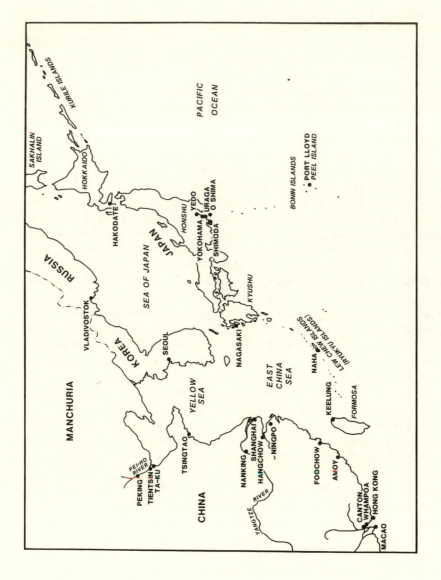

East Asia

palace, feasting at the Regent's residence, and toasting American friendship for the natives, Perry and his party returned to the American ships. During their two-week stay Americans visited Naha frequently, procured a shelter for Americans on shore, and dispatched a party to explore the local area and search for coal on the island. At the same time, other parties surveyed the coastline and harbors of the island. Although they offered no resistance, the passive natives refused to trade or mingle with the Americans and constantly shadowed the visitors.[22]

On June 9th, the *Susquehanna* and *Saratoga* sailed for the Bonin Islands to the northeast. Arriving at Port Lloyd on Peel Island on June 14, Perry found a small colony of thirty-one residents headed by Nathaniel Savoy, a native New Englander who had settled the island in 1830 with a small group from Hawaii. Although he had no intention of using Port Lloyd as a base for his Japanese operations, Perry understood the potential value of the port. It stood directly on the great circle route from Hawaii to the south China ports and would be ideal as a port of supply for American steamers travelling that route. Accordingly, the Americans surveyed the harbor, explored the island for provisions and water, and left a supply of fruit and vegetable seeds as well as farm implements to encourage the residents to increase their agricultural production. Perry himself purchased a small tract of land for a possible waterfront coal depot. He also raised the American flag, drew up a code of laws, and had Savoy elected chief magistrate. Later, Perry would assert an official American claim to the islands. To Washington, he urged the establishment of an open port for the whalers, steamers, and merchant ships of all nations. Recognizing the problems created by a British claim to the islands, Perry recommended an agreement with England to keep the port open. But he also offered to occupy the islands for the United States if the Pierce Administration wished.[23]

After several days Perry returned to Naha to find that the *Mississippi* and *Supply* had been joined by the *Plymouth* and the former ruler replaced by a new ruler and regent. He held a banquet for local officials on the *Susquehanna* and insisted that all goods and provisions taken would be purchased at a fair price by the Americans, thereby placing the Americans on an equal footing with the residents. During his second stay at Naha, Perry drilled his forces in a series of maneuvers on shore and dispatched more parties to collect a wide range of information on the islands. As subsequent events would demonstrate, the Commodore intended Lew Chew and the Bonins to serve as much more than a temporary base for his mission. He believed he had taken the initial steps in establishing two permanent American "ports of refuge and supply" for American whalers, merchant ships, trans-Pacific steamers, and naval vessels. In his judgment both the "honor of the nation . . . and the interest of commerce" demanded such bases. With England already in control of numerous key strategic points in the Far East, the United States must lose "no time . . . in adopting active measures to secure a sufficient number of ports of refuge" along a Pacific "route of a commerce which is destined to become of great importance to the United States. . . . "[24]

After achieving initial success on the Bonins and Lew Chew, Perry sailed in the *Susquehanna* for Japan on July 2, 1853, with the *Mississippi*, *Saratoga*, and *Plymouth*. Six days later, the squadron anchored off Uraga in the entrance to the Bay of Yedo. Immediately the ships were approached by Japanese junks and surrounded by sleek guard boats. Once anchored, the Japanese guard boats attempted, but were prevented, from tying lines to the American ships. Japanese sailors were not permitted to board nor were the first officials who appeared. Finally, a man identified as the Vice Governor appeared and was permitted to board the *Susquehanna*, but he was not received by the Commodore and the conversation was conducted through lesser American officers who informed the Japanese that Perry had a letter from the President for the Emperor. When the Japanese explained that the letter could be received only at Nagasaki, Perry refused. He understood that Nagasaki was well fortified and to proceed there to negotiate would place him on the same inferior footing as the Dutch there. The Americans also demanded the removal of the Japanese guard boats and permitted the Japanese to inspect the awesome gundeck of the *Susquehanna*. The Commodore was off to a good start. He had refused to deal with lesser Japanese officials and placed the United States on an equal diplomatic footing from the outset.

The next day, July 9th, a man identified as the Governor, Kayama Yezaemon, appeared to conduct the negotiations. Again Perry refused this official and negotiated only through subordinate officers. He insisted that his letter from the President be delivered to appropriate authorities at Uraga. If the Japanese refused, Perry emphasized that he would sail directly to Yedo and the royal palace. To underline his claims, surveys of the area and the Bay of Yedo had already begun. Perry also permitted the Japanese to view the elaborately wrapped letter from the President and explained that he would wait only three days before proceeding up the Bay of Yedo. In the interim, the surveys continued and advanced into the vast bay. On the third day Kayama reappeared and another conference through intermediaries was held. Again the Americans emphasized that they would not deliver the letter at Nagasaki. Finally, the Japanese agreed to receive the letter two days later on July 14th in a specially constructed building at Kurihama near Uraga.

At daybreak on July 14th the *Susquehanna* and *Mississippi* steamed into the bay at Kurihama, anchored, and positioned themselves to command Japanese shore fortifications. Since thousands of Japanese troops congregated on shore, Perry sent 250 heavily armed marines and sailors in several launches. Mustering as much pomp and ceremony as possible, Perry included all the officers that could be spared as well as musicians from the two ships. The Japanese met the Americans on shore with elaborate Japanese costumes and banners. The ceremony itself was brief. The American couriers opened the elaborate box containing the American documents and received a Japanese scroll in return. The Japanese reply acknowledged receipt of the President's letter, explained that neither conferences nor entertainment could occur at this spot, and informed Perry that he could now depart. In response the Commodore explained that he would sail in two or three days and would be pleased to convey any messages to Lew Chew or Canton. When the Japanese did not reply, Perry explained that he planned to return the following spring with at least four naval vessels and possibly more. The conference then ended and the Americans returned to the ships without incident. On July 15th Perry transferred to the *Mississippi* and steamed up the bay to Kawaski near the outskirts of Yedo before turning back. A final ceremony was held on July 16th in which small presents were exchanged. The next day the squadron departed for Naha.[25]

Perry based his decision to return to Japan later rather than wait for the Japanese response to the President's letter on several considerations. He understood that the Japanese were unlikely to make an acceptable response without considerable deliberation and delay. At the same time, the squadron's limited provisions, fresh water, and coal restricted the length of his stay in Japanese waters. In addition, the squadron's reinforcement of additional naval vessels carrying some of the presents for the Japanese would not arrive until later. By returning to China Perry could resupply his squadron, add the reinforcements, and address any problems which had arisen in China.[26]

As he returned to Naha Perry could take considerable satisfaction in his initial achievements. He had established contact with the Japanese on an equal basis without provoking an incident or engaging in hostilities. He had insisted on proper respect for his official authority, refused to deal directly with lower Japanese officials, and delivered the President's letter in an appropriate ceremony. He had also refused to permit Japanese to swarm over his ships, insisted that all provisions be paid for, and exchanged gifts with the Japanese only on an equal basis. He had also navigated the Bay of Yedo without hindrance, conducted extensive surveys of the area, and approached the outskirts of the capital. His firmness, careful preparation, and conciliatory manner also left an unmistakable message that he was a determined man who would not be easily diverted by traditional Japanese tactics.

By July 25th, after a rough voyage, the squadron rejoined the *Supply* in the harbor at Naha. Perry was not pleased with the reports he received there. Provisions and food were difficult to obtain, and numerous spies and police continued to plague Americans on shore. At a dinner on July 28th Perry insisted that a free market be established, that Americans be left unmolested on shore, that continued use of the rest house on shore be guaranteed, and that a coal shed be erected for American vessels. When the Regent demurred, Perry replied that unless he received a satisfactory reply within twenty-four hours, he and an American force would again march on the royal palace at Shuri. For effect, he dispatched a carpenter to inspect and repair the sedan chair he had used on his initial visit. However, the next day the Regent complied with each request. The coal shed to be constructed would hold 500 tons and be rented for $10 per month. Perry was now free to depart for China which he did on August 1st.

Perry left Commander John Kelly behind in the *Plymouth* with instructions to cultivate the friendship of the natives in the Lew Chew group, to continue to survey the coast and harbors of the islands, and to visit the Bonins. In October the *Plymouth* sailed to the Bonins and found the small settlement at Port Lloyd to be doing well. Kelly also surveyed the southernmost island of the Bonins, Hala Jima, and claimed the island for the United States.

On his return trip to Hong Kong, Perry met the sloop *Vandalia* which had sailed from Philadelphia in March. At Hong Kong, the squadron was further strengthened. The steamer *Powhatan* and the sloop *Macedonian* arrived in late August, the storeship *Southampton* in September, and the storeship *Lexington* by the end of the year. With ten ships on station, Perry now commanded the kind of squadron he believed necessary to achieve his objectives. His problems, however, were not over in China. American minister Humphrey Marshall wanted the squadron employed to protect American interests during the civil war in China. He sought to have naval vessels stationed at Canton, Shanghai, Amoy, Ningpo, and Foochow. Although willing to protect American interests by having various ships visit these ports, Perry did not intend to be diverted from his primary objective of Japan. At the same time, he learned that both the French and the Russians were in the process of attempting to open relations with Japan. In fact, four Russian naval vessels arrived at Nagasaki in September, 1853, to deliver a dispatch from the Foreign Minister of Russia. Subsequent negotiations with the Japanese to open one or two treaty ports failed and the Russian ships sailed to Shanghai, where they asked to join the American squadron and cooperate with the American mission. Perry denied this request as well as a Russian appeal for eighty tons of coal.[27]

Although he had originally planned to return to Japan in the spring, the arrival of the *Lexington*, the movements of the Russians, and the prospect of new instructions from the United States combined to hasten Perry's departure. By mid-January, 1854, Perry had dispatched part of his squadron to Naha and was himself ready to depart. Unfortunately, on the very day of his departure, he received a letter from Secretary of the Navy J. C. Dobbin instructing him to wait at Macao with a steamer for the arrival of the new American minister to China, Robert M. McLane, who had been ordered to relieve Marshall. The steamer was to be placed under the control and discretion of the new minister until further notice. Undeterred, Perry wrote that he could not detach one of the squadron's three steamers without jeopardizing the mission to Japan. Instead, he would have the *Susquehanna* return from Japan for the use of the minister as soon as the expedition was completed (see pp. 172–174).[28]

On January 20, 1854, the naval steamers joined the rest of the squadron at Naha where they would remain for two weeks. At Naha, Perry found relations with the natives more amicable but protested to the Regent about the difficulty of acquiring provisions and the continued harassment of Americans on shore. He also contemplated American occupation of Great Lew Chew in the event that his mission to Japan failed. On January 25, 1854, he informed Secretary of Navy Dobbin that he intended to occupy and hold the island if the Japanese refused to negotiate or assign a port of refuge for American ships "upon the *ground of reclamation for insults and injuries committed upon American citizens. . . .*" When Perry's proposal reached Washington, Dobbin replied that the President did not want "to take and retain possession of an island in that distant country . . . unless more urgent and potent reasons demanded it than now exist."[29]

By February 13, 1854, the squadron had reached the American Anchorage near Uraga where Perry had prepared for a long stay with adequate provisions, excluding water, for eight months. The Japanese welcomed the Americans hospitably and informed them that five Japanese commissioners had been appointed to negotiate with Perry at Uraga. Thus began several weeks of disagreement over where the formal negotiations would be held. The Japanese insisted on Uraga or Kamakura. Since both harbors offered little shelter from ocean winds and currents, Perry refused and insisted on Yedo. After continued discussions brought no progress on this subject, Perry sailed the squadron up the bay within sight of Yedo. Soon thereafter the Japanese proposed and Perry accepted Yokohama as the site. Here the Japanese erected several buildings for the negotiations and Perry anchored his fleet. In the meantime, surveying proceeded continuously as the Americans thoroughly charted the western section of the bay.

Formal negotiations began with an elaborate ceremony on March 8, 1854, after Perry and an entourage of three bands and 500 sailors, marines, and officers came ashore. The Japanese were represented by five commissioners headed by Chief Commissioner Haykashi Daigaku, the fifty-five-year-old Lord Rector of the University of Yedo. In the initial meeting, the Japanese delivered the Emperor's reply to the President's letter. The Japanese agreed to protect shipwrecked Americans and American ships in distress, and to provide provisions, water, and coal to American ships at one harbor to be selected. However, preparation of that harbor would take about five years. In the meantime, coal would be available at Nagasaki. In addition, the Japanese offered to barter or sell "anything ships may be in want of that can be furnished from the production of this Empire." Perry read the unsigned document and asked that it be signed and delivered to him the next day. Perry then emphasized the importance of concluding a formal treaty between the two nations and presented the Japanese with a copy of the original treaty between the United States and China as well as notes and a letter he had written outlining the advantages of a formal treaty.[30]

Negotiations continued during the rest of March. Having agreed to conclude a treaty, protect shipwrecked sailors, offer refuge to ships in distress, and provide coal, water, and provisions to American ships, the Japanese insisted that the only port to be opened was Nagasaki. After five years another port might be added. In addition, the Japanese informed Perry on March 15th that the Emperor refused to open Japan to commerce as outlined in the American treaty with China. Perry conceded this point but remained adamant on the question of ports. He suggested that five or six ports be opened, and he refused to accept Nagasaki as one of them. Eventually, the negotiators compromised on two ports: Shimoda on the Izu Peninsula on Honshu and Hakodate on Hokkaido along the Taugam Strait. On March 13th, Perry formally presented the American gifts to the Japanese and included a full demonstration of the miniature railroad and telegraph. On the 24th the Japanese reciprocated with gifts of their own and Perry hosted a formal banquet on the *Powhatan* three days later. Throughout the month, relations between the Americans and Japanese remained cordial and virtually free of hostility.

Finally on March 31, 1854, a formal ceremony was held on shore to sign the Treaty of Kanagawa. The agreement specified a "perfect, permanent and universal peace" and a "cordial amity" between the two nations. The Japanese guaranteed protection for shipwrecked American sailors and American ships in distress. The ports of Shimoda and Hakodate were opened immediately to American ships to purchase wood, water, coal, provisions, and other necessities at a fair price. American ships at these ports could also exchange gold, silver, and other articles for Japanese goods under regulations established by the Japanese government. At Shimoda and Hakodate shipwrecked American sailors were also to be permitted to reside temporarily and to move freely within specified areas. The treaty also included a most-favored-nation clause and allowed the United States to send "consuls or agents" to reside at Shimoda anytime after eighteen months.[31]

Although the concessions granted in the treaty did not approximate those enjoyed by the United States in its relations with China, the agreement constituted a dramatic achievement. Not only had Perry achieved the basic objectives outlined in his instructions, but also the Commodore had dealt with the Japanese as an equal and placed diplomatic relations between the two nations on a formal and equal basis. Such a status had never been granted to the Dutch at Nagasaki. If the Japanese commercial concessions proved inadequate, the treaty did provide a basis for the expansion of trade by securing the right for American "consuls and agents" to reside on Japanese soil.

As soon as the treaty was signed, Perry dispatched Commander H. A. Adams in the *Saratoga* to the United States with a copy of the treaty. In the meantime Perry remained in the Bay of Yedo and continued surveying activities until April 18th when he sailed to Shimoda to negotiate the implementation of the treaty while his ships continued to chart and survey. In early May, Perry departed for the second treaty port, Hakodate, where he met with officials, purchased a number of gifts, and oversaw the charting of the harbor and adjacent waters. He returned to Shimoda in June for several weeks and signed an agreement providing for additional regulations there.

Perry then returned to Naha where he intended to sign another formal treaty. Although the Regent did not want to conclude a treaty, he acquiesced under

American pressure and signed a formal agreement on July 11, 1854. It specified that American citizens who came to Lew Chew would be "treated with great courtesy and friendship." Shipwrecked sailors were to be protected, a burial ground was to be provided, "skilful pilots" were to guide American ships into the harbor, and water, wood, and provisions were to be available at reasonable prices. In addition, Americans who came ashore were not to be harassed and were to be free to purchase available goods free from "prohibitory regulations." Missing from the treaty was a clause dealing with the storing and sale of coal. Perry now believed that Port Lloyd offered a far superior coal depot and expected to acquire coal on Formosa and ship it to the Bonins for storage.[32] From Naha, Perry returned to Hong Kong in July and then left for the United States on September 11, 1854, in the British steamer *Hindostan*.

Although contemporary attention focused on the "opening" of Japan, Perry's own goals and achievements were much more extensive than a treaty with Japan. He himself conceived of his mission in broad strategic terms and attempted to provide the basis for an American commercial empire in the western Pacific. In addition to the diplomatic achievements with Japan and the substantial scientific and nautical activities of the mission, Perry sought American maritime superiority in the area. In the Lew Chew islands, Perry had forced a treaty on the Regent at Naha which guaranteed a supply of water, wood, and provisions for American ships, native pilots to guide American captains safely into the harbor, land access for Americans on Great Lew Chew, an American burial ground there, and construction of an American coal shed. In the Bonin Islands, Perry had formally asserted an American claim to the islands, had helped establish a small independent community headed by a native of New England, and had purchased land at Port Lloyd to serve as a naval coaling station. He also dispatched two vessels to investigate reports that shipwrecked American sailors were being held captive on Formosa and to explore coal deposits there. Although no sailors were found, coal was reported to be abundant. The treaty with Japan, then, was but a part of Perry's visionary Far Eastern program.[33]

In the United States, Perry received a hero's welcome and lavish praise for the expedition's achievements. Congress gave Perry a vote of thanks and a $20,000 grant for serving as the diplomatic envoy as well as the naval commander of the expedition. The Commodore received a gold medal from the merchants of Boston and a 381-piece silver service from the New York Chamber of Commerce. In a ceremony in June, 1855, at Newport, the Governor and General Assembly of Perry's native Rhode Island presented him with a large silver salver. In the meantime, Perry had begun work on the official *Narrative* of the expedition with Volume I appearing in 1856 and Volume II in 1857.

Perry also used the period after his return to outline his views of American policy in the Far East in two articles and an address to the American Geographical Society in March, 1856. Like many Americans of his day, Perry predicted a new era of commercial enterprise for the United States in the Pacific. To encourage American commerce, he urged that formal diplomatic and commercial

treaties be concluded with Siam, Cambodia, Cochin China, and parts of Borneo
and Sumatra. Although the recent treaty with Japan exceeded "the most sanguine
expectations," it represented only a "preliminary" step toward a more advanced
commercial agreement which would be concluded once Japan was better prepared
to enter the international community. In addition, Perry endorsed the creation
of a government-supported line of mail steamers from the Pacific ports of the
United States to China, Japan, and the main islands in between. Perry also
reaffirmed the value of naval power in Asian diplomacy. "In all negotiations
with China and other eastern nations," wrote Perry, "the display of a respectable
armed force is necessary . . . in most cases, the mere presence of such force will
answer the purposes desired. . . ."[34]

Although such views were popular during the 1850's, Perry went far beyond
his contemporaries in advocating the creation of a European style empire in the
Pacific. He believed that the United States should take control of Okinawa and
the Bonin Islands. During his voyage, he had taken what he considered to be
the necessary preliminary steps and had even offered to assert control over Naha.
In addition to clearing a route for the Pacific steamship line, Perry believed that
these islands would provide an American base for further expansion while fore-
stalling European encroachment in the region. Perry also wanted the United
States to take the initiative on the "magnificent island" of Formosa by establishing an American colony at the port of Kelung. Once established through
some type of land grant, the American settlement would increase its area, wealth,
and power until it rivaled the ports of Hong Kong and Singapore in importance.
In addition to the rich coal deposits on Formosa, American settlement there
would provide an "entrepôt for American trade" in Asia and give the United
States an excellent "naval and military position . . . directly in front of the
principal ports of China."

Perry also readily accepted the idea of American intervention in the internal
affairs of Asian countries as part of the "responsibilities which our growing
wealth and power must inevitably fasten upon us." In China, he thought the
western nations including the United States should unite "in bringing about a
revolution, civil and military, (and it might be a bloodless one,) which would
place China upon a footing with the most favored nations." Because "the
advance of civilization and the industrial arts" could only be achieved by bringing
the Asian peoples into the "new family of commercial" nations, Perry argued
that "if ever an armed interference of one or more nations . . . could be fully
justified, it would be . . . in bringing by force, if such result were necessary, the
empires of China and Japan into the family of nations."[35]

Perry envisioned continued American expansion in the Pacific as Americans
reached for their ultimate destiny by settling the remote islands of the Pacific
and creating their own "congenial form of government" there. Although not
strictly defined as "colonies," these settlements would undoubtedly be governed
by Americans "with their own constitutions and local laws." At the same time,
Perry well understood that the development of an American empire in the Pacific

would not be a benign process. Forceful military and political action would be necessary to combat European rivalry and establish American supremacy. Eventually, the American people would "in some form or other extend their dominion and their power until they shall have . . . placed the Saxon race upon the eastern shores of Asia." There, predicted Perry, the American "exponents of freedom" would eventually confront the Russian representatives of "absolutism" in a "mighty battle" which would determine "the freedom or the slavery of the world." These visionary ideas, of course, placed Matthew C. Perry far ahead of his time and attracted little serious support in the late 1850's. In this sense, the Commodore's prescience made him much more an ideological contemporary of Alfred T. Mahan's generation than of his own antebellum era.[36]

With its political problems at home, the Pierce Administration failed to capitalize on Perry's achievements in the Far East as his appeals for American control of Formosa, the Bonin Islands, and the Great Lew Chew went unheeded. The East India Squadron soon reverted to its former size so that American consul Townsend Harris was delivered to Japan in 1856 by a single warship, not an impressive squadron. During Harris' tenure in Japan American naval vessels visited infrequently, prompting him to complain about his lack of naval support.

Once Perry departed American naval strength in Japanese waters was only temporarily replaced by the North Pacific Exploring Expedition. The project had been authorized in August, 1852, when Congress appropriated funds for "a survey and reconnaissance for naval and commercial purposes, of such ports of the Behring Straits, of the North Pacific Ocean, and of the China Seas, as are frequented by American whaleships and by trading vessels in their routes between the United States and China."[37] The Senate Committee on Commerce, chaired by William H. Seward, had earlier recommended the expedition as essential "to protect and foster so great a commercial enterprise" as that in the Pacific. Seward hoped the project would stimulate American penetration of the Far East by overcoming the great navigation obstacles in the Pacific and by surveying a direct and safe route from California to China. Along with the mission to Japan and the proposed government-subsidized steamship line to China, Seward considered the exploring expedition a necessary prerequisite to American realization of an "empire of the seas" in the Pacific. The transmission of American commerce, civilization, and religion to Asia would complete a process which had begun nearly four hundred years earlier as European merchants and princes sought to reach China and the Far East. Even the discovery of the New World, according to Seward, was merely "conditional, preliminary, and ancillary to the more sublime result . . . the reunion of two civilizations which, having parted on the plains of Asia four thousand years ago . . . now meet again on the coasts and islands of the Pacific."[38]

The report of the Senate Commerce Committee emphasized the value of the Pacific whale fishery as the primary justification for the expedition. During 1850 and 1851 approximately 299 ships with almost 9,000 men and a total value of $17.4 million had been engaged in Pacific whaling. In April, 1852, a report

from Secretary of the Navy Graham endorsed the Commerce Committee's recommendation. Reiterating the arguments of the Committee, Graham's report
included letters from Lieutenant Maury, Lieutenant Thomas J. Page, Commander
Cadwallader Ringgold, and Commodore Charles Morris, the Chief of the Bureau
of Ordnance and Hydrography, urging the importance of the expedition to the
safety of navigation in the north Pacific and to the "commercial intercourse
between the United States and Asia."[39]

In December, 1852, new Secretary of the Navy John P. Kennedy reported
Commander Ringgold would command the expedition which was to consist of
five ships: the sloop-of-war *Vincennes*, the brig *Porpoise*, the schooner *Fenimore
Cooper*, the steamer *John Hancock*, and the storeship *John P. Kennedy*. Planned
to supplement the Perry Expedition, Ringgold's mission was also intended to
chart the perilous whaling area of the northeastern Pacific as well as to explore
commercial routes in the East Indies and to survey "various lines of navigation
between California and China. . . . " In addition to its commercial and navigation
purposes, Kennedy assigned a hydrographer, an astronomer, a botanist, and a
naturalist to help collect as much scientific information as possible.[40]

In his official instructions to Ringgold, Kennedy emphasized that the "great
object of the Expedition is for the benefit of commerce and navigation, and
particularly that of the Whaling interest of the Country." The Commander was
"to extend the bounds of science and promote the acquisition of knowledge."
During the expedition, the Commander was not to violate the rights of other
nations or native peoples, but to protect American rights "by persuasive yet firm
measures," and to resort to force only as a last resort. "The Expedition is not
for conquest but discovery. Its objects are all peaceful; they are to extend the
empire of commerce and of science. . . . "[41] With him, Ringgold carried a number
of scientific works, a pamphlet on the commerce of the Orient by A. H. Palmer,
and a letter from Commander James Glynn who had rescued stranded American
whalemen from Japan in the *Preble*. Based on his experience, Glynn had outlined
"a field for original discovery" which included a direct trade route from China
to California via the southern islands of Japan and the Bonin Islands.[42]

In June, 1853, Ringgold and his squadron sailed from Hampton Roads en
route to the Cape of Good Hope and Hong Kong, where all had arrived by June,
1854. Unfortunately, the expedition encountered delay, confusion, and frustration in the next few months. Repairs were required. Then the *John P. Kennedy*
was transferred to the East India Squadron which needed ships to protect American interests in China during the Taiping Rebellion. In the meantime, liquor
and disease had taken its toll on the crew and its commander. After suffering a
mental breakdown, Commodore Ringgold was replaced in August, 1854, by
Lieutenant John Rodgers, the forty-two-year-old son of a preeminent American
naval figure of an earlier age. In his twenty-six-year career, Lieutenant Rodgers
had served on several squadrons, worked on the coastal survey between 1849
and 1855, and was himself on the way to a distinguished naval career. Once
appointed, Rodgers hastened to regain the expedition's lost initiative and reaffirm

its commercial purpose. "No one but ourselves," wrote Rodgers, will "survey the particular fields of our commercial enterprise. Our ships from San Francisco to China and our Whalers in the Pacific, and waters which empty into it, whiten the Ocean. For them, if I judge rightly, was this expedition fitted out."[43]

During the fall of 1854 the *John Hancock* and the *Fenimore Cooper* engaged in various diplomatic and surveying activities along the Chinese coast while the *Vincennes* surveyed portions of the Bonin Islands, Okinawa, and Kagoshima Bay in southern Kyushu. At the main harbor of Naha on Okinawa, Rodgers objected to the cool reception he received and to the fact that the treaty recently concluded by Perry was not being observed. Local authorities had failed to provide a pilot to guide the *Vincennes*, had allowed marker buoys set up by Perry to drift out of place, and made it difficult for the Americans to secure wood, water, and provisions. After an audience with the Regent proved ineffective, Rodgers decided on "a display of energy" to reverse the "long course of evasion, of subterfuge, [and] of practical refusal to abide by the treaty." With a field piece and an armed force of one hundred marines and sailors, he marched to the royal palace at the capital of Shuri. The show of force had its desired effect. After a meeting with local officials, adequate provisions and wood were provided, the bills were paid, and a pilot boat waited to guide the *Vincennes* on its way.[44]

By January, 1855, the *Vincennes*, the *John Hancock*, and the *Fenimore Cooper* had returned to Hong Kong to prepare for the most challenging part of their journey, the survey of the Japanese coastline and the islands of the North Pacific. Under Article 10 of the Perry Treaty with Japan in 1854, American vessels had the right to enter Japanese ports in case of distress. Commodore Rodgers now claimed the authority to survey Japanese coastal waters as "necessary and proper to the enjoyment of the right." Rodgers explained in a dispatch to the Japanese that to "tell a friend that he might enter the nearest harbor" in case of distress and then "to hide from him the position of the harbor, and the way to enter it, would seem like more mockery than good faith." In February, the *Fenimore Cooper* under the command of Acting Lieutenant William Gibson sailed to Naha, then proceeded north to chart the rocks and island shores south of Kyushu, and arrived in Hakodate in early June. In the meantime, the *Vincennes* and the *John Hancock* sailed from Hong Kong to the Island of Ooshima, past Kyushu to the treaty port of Shimoda in early May, and on to Hakodate in June.[45]

At Shimoda, the Japanese denied permission for Rodgers to explore the coastline north of Yedo Bay. Rodgers, however, decided to proceed without permission and dispatched the small launch *Vincennes, Jr.* to survey the 450-mile coastline. Under the command of Lieutenant John M. Brooke, a protegé of Maury, a fifteen-man crew conducted an extraordinary exploit as they camped along the shore and risked great peril to compile a large amount of invaluable information. After a twenty-one-day voyage the *Vincennes, Jr.* joined the squadron at Hakodate on June 16, 1855.[46]

In his dealings with the Japanese Rodgers asserted American rights embodied in the 1854 treaty as aggressively as he could without creating a diplomatic incident or armed confrontation. He appealed for permission to survey the Japanese coast and then dispatched the launch of *Vincennes, Jr.* to conduct the survey when permission was denied. Rodgers claimed the right for the party to camp along the Japanese shore under the treaty clause which permitted mariners to land in emergencies which endangered their vessels. He also supported the appeal of ten Americans to reside at Shimoda for an indefinite period after their merchant vessel departed on a chartered cruise to Petropavlovsk, Russia. At Hakodate Rodgers petitioned on behalf of American merchants for permission to reside on shore in order to conduct a legitimate trade with American whalers who touched there. And in Shimoda and Hakodate where the treaty permitted Americans to reside "temporarily," Rodgers argued that the permission to live "must give all the means of living . . . it intends protections, and permission to reside in houses and to buy food." In each case Japanese authorities denied these requests. As he had in his request to survey Japanese waters, Rodgers based his requests on the diplomatic "rule in the interpretation of treaties amongst nations, . . . that any right conferred involves the session of such powers as are necessary and proper to the enjoyment of the right. . . ." Or as he put it on another occasion, "When a treaty gives a thing, it gives every thing which is necessary to the enjoyment of the thing given."[47]

In spite of the fact that his interpretation stretched the meaning of the treaty, Rodgers reported to Washington that the Japanese were not acting in good faith. Their consistent denials of his requests demonstrated that they had no "intention of abandoning the seclusion which has so long been the policy of their nation." If they could discourage navigation of their coastal waters, prevent trade with foreigners, and prohibit foreign residents, the Japanese could retain their seclusion in spite of the treaty. Recognizing this, Rodgers recommended that the United States maintain a naval presence in the area and keep diplomatic pressure on the Japanese by seeking a reinterpretation and revision of the existing treaty. A vice consul was needed to assist the American consul at Shimoda and an official should be sent to Hakodate along with a "man of war with a judicious Commander" to mediate between the Japanese and whalers who provisioned there. A series of changes was needed to regularize the currency exchange and permit trade. The harbor of Yedo should also be substituted as a treaty port for the inferior harbor at Shimoda. Given the difficulty of securing provisions at Hakodate, Rodgers even suggested that some of the fertile fields in the area be leased by the United States "at a price fixed by us" and cultivated "in our own manner."[48]

Having done all he felt he legitimately could do to assert American commercial rights, Rodgers and his squadron left Hakodate in late June, 1855. The *Fenimore Cooper* proceeded north and then west along the Aleutians before turning south to San Francisco. The *Vincennes* sailed along the Kuriles and the coast of Siberia into the Bering Sea where Brooke, and a small party were left to chart in a small boat. The *Vincennes* then sailed into the Arctic before returning to pick up the Brooke party and proceed down the northwest coast to San Francisco. The *John Hancock* sailed into the Sea of Okhotsk along the west coast of Kamchatka to chart the northern approach to the Amur River and search unsuccessfully for coal before departing for San Francisco. By October, 1855, the three ships had all arrived at San Francisco where they received word that all funds for the expedition were exhausted. The *Vincennes* was to return to the east coast while the other two ships were to remain on the west coast.

Of the work which remained unfinished, the failure to conduct an immediate survey of a route to China was the most regrettable to Rodgers. "I think the Pacific Rail Road, and Steamers to China, will turn the tide of commerce this way," he wrote to the Navy Department on January 29, 1856. "We shall carry to Europe their teas and silk, from New York. I believe that this result is inevitable, and . . . the time of its attainment will be shortened by accelerating . . . the passage to China." Rodgers argued that a proper survey would greatly reduce sailing time "by pointing out the position of real dangers and by crossing imaginary ones from the Chart. . . . " Noting the dominance of the United States, Rodgers declared that "the route to China must be surveyed by the United States. The outlay cannot be avoided." In expressing his views, Rodgers had helped prepare the way for just such a naval enterprise two years later.[49]

The results of the Rodgers Expedition were considerable. A wealth of scientific, commercial, and nautical information was collected. Most important were several dozen charts of the North Pacific made by the three ships. These charts proved invaluable to American mariners in the Pacific and remained in use well into the twentieth century. The expedition's work in the northeastern Pacific confirmed the danger and difficulty of navigation in the area, thereby documenting the need for additional surveys. The experiences of the expedition at Shimoda and Hakodate demonstrated the evasiveness and determination of the Japanese to remain as elusive as possible. The tenure of Townsend Harris further documented many of the problems detailed by Rodgers. Clearly, a naval presence and constant diplomatic pressure were essential if the treaty was to operate as the Americans envisioned.

A footnote remained to be written to the work of the North Pacific Expedition. In April, 1858, Secretary of the Navy Toucey ordered Lieutenant John M. Brooke to complete the work of the expedition by surveying the sea lanes from California to China. The young Virginian had joined the navy in 1841, graduated from the Naval Academy in 1847, worked with the coastal survey, and served at the Naval Observatory from 1851 to 1853. There he invented a useful deep sea sampling device and returned after the North Pacific Exploring Expedition to help prepare its numerous charts. Brooke's detailed instructions specified that he determine the precise position of numerous reported navigation obstacles in the Pacific, chart dangers to navigation along the islands south of Japan, and survey prominent points along the Japanese coast. Toucey also instructed Brooke to look for possible guano islands and to select the best places for coal stations.[50] To accomplish his mission Brooke received command of the *Fenimore Cooper* and a crew of twenty men. Sailing from San Francisco in September of 1858, Brooke reached Honolulu in early November. From the Hawaiian Islands, he surveyed extensively, proved that many reported navigation obstacles did not exist, discovered a seal rookery and guano deposits on French Frigate Shoals northwest of Hawaii, and claimed the reefs for the United States. In 1859 Brooke worked farther west, reaching Guam in April and Hong Kong in May. The next month, Brooke sailed for Japan and surveyed the waters of Okinawa en route. After arriving at Kanagawa Bay in August, the work of the expedition was cut short by the loss of the *Fenimore Cooper*. After six land-bound months in Japan, Brooke returned to San Francisco in March, 1860. By fixing the precise position of various navigational dangers and determining that many others did not exist, the expedition provided a considerable amount of invaluable information. Unfortunately, the outbreak of the Civil War and Brooke's resignation to join the Confederacy prevented completion of many of the charts prepared by the expedition.[51]

9.

Neutrality and Noninterference for the East India Squadron

The Chinese "must be taught to respect us, but that lesson should ever be given with generous forebearance and the studied avoidance of unnecessary collision. You will be careful not to become entangled with the controversies and difficulties . . . between other Powers and the Chinese. Our countrymen have large interests in China. Protect them.
Secretary of the Navy James Dobbin to Commodore James Armstrong, 1857

Although many Americans expected the Treaty of Wanghia to initiate a new era of commercial opportunity, missionary activity, and diplomatic stability, American merchants, missionaries, diplomats, and naval officers in China found the next fifteen years to be just as frustrating as the previous decade had been. Internal upheaval compounded the problem of dealing with Chinese officials who from the American viewpoint remained as unreasonable and intransigent as ever. In addition, the United States responded to the difficult situation in China with a policy that was ambiguous, confused, and inconsistent. For the East India Squadron the period was frustrating and difficult. Once a commercial agreement was concluded the navy usually played a supplemental diplomatic role by visiting major ports, showing the flag, and responding to the periodic problems and crises which arose. In China, however, a constant naval presence remained essential to the conduct of diplomacy. The involvement of the navy in what were basic diplomatic activities had a negative effect on the navy's commercial role in the Far East. Since the small squadron was almost constantly required in Chinese waters, naval vessels could not play an effective, much less expansive, role in the East Indies and southwestern Pacific. At the same time, the navy's commercial role in China was also restricted by Chinese resistance to further foreign penetration and by an American policy which eschewed aggressive commercial or diplomatic objectives in China.[1]

The Treaty of Wanghia failed to place Chinese-American commercial and diplomatic relations on a stable and amicable basis for several reasons. First, the Americans and the Chinese viewed the treaty in very different ways as a result of their respective cultural perspective and diplomatic tradition. In 1845 President Tyler predicted that the treaty would place ''our relations with China on a new footing eminently favorable to the commerce, and other interests of the United States.''[2] Although many observers in the United States and Americans in China did not share the President's optimism, they held a general expectation that the treaty would provide the foundation and framework for stable diplomatic and commercial relations between the countries. Like other nations in the Western Hemisphere and Europe, the United States assumed that both parties signed such diplomatic agreements to insure a system of diplomatic intercourse, a means of resolving various disputes, and a forum for expanding commercial contact on terms that would be mutually beneficial to both nations. In short, the Treaty of Wanghia, like the treaties which China signed with various European nations, was viewed in the United States as well as Europe as a means of bringing China into the Western World.

The Chinese, however, held no such view of the treaties they signed. To them, these western diplomatic agreements represented a way to accommodate the western nations and bring them within the Chinese world. As an adaptation of the previous ''tribute system,'' the ''treaty system'' in the period before 1860 represented a way to bridle and control the powerful ''barbarians.'' According to historian John K. Fairbank, the western powers ''did not realize how closely the treaty system was built within the framework of Chinese tradition.'' Westerners viewed the main features of the new order to be designated treaty ports for foreign residence and trade, the principle of extraterritoriality, nonprotective tariff duties enforced equally on the merchants of each nation, and the equal foreign privileges guaranteed by the most-favored-nation principle. However, these characteristics ''were all well within the Chinese tradition.'' Of particular note, the most-favored-nation principle ''originated in the imperial desire to show a superior impartiality to all non-Chinese, the better to play off one barbarian against another while treating them with the same condescending benevolence.'' In short, while westerners took the treaties as a ''charter of privileges'' to be expanded at every opportunity, the Chinese viewed the same treaties as a ''charter of limitations that set boundaries which the foreigners could not overstep without endangering their commercial profits.'' The result of such a contradictory perspective would be misunderstanding, hostility, and tension between Chinese officials and western diplomats during the late 1840's and 1850's.[3]

In addition to the problem with the new treaties, internal conditions in China complicated and confused relations with the western nations. Early in 1850 Emperor Tao-Kuang died and was succeeded by his twenty-year-old son, Emperor Hsien-feng. The new Emperor was an arrogant, determined man who resolved to rebuild the declining empire. In addition to a series of domestic reforms, Hsien pursued an uncompromising foreign policy and dismissed proponents of appeasement and compromise with the western nations. These officials included China's most experienced and knowledgeable "barbarian" experts, men who understood that stubborn resistance in the face of superior western power would only lead to the kind of political and military disasters which China experienced in the Opium War. The new guide of Chinese foreign policy was Yeh Ming-ch'en who pursued an intransigent and militant foreign policy until a series of setbacks forced a shift to a policy of appeasement in the late 1850's. In other words, the errors made and the lessons learned by one Chinese regime during the late 1830's and 1840's had to be repeated by another regime in the 1850's.[4]

Further complicating Chinese relations with the outside world was the Taiping Rebellion which began in 1850. The movement was led by Hung Hsiu-ch'üan, a self-baptized Christian from south China. After a conversion experience in 1837, Hung studied various Christian tracts, began to preach his personal version of Christianity, and subsequently attracted a large group of followers. In the mid–1840's he organized his converts into the "Society of Worshippers of God." In 1850 Hung mobilized widespread peasant discontent in the south and led his followers into open rebellion in Kwangsi Province. With the imperial government unable to suppress the movement, success came quickly. The rebels captured the large city of Yung-an in Kwangsi and moved north to challenge the dynasty. By 1853 the Taipings had won an impressive series of victories, gained control of a huge land area, and captured numerous towns, including the city of Nanking, where Hung established the capital of his heavenly kingdom. By the time it was finally defeated in 1864 the Taiping Rebellion would engulf sixteen provinces, destroy hundreds of cities, and result in the death of an estimated 20 million Chinese.

By shaking the internal stability of China, the rebellion also disrupted commercial and diplomatic relations with the western nations. It threatened foreign commerce and spurred piracy along the Chinese coast. At the treaty ports, lives and property were periodically endangered. Trade ceased for periods at Canton and Shanghai. In Shanghai, fighting between the rebels and imperial forces destroyed the existing customs system and led to the creation of a Foreign Inspectorate of Customs. Canton was also a heavily contested area with strong rebel support. Here a series of anti-foreign riots and clashes occurred throughout the decade. The rebellion created numerous situations which led directly to foreign military involvement for brief encounters or for extended periods, such as the British campaign which led to the conquest of Canton. In such a climate the already difficult task of diplomats was increased as they attempted to stabilize commercial and diplomatic contacts between the Chinese and their respective western nations.[5]

American relations with China were further confused by the American government. In some circles in the United States there was considerable interest in Chinese affairs, and periodic pressure could be exerted on Congress and the President by commercial lobbyists, missionary groups, and individual politicians.

However, China was viewed as neither vital nor central to American diplomacy in the 1850's. Once the Treaty of Wanghia went into effect, most observers believed that American objectives had been achieved. Presumably the treaty would permit sufficient opportunities for American merchants and missionaries. Other than the presence of a few naval vessels and a small diplomatic establishment, nothing additional needed to be done. Instead, Americans focused their attention after the Mexican War on Europe, the Caribbean, and South America until the sectional crisis of the 1850's pushed foreign policy aside. As a result, America's China policy remained vague but committed to the traditional objectives of diplomatic neutrality and a commercial open door for Americans and territorial integrity for China. The State Department dispatched its commissioners with very general instructions which did not address a number of specific issues in China. For example, to what extent should the United States cooperate with England and other European powers on treaty issues of mutual interest? To what extent should American officials attempt to assist the Chinese resist British pressure and aggression? How strictly was American neutrality to be maintained during the Taiping Rebellion? In addition to their brevity and omissions, instructions from the State Department often were marked by inconsistencies which resulted from a lack of understanding of conditions in China. Hence, American diplomats were ordered to seek the settlement of outstanding American claims against China and to press for treaty revision, but they were also instructed not to use naval pressure or intervention to achieve these objectives.

In the absence of firm direction from Washington, various diplomatic and naval officials in China assumed responsibility for shaping American diplomacy in China. A decentralized approach might have worked if one or two individuals had been able to provide continuity. However, nine different men served as commissioner or acting commissioner between 1846 and 1860. Of these Humphrey Marshall, Robert McLane, Peter Parker, William Reed, and John Ward were the most important, but none of these men served in China for more than two years. Parker actually served six different interim terms as chargé. Intensifying the problem of leadership was the experience of the commissioners. The appointment was neither prestigious nor coveted, and it attracted neither the interest of the nation's best qualified diplomats nor the concern of its most influential politicians. On several occasions the appointment was declined. As a result, only Dr. Peter Parker combined interest, knowledge, and first-hand experience in China. As an active medical missionary in China since the mid–1830's, Parker had strong ideas about American interests and policy. Unfortunately, his recommendations as commissioner from 1855 to 1857 ran contrary to basic American policy in China and he was finally recalled in 1857.[6]

Another serious problem that weakened American diplomacy in China was the lack of cooperation and coordination between various commissioners, naval officers, and consular officials. These officials often acted independently of the Commissioners and, at times, undermined the judgments and policies of individual Commissioners. In fact, the American diplomatic and consular establishment in China was understaffed, poorly funded, and professionally incompetent. Consuls in China were unpaid volunteers, most of them merchants, who usually had no staff support. The diplomatic legation, which was located at Macao through most of the period, lacked anyone fluent in both English and Chinese, did not have an American flag, and did not own enough legal reference material for necessary research. Even Peter Parker had to rely on a Chinese assistant who did not speak "one word of the English language."[7]

In spite of the confusion and inconsistency which marked American diplomacy, the United States charted a general policy of neutrality, commercial equality for Americans, and territorial integrity for China. By the early 1850's the focal point of this policy became the need for revision of the Treaty of Wanghia. Chinese intransigence and domestic upheaval resulted in violation of parts of the existing treaty, disruption of American trade in China, and prevention of the kind of commercial opportunity America expected from the treaty. Although treaty revision was guaranteed after twelve years by the Cushing agreements, Chinese attitudes and actions made it clear that revision would only occur involuntarily. After 1853, then, the specific goal of each commissioner to China was treaty revision, but the means of reaching this goal were left undefined by the State Department.

The situation finally came to a head during Peter Parker's term as commissioner. With the outbreak of the Arrow War in 1856 England was again at war with China in an attempt to impose its commercial demands, open Canton to foreign residence, settle outstanding grievances with the Chinese, and rewrite the treaties of the 1840's. The outbreak of war confronted the United States with a choice of either cooperating with the British in conflict with China to insure American interests in the peace settlement or supporting China in order to resist British aggression and demands. As commissioner, Parker's instincts and long experience with China led him to urge close cooperation and joint diplomatic initiatives. At one point in 1856 he recommendend a joint military expedition with the French and British to the Pei-ho River. On December 12, 1856, he outlined a "last resort" policy to the outgoing Pierce Administration which Parker believed would settle all American claims and result in complete revision of the existing treaty. If the Chinese refused to negotiate with a mission of American, British, and French diplomats at Peking, then the French should take temporary control of Korea, the British of Chusan, and the Americans of Formosa. Only when outstanding grievances were settled would the possessions be restored to China. Two weeks later Parker requested extensive naval support for his joint program.[8]

In the United States, Parker's desire for a more aggressive and cooperative policy coincided with pressure from the China merchants in Boston who in Attorney General Caleb Cushing had a sympathizer and politician experienced in Chinese affairs on the Cabinet. Traditionally opposed to an aggressive American policy of intimidation and cooperation with England and France, these men now shifted their position and urged a new policy. In the opinion of R. B. Forbes, a leading member of Russell and Company, the time had come to act in concert with England and France, exert necessary military pressure, and demand a new permanent treaty.[9]

President Franklin Pierce and Secretary of State William L. Marcy demurred because they believed that close cooperation with France and England would lead to war with China and even a limited war was unlikely to win the authorization of Congress. Accordingly, Marcy warned Parker in early February that British goals in China exceeded those of the United States. He also expressed his concern that some Americans in China had already been drawn into the conflict and that American naval vessels had acted indiscreetly prior to the Barrier Forts incident in November, 1856 (see pps. 180–182). Several weeks later, the State Department received Parker's December 12, 1856, dispatch which proposed joint military action with England and France. Marcy responded immediately and emphasized to Parker that his plan was inconsistent with American policy. The "last resort" strategy, wrote Marcy, would mean war, "and the Executive branch of this government is not the war-making power." Although the President might increase American naval forces in China, he would "not do it for aggressive purposes."[10]

When the incoming Buchanan Administration chose to continue the policy outlined by Marcy, Parker's days in China were numbered and he was recalled in April, 1857. With Parker's recall came a change in the way the government conducted its China policy. When William B. Reed was appointed as Parker's replacement, he received the most detailed and specific set of instructions yet issued to a commissioner to China. In these instructions, Secretary of State Lewis Cass outlined the nature of American neutrality in China, the extent to which Reed might cooperate with the British and French, and the conditions under which the navy might interfere. From here on, the administration exerted relatively firm control of American diplomacy.[11]

The situation in China and the lack of a clearly defined diplomatic policy by the United States, then, created a very ambiguous and difficult environment in which the East India Squadron had to operate. In fact, China presented a unique challenge to the commanders and officers of the East India Squadron in the decade and a half before the Civil War. In Europe, the Mediterranean, and most areas of the Western Hemisphere, traditional forms of western diplomacy prevailed. Day-to-day diplomatic and commercial matters were handled by diplomats and consular officers in accord with existing treaties and long-standing procedures. In this way, diplomatic relations were conducted, port duties paid, tariffs collected, ships registered, and claims settled. When more serious disputes arose, procedures existed to resolve most differences. With established diplomatic process, the navy played a significant but secondary and irregular role. In addition to transporting some diplomats, visiting major ports, and showing the flag, naval vessels intervened to preserve American interests or protect American lives or property in a trouble spot and occasionally naval officers served as diplomats to negotiate a treaty or resolve a dispute. In more remote and less civilized regions along the west African coast or in the Indian and Pacific Oceans, the navy played a more direct diplomatic role because of the absence of western diplomatic protocol and the direct relationship which often existed between effective diplomacy and military might. In such areas the navy helped expand American commercial opportunity by negotiating treaties with local authorities, protecting American merchants from hostile natives, combatting pirates, responding to outrages on the American flag, and charting local waters.

China, however, presented different problems for the navy in the late 1840's and 1850's. Here diplomacy and naval activity had to be closely tied. In spite of the treaties they had signed in the mid–1840's, the Chinese did not abandon their hostility to foreigners nor did they observe traditional or regular forms of diplomacy. Western diplomatic representatives were not received or permitted to reside in Peking. Instead, they were dealt with on an irregular basis in the treaty ports. Some American commissioners had difficulty even making official contact with Chinese authorities. As a result, the naval vessels were needed to provide transportation for American commissioners as they moved from port to port because overland transportation was usually not possible. Moreover, once a commissioner had been received, naval vessels remained essential because the Chinese had no intention of adhering to the letter of the existing treaty unless they were pressured to do so. Only the navy could provide the symbol and reality of American power to combat Chinese procrastination and resistance. "The efficiency of the commissioner essentially depends on his ability *to coerce,*" wrote Humphrey Marshall in 1853. "When an armed steamer casts her anchor in front of a Chinese city—especially in one of the five ports—her presence seems to bring into active exercise sentiments of justice to which, under other circumstances, the mind of the Chinese is utterly dead." Two years later, acting commissioner and commodore Joel Abbot wrote that his diplomatic authority and "command of the 'dogs of war,' has had a most excellent effect" in resolving difficulties at Shanghai.[12]

This situation produced a difficult and sharply restricted commercial role for the navy in China during the 1850's. On the one hand, Chinese determination to resist further western penetration precluded various naval initiatives in support of American commercial expansion in China. For example, the navy could not compile the kind of geographic and economic information it did in other regions, nor could naval vessels chart and explore the main river basins of China because access to the coastal interior was rigidly controlled. On the other hand, the navy's direct role in American diplomacy in China was also severely restricted. Although the situation involved the navy directly in diplomatic activity, the U.S. government never attempted to use the navy as a strong arm of an aggressive China policy designed to expand American commercial activity there. Instead, the navy's role was to protect existing American treaty rights and to defend American property and lives from periodic outrages and attacks.

In this sense American naval policy in China closely reflected the character of American foreign policy in China. In the 1850's the U.S. government never outlined or supported an aggressive diplomatic role for the East India Squadron because the government itself did not pursue an expansive or imperialistic China policy. Instructions from the State and Navy Departments made it clear that American policy was still to be one of neutrality, nonbelligerency, and noninterference in China. Although commissioners could theoretically use the navy to conduct diplomacy, they could not use naval vessels to force the Chinese to observe the terms of the existing treaty, to coerce intransigent Chinese officials to rewrite the treaty, or to join with British and French forces in joint military action. The Chinese "must be taught to respect us, but that lesson should ever be given with generous forbearance and the studied avoidance of unnecessary collision," wrote Secretary of the Navy Dobbin to Commodore James Armstrong in 1857. "You will be careful not to become entangled with the controversies and difficulties . . . between other Powers and the Chinese. Our countrymen have large interests in China. Protect them."[13]

The most serious immediate obstacle to effective naval diplomacy in China was the lack of cooperation between diplomatic officials and naval officers. In the late 1840's and early 1850's there was virtually no coordination between diplomatic policy and the East India Squadron. American diplomats received assurances from the State Department that they would have adequate naval support. Although several previous incidents underlined the problem, it became serious with the arrival of a new commissioner in January, 1853. Humphrey Marshall was a West Point graduate, Kentucky lawyer, and former congressman who brought a much exaggerated sense of his own importance to China. After being conveyed in the *Saratoga* to Canton where the Chinese refused to receive him, Marshall requested use of the steamer *Susquehanna* from Commodore Aulick, to proceed to Nanking and demand that he be received. Aulick who was under orders to remain in the Hong Kong area pending his replacement as commander of the squadron, removed the *Saratoga* from Marshall's control and refused to grant him use of the *Susquehanna*. In the conflict which ensued, Aulick asserted his right and duty as commander to judge what was in the national interest in accord with his instructions from the Secretary of the Navy. Significantly, Aulick did not explain his decision on the basis of his orders to wait for a replacement, but rather on the basis of his prerogatives as commander of the squadron. Subsequently, Aulick's conduct in this dispute was affirmed by Secretary of the Navy Dobbin who declared his presumption that naval officers would always "lend the aid of his force" to protect American interests and honor overseas, but emphasized that "our Ministers abroad have no right to control the movements of a naval force without instructions from the Department. . . ."[14]

After Aulick's departure for the United States, Marshall requested and received use of the *Susquehanna* from Commander John Kelly to travel to Shanghai. This decision by Kelly, however, upset Commodore Perry who arrived in Hong Kong in March to find the war steamer missing. Intent on his mission to Japan, Perry was determined to use all available ships to augment his naval force rather than permit his objective to be threatened by leaving ships on the China station. Marshall disagreed. He was determined to be received by the Chinese or to proceed to Peking and establish diplomatic residence there. For such a bold stroke he would require strong naval support. At Shanghai, foreign interests were also jeopardized by the Taiping Rebellion in 1853, and American merchants there urged American naval support.[15]

Perry was not to be deterred. He rejected Marshall's plan, the appeals of the merchants, and an Imperial Chinese request for assistance against rebels and ordered the *Susquehanna* to prepare for departure. His only concession was to leave the *Plymouth* behind temporarily with orders to join the squadron later. After months of frustration, Marshall was enraged. He declared Perry's action to be "impolitic, unfair to the American owners . . . and *grossly unjust and injurious to me.*" He had literally been "*put ashore and abandoned by his country's flag. . . .*" More important, he reported to the State Department that a diplomatic representative could not perform his duties under such conditions. If Perry could withhold use of a ship under his command from taking Marshall to the court to which he was accredited unless it was done in a manner which Perry approved, then he by definition asserted a "right to supervise the action of the Commissioner, and to render co-operation of the naval force . . . solely dependent upon the approval of the course of the Commissioner by the naval commander!" If sustained, such a pretension suggested "the propriety of managing diplomatic relations with foreign countries through the instrumentality alone of the commodores of the navy, whose education and habits fit them peculiarly for the discussion of questions of international law."[16]

When Perry returned to China after his first trip to Japan in the summer of 1853, he was no more willing to cooperate with Marshall and get the navy involved in the Chinese situation than he had been prior to his departure. On his return he bypassed Shanghai completely and went directly to the Canton area. Here, in September, he refused another request for naval support during an uprising at Canton in which local rebels ousted local officials and were then confronted by an Imperial army. In November, in response to requests from the American merchant community at Canton, Perry refused to leave any of his ships behind but chartered a small steamer and stationed it near Canton.[17]

Perry explained his conduct by emphasizing that his instructions from both the State and Navy departments did not specify that he deal with any problems in China save the settlement of outstanding claims. To the Secretary of the Navy he noted that in "no navy in the world, serving on foreign stations . . . has an ambassador, resident minister, or consul, the slightest right to interfere. If it were so, the commanders of such forces would find themselves entirely powerless to effect any object of usefulness." Although he affirmed his willingness "to advise with and to act in concert, so far as may be practicable, with these functionaries," only the naval commanders could "judge the fitness of their ships for particular service. . . ."[18]

What renders the Marshall-Perry dispute particularly instructive about American diplomacy in China is the fact that Perry had made a number of diplomatic policy judgments in reaching his decision to take all available ships to Japan. Unfortunately for Marshall, these judgments conflicted with the commissioner's. First, contrary to Marshall's assessment and the appeals of American merchants in Shanghai, Perry concluded that American lives were not seriously endangered. Second, Perry believed the reigning dynasty was destined to fall to the rebels and it was in the interest of the United States for that to occur. Marshall did not agree. He supported the dynasty and thought the chances for stability in China would be enhanced by a rebel defeat. Finally, Perry believed that U.S. interests were best served by neutrality and inaction, not periodic naval intervention. "If we remain quiet," Perry reported in August, 1853, "our relations with the Tartar government, should it triumph, cannot be in the least affected; and should the revolutionary party succeed, we shall be greatly the gainers. Therefore, for the present, the exercise of a 'masterly inactivity' is our best policy. . . . "[19]

This assertion of authority and judgment in the realm of diplomatic activity particularly angered Marshall. Perry was not only exerting control over the squadron but was also making policy judgments on questions which were within the scope of the Commissioner's authority. On October 30, 1853, Marshall complained that clear lines of authority had to be established between American naval and civilian officials in China. Otherwise, if Perry's view prevailed, "there will be no sphere of action for civil officers, except as assistants to the *naval diplomatists.*"[20] Humphrey Marshall was an autocratic, vain, and arrogant man who alienated many people he came in contact with. As such, he was ill-suited to seek cooperation with men like John Aulick and Matthew Perry who could be equally unreasonable and uncompromising. In Perry's case, his single-minded determination to use all available resources to achieve his goals in Japan rendered him relatively insensitive to the situation in China. But the clash between Marshall and Commodores Aulick and Perry was not merely a personality clash. It exposed recurring and difficult problems of authority, judgment, and coordination between the naval commanders and diplomats in China.

American commodores and commissioners continued to disagree periodically over the use and disposition of naval forces as well as questions of authority and policy. After 1854, however, conditions improved. The State and Navy departments cooperated and sent instructions to their respective officials which stressed the need to cooperate and consult closely on affairs in China. In some instances, the squadron was placed at the disposal of commissioners subject to certain limitations on how it might be used.[21] Closer cooperation did not necessarily result in more effective naval diplomacy in China because the size and broad duties of the East India Squadron always restricted the extent of its activity along the Chinese coast and in the five treaty ports. From the end of the Mexican War through the 1850's, the squadron usually consisted of three or four vessels. At times no naval vessels were present on the Chinese coast. In 1856, shortly after Commissioner Peter Parker arrived from the United States with instructions which placed the squadron at his disposal, he discovered that no ships were available to him. The *Powhatan* and *Macedonian* had departed for the United States, the *Vandalia* had sailed to Manila, and the *San Jacinto* and *Levant* had not arrived. When the *San Jacinto* did arrive in June, Commodore James Armstrong carried orders to convey Townsend Harris directly to Japan.

Moreover, the few ships of the squadron were expected to cruise a vast area which stretched from Australia to the Arctic and from the 180th meridian to the Indian Ocean. Within this vast area, commanders of the squadron were instructed to protect American trade, guard the nation's valuable whale fisheries, enlarge the "opportunities of commercial intercourse," and collect nautical, social, political, and commercial information.[22] Although the central point on the station was Hong Kong, it was very difficult for commanders to observe their instructions and simultaneously permit the concentration of the squadron's few vessels at any one point in China for an extended period of time. When additional ships were dispatched to the area, they were under special instructions. In 1853–1854 the ships under the command of Perry were used to advance his expedition to Japan. Between 1854 and 1856 the four ships which comprised the North Pacific Exploring Expedition were used almost entirely for exploration and surveying of the North Pacific, not to deal with Chinese diplomacy.

As a result, American diplomats in the 1850's requested and pleaded with the State Department to send additional naval vessels to China. In the wake of the Perry expedition in November, 1854, Robert McLane suggested a similar approach to achieve treaty revision with China. He recommended that a letter be forwarded from the President to the Emperor and that a naval force comparable to Perry's be dispatched to convey the letter to Chinese officials at Peking. Probably realizing the futility of his request, the frustrated McLane then left for France in December and never returned to China. In December, 1856, after the Chinese continued to refuse a revision of the treaty, Peter Parker wrote specially to the Secretary of State to convey his "irresistible conviction of the indispensable necessity of a much larger United States naval force in China. . . . *A force not less efficient and imposing than the Japan expedition of 1853–54 is most desirable, not to say indispensable.*"[23] In response, the U.S. government refused to increase substantially the number of ships in the squadron although an increased number of steam warships were sent to China in the late 1850's and, in some cases, American officials were permitted to charter an additional steamer. Steamers were particularly valuable in China because their independent power source and shallow draft allowed them to maneuver freely in the treaty ports, travel the rivers of China, and combat pirates along the coast.

Although naval and diplomatic officials in the United States remained concerned about affairs in China, the decision to restrict the size of the East India Squadron made good sense. Developments in Europe, the Mediterranean, Latin America, and the Caribbean were viewed as more vital and more pressing than the situation in China. In addition, U.S. economic interests and commerce in these areas far surpassed trade with China or even all of Asia. The popular imagination in some American circles might have been excited by the promise of unlimited trade with China and the Orient, but the reality during the 1850's was sobering. The value of merchandise imported to the United States from China represented only 3 or 4 percent of the total value of the U.S. imports during the decade 1851 to 1860. Although the volume of trade increased sharply, actual imports from China as a percentage of the American total decreased from the 5 percent figure of the decade 1841 to 1850. Moreover, from 1850 to 1860 exports from the United States to all of Asia comprised only a little more than 2 percent of total American exports. In contrast, U.S. trade with Europe and Latin America constituted a much higher figure and a much more vital interest. Intensifying the problem was the fact that the U.S. Navy remained small during the 1850's in comparison to the nation's far-flung commercial interest.[24] During the 1850's, approximately forty naval vessels served each year in six squadrons including the Home Squadron which had responsibility for the Caribbean. Given its diplomatic and commercial importance, then, the East India Squadron was treated fairly receiving its share of available ships and probably more than its share of steamers.

Naval leadership also hampered effective naval policy in China. The station was neither popular nor prestigious. Conditions were difficult, disease a constant threat, and rewards small. Perry initially preferred command of the prestigious Mediterranean Squadron to the Japanese Expedition until he learned that he could practically set his own terms. Other than Perry, the commodores in China were not the navy's most outstanding and did not distinguish themselves. James Biddle was humiliated by the Japanese. Philip F. Voorhees, who had been twice court-martialed earlier in his career, accomplished little in Asia in 1850. He carried on a running feud with special diplomatic agent Joseph Ballestier, returned to the United States long before he was authorized to do so, and received a censure from the Navy Department. By the time he arrived at Hong Kong, John Aulick was reprimanded for previous conduct and ordered to remain in the area pending arrival of his replacement. Joel Abbot, James Armstrong, and Josiah Tattnall were all capable men who served as commodore in the period from 1854 to 1859. However, each was unpopular with various individuals or merchants in China and each became the focus of controversy and criticism. Between 1845 and 1860, nine different men served as commanding officers of the East India Squadron; none served as commander on station for as long as two years. In addition, on several occasions the squadron was without a commanding officer, once for more than a year.

Given these problems, it is not surprising that most naval officers in China played a restrained role in attempting to implement American policy. Their relations with State Department officials were usually tentative and formal, the policy of their government in China was vague and uncertain, their own instructions were general, and the size of their squadron was barely adequate. In addition, they faced a confusing, uncertain situation in China which they did not understand and were not in contact with long enough to develop sufficient expertise. Not only were affairs in China hard to understand, but the subtleties of European objectives were difficult to follow. As a result, American naval officers helped shape the nation's China policy by being more cautious and more determined to avoid naval intervention than American diplomats and merchants in China.

This caution was well reflected in the problem of treaty revision. Because of the internal situation in China and the manner in which the Treaty of Wanghia was operating, a central goal of American policy after 1853 was the substantial revision of the treaty. Although explicitly guaranteed by the treaty after twelve years, revision was ignored and resisted by the Chinese. By late 1856 Chinese behavior made it clear to all observers that the Chinese would negotiate only when compelled to do so. It was this situation which Parker responded to in December, 1856, when he proposed close American cooperation with the English and French, a joint military expedition to the Pei-ho, and the temporary occupation of Chinese territory as a "last resort" to force treaty revision. This recommendation assumed an aggressive role for the navy, and Parker accordingly requested that the squadron be enlarged.[25]

In early 1857 the State Department rejected this proposal and recalled Parker in April. His replacement, William Reed, carried detailed instructions which reaffirmed American neutrality and nonbelligerency and specified very limited cooperation with England and France because the United States was not at war with China and did not seek territorial possessions or political influence in China. It sought only to expand its commercial privileges and to protect American lives and property. Although the State and Navy departments cooperated to place the squadron at Reed's disposal, he was not authorized to use the navy to force treaty revision. In the event that "firm representations" to Chinese reason and justice failed, Reed was to request his government "to determine upon the course to be adopted. . . . "[26]

As a result, treaty revision was eventually achieved with little support from the American Navy. When 6,000 allied troops attacked Canton in December, 1857, and later captured Imperial officials there, American forces did not participate. In May, 1858, a joint allied naval force entered the Pei-ho River, attacked the Chinese forts at Ta-Ku, and captured the city of Tientsin. Again American naval forces did not participate, and Commissioner Reed was transported to Tientsin in the Russian steamer *Amerika*. Once Tientsin fell, the Chinese bowed to the inevitable and, in the next month, negotiated comprehensive new treaties with England, France, and the United States. In addition to guaranteeing all the old privileges detailed in the Treaty of Wanghia, the Treaty of Tientsin provided new concessions which opened China for free trade to all western nations. In this process, European determination and military power had been critical. The position of the United States was commonly likened to that of a jackal waiting to share the bounty of a hunt conducted by others. Although this posture has subsequently been criticized by some, it served the United States very well in the 1850's.[27]

The navy cooperated fully in this strategy. In April, 1858, when the *Mississippi* had been ordered to accompany the allied fleet from Shanghai to the mouth of the Pei-ho, Captain William Nicholson received explicit orders from Commodore Josiah Tattnall not to participate in any fighting. In the event that Commissioner Reed landed and travelled to the interior, Nicholson was to provide support, but he was warned "not to involve yourself with hostilities with or to make any hostile demonstrations towards the Chinese unless your own judgment on these points shall concur with that of Mr. Reed." Although a special company of riflemen was created and trained to accompany Reed up the Pei-ho, its services were not used. In anticipation of the allied action against the Ta-Ku forts, Reed explicitly warned Captain S. F. Du Pont against action when the *Minnesota* arrived. Under "no circumstances (except what is most improbable, a wanton attack, imposing a necessity of actual self-defense) must there be any violation of our absolute neutrality."[28]

Privately, American naval officers resented their bridled condition. Anxious to participate in the action, they were subjected to the sarcasm and scorn of the foreign diplomats and naval officers. James D. Johnston, an officer on the *Powhatan*, noted that Tattnall's "patriotic and professional pride revolted at the idea of appearing among the large number of English and French men-of-war anchored off the mouth of the Pei-ho, in the character of a passive spectator— or, 'Jackall to the British lion'—with which opprobrious epithet . . . the press in China had stigmatized the position assumed by the Government of the United States in its diplomatic intercourse with the Chinese." But chafe at his role as he might personally, Tattnall did not express his resentment in his official correspondence, and only briefly did he shed his neutral role in 1859 at Pei-ho.[29]

Naval officers spent a great amount of time during the 1850's cruising the Chinese coast, visiting the treaty ports, displaying the flag, and transporting American diplomats from port to port. Naval officers also had to deal continually with the problem of piracy which became especially rampant after 1847. Concentrated in the South and especially in the Canton estuary, innumerable pirates preyed on all forms of coastal shipping. The Taiping Rebellion intensified the problem by rendering government officials virtually helpless in confronting or controlling the problem. In addition, the navy was poorly equipped to combat piracy. Naval vessels were generally too heavy, slow, and deep draught to operate in the shallow bays, shoals, inlets, and estuaries used by the pirates. Only small steamers could deal effectively with the marauders and they were too few to have an impact on the problem. On occasion Anglo-American cooperation brought better results. In 1855, for example, a joint raid by the steamer *Powhatan* and British *Rattler* resulted in a prolonged battle and the death of between 600 and 2,000 pirates.[30]

Throughout the decade local riots, clashes between Chinese and foreigners in the treaty ports, and battles between Taiping rebels and government forces presented American diplomats and naval officers with continuous decisions on whether American military forces should be used. For the most part American naval officers were very cautious and reluctant to commit forces under their command to any action in China. Although they readily moved naval vessels, if they were available, to a troubled spot, these same officers interpreted American neutrality in strict terms once the ships had been dispatched. For their caution several American commanders won sharp criticism from beleaguered American merchants and consular representatives as well as American commissioners.

In late 1854 fighting for Canton spread to the Canton River which became the scene of a number of naval encounters between rebels and imperial forces. On December 29th one of these naval battles occurred close to the foreign settlement and was witnessed by Commodore Joel Abbot, a forty-two-year-old naval veteran who had not been promoted to Captain until 1850. After serving as one of Perry's commanders, Abbot stayed on as Commodore of the East India Squadron. In China he proved to be a capable and prudent officer who avoided precipitous actions. Although the *Powhatan* and *Macedonian* were anchored at Whampoa they did not intervene. American merchants demanded strong naval action to break what they claimed was a virtual blockade and to protect American property. Acting through Vice Consul Robert Sturgis, they accused Abbot of inaction and rebel sympathy. Abbot refused to act and emphasized that he would protect American lives and property but that he would also preserve American neutrality. He emphasized that his own views as well as his duty, "preclude me from breaking our neutrality, from waging war without proper authority, and from becoming a mere partisan of the Imperialists in putting down the rebellion. ..." He went on to add that neither the U.S. government nor the American people would justify the use of "their Naval Forces being used in assisting to quench even the faintest spark of freedom."[31]

Acting chargé Peter Parker joined with the British commander, Admiral Sir James Stirling, to demand that the rebel junks not impede foreign trade on the river. After the rebel commander complied, Parker sent another message cautioning that rebel ships not engage imperial forces near the foreign anchorage at Whampoa. To this last request, Abbot objected. In a letter to Parker, he noted that such a request was an unneutral act because it would provide a refuge for imperial forces if observed by the rebels. Fortunately for the Americans, these issues were never joined. After the rebel commander divided his forces, they were destroyed by imperial ships and the potential crisis passed.[32]

Although Parker agreed with Abbot's response, the merchants and Vice Consul Sturgis did not. They held a meeting and protested Abbot's lack of action. Because they now favored imperial forces, they wanted Abbot to use his warships to drive the rebels from the river. Unlike Abbot, they viewed the rebels as lawless pirates whose triumph would create chaos in Canton, disrupt trade there, and sever all commerce with the interior. Their complaints were ultimately conveyed to the State Department in a dispatch from Vice Consul Sturgis. Although Abbot admitted his sympathy for the rebels, he believed that a "covert plan" existed to have American naval forces used against the rebels and he determined "to maintain a strict neutrality" by refusing to use his forces against the rebels. Privately, Abbot wrote to his son about his fears that "newspaper misrepresentations'' in the United States would undermine his position unless he sent prompt and full dispatches to the Navy Department.[33]

When American forces did intervene, those incursions were brief and intended to resolve an immediate crisis or outrage. Once the problem was resolved, American forces withdrew. In early 1854 rebel forces controlled the walled city of Shanghai and were under siege by imperial troops. The fact that the foreign compound at Shanghai was located adjacent to the walled city complicated the situation. Chinese imperial forces were not allowed to enter or pass through the foreign settlement which was governed as an autonomous British protectorate by a Committee of Cooperation. Accordingly, rebels did not fortify the northern section of the walled city which bordered on the foreign settlement and traded freely with the foreigners for supplies and military equipment. Imperial forces objected to this situation and on one occasion in 1853, several hundred entered the foreign settlement before they were repulsed by British marines. Although they did not attempt to enter again, imperial forces set up a military encampment on the western fringe of the settlement. Here, in early 1854, an atmosphere of tension and distrust reigned. While imperial officials resented the failure of foreign officials to stop the supply of war material to the rebels, foreigners were upset by roving bands of uncontrolled imperial soldiers who threatened and periodically robbed residents. The situation came to a head in early April, 1854, when the British organized a military force of 400 men to disperse the threat. Included were American men from the *Plymouth* under the command of Commander John Kelly. On April 3rd and 4th in the Battle of Muddy Flat, this force engaged a much larger imperial force and forced it to retreat from the threatening encampment. As soon as the crisis passed, American forces withdrew and Commissioner McLane devoted his efforts to the preservation of strict neutrality.[34]

More serious was the Barrier Forts episode in November, 1856. On October 8th the so-called Arrow War began at Canton when Chinese imperial troops boarded the lorchna *Arrow*, removed twelve Chinese crewmen, and allegedly lowered the British flag. Although the ship's British registration was questionable, the British consul insisted that the ship was subject to British control and lodged an official protest. When negotiations failed to resolve the incident, the British began to capture and dismantle some of the forts near Canton. In expectation of Chinese reprisals on the foreign settlement, the American consul at Canton contacted the senior naval officer present and asked for assistance. Commander Andrew H. Foote of the *Portsmouth* had earned a reputation as an able and energetic officer, and he dispatched eighty men and a cannon to defend the American factories. When the *Levant* arrived at Hong Kong shortly afterward, Foote obtained sixty-nine additional men for the American force at Canton.[35]

In the meantime, British efforts to resolve the dispute to their satisfaction failed and they began to shell Canton on October 27th. Two days later, a British force stormed the city and ransacked the imperial commissioner's residence. Although the American community remained neutral, American Consul James Keenan allegedly joined the British attackers, entered the city, displayed the

American flag, and fired his revolver at one of the Chinese. Keenan denied reports of his participation, but Chinese officials believed that the Americans aided the British in the attack. When the storming of Canton had no effect on the Chinese, the British continued to shell the city periodically and to clear the river of imperial junks.[36]

At this point Commodore James Armstrong and Commissioner Peter Parker arrived at Hong Kong. Armstrong had been born in Kentucky in 1794, entered the navy in 1809, and had not been promoted to Captain until 1841. In command of the East India Squadron, he proved to be a careful and conscientious officer. Along with British and French forces, American forces still held defensive positions near the foreign factories, but they were under specific orders from Commander Foote not to fire unless American rights were invaded. After leaving Parker at Macao, Armstrong arrived at Whampoa on November 12th to evaluate the situation. Here he was informed by the imperial commissioner that Americans and their protective force should be withdrawn. Armstrong refused and dispatched additional arms and marines to Canton, an action which had the full support of Commissioner Parker. After taking this step Armstrong decided to reevaluate the situation and ordered Foote to join him from Canton. The conference led Armstrong to realize that the presence of American troops at Canton increased the probability of American involvement in the emerging Anglo-Chinese War. With no resolution of the conflict in sight, Armstrong judged that American neutrality would be served most effectively by the withdrawal of American forces from Canton and the stationing of a warship near the city in case American residents needed to be evacuated.[37]

Ironically, this decision to withdraw American troops led directly to hostilities. On November 15th Foote left Whampoa for Canton to prepare for the troop removal. As he approached the huge fortresses commanding the river approach to Canton, his boat drew fire and he returned to the *San Jacinto* and reported the incident to Armstrong. Believing that the American flag had been insulted, Armstrong eschewed a diplomatic protest and prepared for action. The next day, a small steamer was sent to retrieve the forces at Canton and a small boat from the *San Jacinto* sent to take a sounding. The Chinese again fired and killed the coxswain of the sounding boat. Because the *San Jacinto* drew too much water, Armstrong had to rely on his other two warships. Although the *Levant* grounded, the *Portsmouth* approached the forts, opened fire, and silenced the fortresses after an hour of fierce shelling. After a day's respite in which both American ships grounded, Armstrong attempted to resolve the conflict by demanding an explanation and an apology from the Chinese officials within twenty-four hours. After he learned that the forts were being repaired, Armstrong renewed hostilities on November 20th Two days later, American forces had captured all five forts with losses of 7 killed and 22 wounded in contrast to Chinese losses of more than 160 killed. By December 6th American forces had destroyed the battlements and spiked the mounted guns of the forts. They then withdrew to Whampoa.[38]

Of significance is the fact that the episode ended here. Chinese officials were anxious to close the dispute and sent a conciliatory message to Armstrong rather than have the Americans join with the British at Canton. In fact, a joint effort was precisely what the British suggested to Parker and Armstrong. On November 21st Parker declined a British offer for the United States to join in the occupation of Canton and to demand direct access to Chinese officials there. On November 24th Armstrong refused to join the British in naval action against the Chinese along the Canton River. As far as Armstrong was concerned, the Barrier Forts action had been conducted to redress an insult to the American flag and to assist existing negotiations. Once those objectives were achieved, he and Parker were anxious to resume American neutrality. Although the State Department apparently misunderstood the incident and viewed Armstrong as the aggressor, the Navy Department sustained the commodore's action. Armstrong had acted in a decisive but restrained manner to uphold American prestige and preserve American neutrality. According to Parker, the episode had precisely the right impact. "This is the first blow that has ever been struck by our navy in China," he reported to the State Department, "and it has been done in a manner calculated to secure for it an important prestige in the mind of this haughty government."[39]

American naval officers were also cautious about their involvement in imperialistic ventures such as the scheme to acquire Formosa in 1857. Soon after he recommended that the United States take temporary possession of Formosa as a "last resort" to force treaty revision, Peter Parker became involved in a plan to occupy the island permanently. Because Formosa was strategically located on a route from the south China coast to California and contained rich coal deposits, the island had held the interest of Americans for some time. During his expedition Commodore Perry sent a special detachment to explore and examine the value of the island. Upon his return to the United States, Perry actively argued the importance of Formosa to American interests. In addition, American commercial pressure for some action by the United States was growing by 1855. Particularly active were commercial partners Gideon Nye and William Robinet who lobbied available American officials for decisive action.[40]

In February, 1857, Nye sent a letter to Parker outlining the situation on Formosa and recommending that an independent colony be established with guaranteed protection from the United States. Given the threat of natives on the island to foreigners and frequent rumors that shipwrecked sailors were killed or imprisoned, Nye argued that the Chinese government had abdicated its sovereignty by failing to control the population. Nye's proposal suited Parker's own mood and ideas about American policy well, and he forwarded the letter to the State Department with his endorsement.[41] At the same time, he met with Commodore Armstrong on February 28, 1857, to discuss the situation. Apparently, both men agreed that the acknowledged principles of international law would justify American occupation of Formosa as a legitimate response to outstanding American claims and grievances against China. They also concurred that Formosa was "a most desirable island" which would be "particularly valuable to the United States," but that the existing American naval force made such a venture "impractical." It simply was not large enough to resist a determined Chinese attack. In spite of his sympathy for the project, Armstrong made no commitments about naval support and did not petition the Navy Department for a larger force. In fact, he did not mention the proposal in his dispatches. He did, however, agree to dispatch a marine captain to the island to investigate rumors that ship-wrecked Americans were imprisoned there. "Such a step," Armstrong informed Parker, "may be necessary to legitimate a prior American foothold in case our government should look to future reprisals and occupancy."[42]

In the meantime Parker continued to receive information, reports, and rec-ommendations from Nye and Robinet. The Commissioner, in turn, forwarded this information along with his own strong recommendations for American action to the new administration in Washington. In Parker's mind, what began as a plan to establish an independent American colony on Formosa quickly became an opportunity for annexation by the United States. On March 10, 1857, Parker observed that because Formosa would probably not remain part of the Chinese empire for long, it was obvious that the United States should possess the island, "particularly as respects the great principle of balance of power. Great Britain has her St. Helena in the Atlantic, her Gibraltar and Malta in the Mediterranean, her Aden in the Red Sea, Mauritius, Ceylon, Penang, and Singapore in the Indian Ocean, and Hong Kong in the China Seas. If the United States is so disposed, and can *arrange* for the possession of Formosa, England certainly cannot object."[43]

In fact, such visions of territorial empire in Asia were chimerical. Both the outgoing and incoming administrations rejected American intervention or oc-cupation of Formosa. By early May Parker had received his government's re-sponse and he was on his way out as commissioner. Significantly, Armstrong's status was not affected by these events. Although he was not entirely candid with the Navy Department on Formosa in his dispatches, he was scrupulous not to involve or place the navy in a situation where it might be involved without explicit instructions from Washington.

The most serious breach of neutrality by the American Navy occurred in June, 1859, during a British assault on the Ta-Ku forts near the mouth of the Pei-ho River. Earlier in 1859 American, British, and French diplomats had attempted to exchange ratifications of the Tientsin treaties with the Chinese and to establish their respective diplomatic residences in Peking. As usual, the Chinese responded with evasions, passive resistance, and prevarication. The American Commis-sioner, Georgian John E. Ward, responded by renewed diplomatic initiatives in June. In contrast, the British and French were not as patient, charged the Chinese with bad faith, and prepared to go directly to Peking. In early June the British admiral ordered his naval forces to the Pei-ho and the British warned that full responsibility for any resultant trouble would rest with the Chinese. When the British arrived on the Pei-ho, they found barriers obstructing the mouth of the river and the forts rebuilt. Contact with the Chinese brought a refusal to remove the barriers and instructions for the foreigners to proceed up the coast to Pei-t'ang where they were to be received. Several days later, on June 21st, Ward and Commodore Josiah Tattnall arrived in the *Powhatan* with the small chartered steamer *Toeywan* in tow. On June 24th the *Toeywan* entered the river but ran aground near the forts. In spite of British assistance, the steamer was not refloated until high tide.[44]

That same evening the British began to remove the barriers and attacked the forts the afternoon of the next day. The Chinese, however, were well prepared and registered an unprecedented victory over the British. In the battle, the British suffered heavy casualties, lost their flagship, and were forced to withdraw after a costly assault on the forts. In addition to their Admiral, who was seriously wounded, the British suffered more than 400 killed and wounded compared to several dozen for the Chinese.

Although he began as an observer, Commodore Tattnall did not stay neutral long. During the fighting, he searched for the wounded British Admiral who had his own barge sunk and its coxswain killed. American sailors also helped the British load their guns and towed a flotilla of British launches into position for a land assault. Done with the full approval of Commissioner Ward, Tattnell allegedly exclaimed that "blood is thicker than water" in explaining his order and gave orders to have his executive officer prepare a 200-man armed landing party, although this force was not used.[45]

In Washington, the Buchanan Administration was not pleased by the incident. Although warm praise and expressions of appreciation from the British no doubt helped the situation of Ward and Tattnall, subsequent dispatches approved their action at Pei-ho unenthusiastically. Secretary of the Navy Isaac Toucey tersely informed Tattnall that "Your course as indicated in your despatch meets with the approbation of the Department." American missionary and interpreter S. Wells Williams summarized the situation well when he noted that, although the Secretary of the Navy had approved his actions, Tattnall well understood "that an act may be approved after it has been committed which would have been differently criticized beforehand."[46]

Whatever the explanation for his actions, Tattnall had seriously compromised American neutrality by sympathizing openly and assisting the British assault. Ironically, this violation of neutrality did not have a significant impact on Chinese-American relations. The Chinese resented the incident, but they chose to ignore it officially. Instead, they made Ward's diplomatic mission more difficult than necessary. Shortly after the battle, Ward arrived at Pei-t'ang in July and was received by Chinese officials before continuing on to Peking. But the Chinese helped make his overland trip very uncomfortable, placed him under virtual house arrest in Peking, and insisted that he perform the kowtow. When Ward refused, the actual exchange of ratifications for the Treaty of Tientsin ended up being made on the Chinese coast, not in the capital.

Although conditions in China did not improve markedly, there were no more potentially serious incidents in the two years which remained before the Civil War. When the call came in 1861 for the ships of the East India Squadron to return to the United States, it marked the end of a frustrating but fascinating epoch in naval history. Not only would conditions be different when American naval vessels returned to China after the war, but the ships there would also be part of an entirely different unit, the Asiatic Squadron.

10.
Conclusion

By the late 1850's the Buchanan Administration seemed prepared to embrace a naval policy commensurate with its aggressive diplomatic objectives in the Western Hemisphere. Although it defended its naval initiatives in terms which were compatible with traditional American attitudes on the navy, the administration sought a much expanded naval force capable of controlling the waters of the Caribbean and of intervening in the affairs of other nations in Latin America. In December, 1857, Secretary Toucey criticized the idea of an "overgrown naval establishment" and emphasized that it was "not the policy of our Government to maintain a great navy in time of peace." But just a year later Toucey recommended nineteen small steam warships capable of "entering the rivers and harbors of all foreign countries, as well as our own." The waters of the Caribbean "should be made to swarm with these floating fortifications."[1]

Buchanan also made a serious effort to acquire naval bases from Santo Domingo and New Granada (Colombia). When these efforts failed, he pursued a dubious arrangement with a private company in an unsuccessful attempt to secure bases in Panama. In addition, Buchanan created a large naval squadron to resolve a minor diplomatic dispute with a weak, landlocked nation in South America. In so doing the President was not so much attempting to intimidate an offending Paraguay as he was sending a message to other nations about the ability and the willingness of the United States to assert and defend its interests in the Western Hemisphere. The President's requests to Congress for authority to intervene in Central America and Mexico as well as his determination to acquire Cuba also presaged an aggressive diplomatic role for the navy in the region.

In fact, the sectional crisis of the late 1850's precluded a transformation in the navy's peacetime role as naval policy became yet another victim of domestic turmoil. When politicians addressed naval issues, they now spoke in the rhetoric of sectionalism. Traditionally, proponents of a strong peacetime navy had been concentrated in the maritime districts of the middle and upper Atlantic seaboard. Pro-navy supporters had also tended to favor the construction of large warships because they were well adapted to duty on the high seas and symbolized the nation's pretensions to status as a first-class power. Although pro-navy forces gradually recognized the need for more small warships, the situation changed dramatically in the 1850's as more and more southerners pressed for additional small steam warships. Southerners realized that the creation of an empire in the Caribbean would require a strong navy which could operate actively in the shallow waters of the region. In addition, the fear that the powerful English Navy would wreck havoc in wartime by penetrating southern waterways, landing troops, and freeing thousands of slaves combined to create strong support in the South for a larger navy. Southern anxieties intensified during the Anglo-American war scare of 1858 when a naval conflict in the Caribbean seemed imminent and southern vulnerability was never more apparent.

The importance of the navy to the South was reflected in the fact that both the House and the Senate Naval Affairs Committees were chaired by southerners, Representative T. S. Bocock of Virginia and Senator Stephen R. Mallory of Florida, and Buchanan's Secretary of the Navy was a doughface, or a Northerner with southern principles. In the late 1850's the department and its southern supporters in Congress sought small, light, fast, well-armed steamers tailored to the Caribbean and the Gulf of Mexico but relatively worthless on the high seas in any war with England or France. Congressional measures in 1857, 1858, and 1859 for naval expansion specified steam driven sloops-of-war or small, light steamers. In Congress by this time it was relatively easy to collect southern votes to build or purchase light steamers, but anti-slavery northerners objected. Although traditional supporters of the navy did not oppose the construction of smaller warships *per se*, they well understood southern expansionist intentions in the Caribbean. The degree to which the navy had become embroiled in sectional politics was highlighted in 1860 when abolitionist Senator Henry Wilson of Massachusetts introduced a measure to build five steam sloops for the express purpose of suppressing the slave trade. The Naval Affairs Committee, chaired by Mallory, amended the measure to authorize construction of seven light steamers without specification as to their use. On the floor, Wilson then attempted to reamend the measure but failed by a vote of 18 to 25 and the whole measure was lost. Debate on the issue found anti-navy Senators criticizing Wilson for using the suppression of the slave trade as a pretext for increasing the navy. At the same time, some southerners who had previously supported the construction of small steamers now opposed both Mallory's and Wilson's proposals because they feared a genuine effort to suppress the slave trade. Thus entangled in sectional politics, the navy had little hope of addressing its legitimate peacetime needs.[2]

Between 1829 and 1860 the navy's sphere of activity and range of responsibility had increased dramatically in response to the tremendous growth of American commerce and economic activity overseas. The development of a maritime commercial empire had created two types of pressure for increased naval support. From within the United States, interest groups and their political spokesmen demanded naval assistance as they sought to protect the far-flung whale fisheries, open new markets, identify new navigation routes, and expand existing markets in remote areas. Since they represented a diverse array of interests, these proponents of a strong, active, commercially oriented navy never constituted a unified, pro-navy lobby in the antebellum United States, nor did they articulate a broad conceptual argument for a powerful modern navy. Instead, these forces tended to support specific naval activities or demand naval protection for a specific interest.

Overseas, the acceleration of American commercial activity inevitably created numerous situations which required a naval response. In remote areas, warships had to be available to prevent attacks on American merchant ships, to guarantee commercial equality for Americans, to conduct basic diplomacy, and, at times, to protect American lives and property. Although some diplomatic confrontations with established nations occurred over commercial questions during the period, the main problems arose in remote areas and with nonwestern countries such as China and Japan where diplomatic and commercial activity required active naval support.

The fact that the expansion of the navy's role occurred in response to an array of internal pressures and external demands meant that the increase in responsibility was not the result of a conscious change in the naval policy of the government or of either major political party. Although individual initiative played an important role in naval development during the period, the individuals most interested in transforming the navy tended to be in positions of limited authority. A man like Matthew F. Maury could propose and shape specific naval ventures, but he was not in a position to influence the government's fundamental naval policy. And individuals like Abel Upshur or Isaac Toucey who wished to transform the peacetime navy, either occupied their positions for a short time or were part of an administration overwhelmed by domestic political turmoil.

In short, while the navy was playing a more and more active peacetime commercial role between 1829 and 1860, most traditional American assumptions and attitudes about the professional military, in general, and the navy, in particular, remained in place. Americans took pride in their navy and extolled it publicly, but they still expected it to remain small and worried periodically about its potential threat to their republican institutions. With its aristocratic image, the navy also served as a whipping boy for some politicians to use in their appeals for egalitarian reforms. Even those individuals who supported naval expansion and the concept of a strong modern navy readily denied that the U.S. Navy should be modeled after those of the European powers or challenge them for control of the seas. With few exceptions, the individuals who demanded a stronger navy argued the need for a naval response to a specific threat, economic interest, or political objective. In addition, the senior naval officers of this period were neither trained nor inclined to redefine the strategic or diplomatic role of the navy. Although the navy did not lack impetuous or aggressive officers, they rarely thought in broad strategic or diplomatic terms. In fact, given their considerable latitude in reacting to various situations, one is struck by the narrow context in which most naval officers defined their actions and the considerable restraint most exercised on such difficult assignments as the East India Station. In this period, the only senior naval officer who viewed the potential role of the navy in terms which presaged those of Alfred Mahan's generation was Matthew C. Perry, and his views set him apart from his peers.

The navy's expanded role, then, resulted not from a change in the nation's naval policy, but from an operational redefinition of its responsibility to protect American commerce. The Presidents and Naval Secretaries of the 1850's still spoke of the "protection of commerce" as the primary peacetime duty of the navy, just as Jackson and his Secretaries had, but the practical meaning of that term had now been transformed. Americans now expected the navy to play an active, positive, and expansive part in the growth of their burgeoning maritime empire. And by 1860 the navy could point with pride to a considerable list of peacetime achievements which would have been virtually impossible to foresee just thirty years earlier. In retrospect, many of these accomplishments were less dramatic than the wartime exploits of the navy in the War of 1812 and the Civil War, but they nonetheless had a substantial and lasting impact on the growth of American commerce in the Caribbean, South America, the Far East, and the Pacific Basin.

Notes

CHAPTER 1

1. Summary accounts and interpretations of peacetime naval activities and policy in this period include William R. Braisted, ''Naval Diplomacy,'' in Alexander DeConde, ed., *Encyclopedia of American Foreign Policy*, 3 vols. (New York, 1978), II: 668–678; Dudley W. Knox, *A History of the United States Navy* (revised edition, New York, 1948; original edition, 1936); Harold and Margaret Sprout, *The Rise of American Naval Power, 1776–1918* (revised edition. Princeton, N.J., 1966; original edition, 1939); Charles O. Paullin, *Diplomatic Negotiations of American Naval Officers, 1778–1883* (Baltimore, 1912); David F. Long, ''The Navy Under the Board of Navy Commissioners, 1815–1842,'' and Geoffrey S. Smith, ''An Uncertain Passage: The Bureaus Run the Navy, 1842–1861,'' both in Kenneth J. Hagan, ed., *In War and Peace: Interpretations of American Naval History, 1775–1978* (Westport, Conn., 1978), 63–78, 79–106. An excellent collection of primary sources on the navy's peacetime diplomatic and commercial activities before the Civil War is contained in K. Jack Bauer, ed., *The New American State Papers, 1798–1860; Naval Affairs*, 10 vols. (Wilmington, Del., 1981), vols. 2, 3, 9. Essays on aspects of the navy's role are contained in Clayton R. Barrow, Jr. ed., *America Spreads Her Sails; U.S. Seapower in the 19th Century* (Annapolis, Md., 1973).

2. Harry Bluff [Matthew F. Maury], ''Scraps from the Lucky Bag,'' *Southern Literary Messenger*, VII (1841): 23–24. The administrative problems of the department are discussed in Leonard D. White, *The Jacksonians: A Study in Administrative History, 1829–1861* (New York, 1954), 213–250; and in Charles O. Paullin, *Paullin's History of Naval Administration, 1775–1911* (Annapolis, Md., 1968), 159–247. This volume reprints a series of articles which appeared in the early twentieth century.

3. George Rogers Taylor, *The Transportation Revolution, 1815–1860* (Torchbook edition, New York, 1968; original edition, 1951), Appendix A, 444–445, 440–441; Alexis DeTocqueville, *Democracy in America*, Phillips Bradley, ed., 2 vols. (Vintage edition, New York, 1945; original edition, 1835), I: 447. For additional statistics on the growth of American foreign trade, see Douglas C. North, *The Economic Growth of the United*

States, 1790–1860 (New York, 1961), Appendix III, 267–291; and J. Smith Homans, Jr., *An Historical and Statistical Account of the Foreign Commerce of the United States* (New York, 1857). Statistics on the foreign commerce of the United States are available in *Historical Statistics of the United States; Colonial Times to 1970*, 2 Parts (Washington, D.C., 1975), 2: 858–907. In this study, when possible, I have used the appendices in Taylor, *The Transportation Revolution*, because the figures cited there are complete to the last digit while those in *Historical Statistics of the United States* are rounded to the nearest one-thousandth.

4. *Historical Statistics of the United States*, 2: 904, 907.

5. *Congressional Globe*, 31st Congress, lst Session (1849–1850), Appendix, 262.

6. James D. Richardson, ed., *A Compilation of the Messages and Papers of the Presidents, 1789–1902*, 10 vols. (Washington, D.C., 1903), II: 459.

7. See, for example, Sprout, *Rise of American Naval Power*, 149.

8. A detailed analysis of the debate on the Revenue Bill is in Craig L. Symonds, *Navalists and Antinavalists: The Naval Policy Debate in the United States, 1785–1827* (Newark, Del., 1980), 199–213.

9. *Annals of the Congress of the United States*, 14th Congress, 1st Session (1815–1816), 749, 872, 757.

10. Ibid., 792, 776, 829.

11. Ibid., 849.

12. Ibid., 916–917. John Randolph, for example, was one of the sharpest opponents of the Revenue Bill, but nevertheless acknowledged the need for a strong navy, Ibid., 843.

13. D. Jack Bauer, "Naval Shipbuilding Programs, 1794–1860," *Military Affairs*, 29 (1965): 29–40. See also Symonds, *Navalists and Antinavalists*, 199.

14. Ibid., 224–231.

15. William Appleman Williams, "The Age of Mercantilism: An Interpretation of the American Political Economy, 1763 to 1828," *William and Mary Quarterly*, 3rd Ser., 15 (1958): 419–437 as cited in Armin Rappaport, ed., *Essays in American Diplomacy* (New York, 1967), 62–74. See also Richard W. Van Alstyne, *The Rising American Empire* (New York, 1960), 99; Howard Kushner, *Conflict on the Northwest Coast; American-Russian Rivalry in the Pacific Northwest, 1790–1867* (Westport, Conn., 1975), 45–58.

16. Taylor, *Transportation Revolution*, 129. See also Emery R. Johnson et al., *History of Domestic and Foreign Commerce of the United States*, 2 vols. (reprint edition, New York, 1967; original edition, 1915), II: 297–298.

17. Symonds, *Navalists and Antinavalists*, 222; Russell F. Weigley, *The American Way of War: A History of United States Military Strategy and Policy* (New York, 1973), 61.

18. *Niles National Register*, 19 April 1823 as cited in David F. Long, *Nothing Too Daring: A Biography of Commodore David Porter, 1780–1843* (Annapolis, Md., 1970), 204.

19. Gardner W. Allen, *Our Navy and the West Indian Pirates* (Salem, Mass., 1929); Francis B. C. Bradlee, *Piracy in the West Indies and Its Suppression* (Salem, Mass., 1923); Richard Wheeler, *In Pirate Waters* (New York, 1969); David F. Long, *Sailor-Diplomat; A Biography of Commodore James Biddle, 1783–1848* (Boston, 1983), 93–111.

20. Long, *Porter*, 203–255; Raymond Shoemaker, "No One Died at Fajardo: The

Strange Court-Martial of David Porter,'' Paper delivered at the Sixth Naval History Symposium; Annapolis, Md., September 30, 1983.

21. Edward B. Billingsley, *In Defense of Neutral Rights: The United States Navy and the Wars of Independence in Chile and Peru* (Chapel Hill, N.C., 1967); T. Ray Shurbett, "Chile, Peru, and the U.S. Pacific Squadron, 1823–1850," in Craig L. Symonds, ed., *New Aspects of Naval History* (Annapolis, Md., 1981), 201–210.

22. Robert G. Albion, "Distant Stations," *United States Naval Institute Proceedings*, 80 (1954): 265–273. Studies of the individual squadrons and their activities are George M. Brooke, "The Role of the United States Navy in the Suppression of the African Slave Trade," *American Neptune*, 21 (1961): 28–41; James A. Field, Jr., *America and the Mediterranean World, 1776–1882* (Princeton, N.J., 1969); Donald W. Griffin, "The American Navy At Work on Brazil Station, 1827–1860," *American Neptune*, 19 (1959): 239–256; Robert Erwin Johnson, *Far China Station: The United States Navy in Asian Waters, 1800–1898* (Annapolis, Md., 1979); Robert Erwin Johnson, *Thence Round Cape Horn: The Story of United States Naval Forces on Pacific Station, 1818–1923* (Annapolis, 1963); James M. Merrill, "The Asiatic Squadron: 1835–1907," *American Neptune*, 29 (1969): 106–117; Raymond L. Shoemaker, "Diplomacy from the Quarterdeck: The U.S. Navy in the Caribbean, 1815–1830," in Robert W. Love, Jr., ed., *Changing Interpretations and New Sources in Naval History* (New York, 1980), 169–179.

23. Kushner, *Conflict on the Northwest Coast*, 43–62; Samuel Flagg Bemis, *John Quincy Adams and the Foundations of American Foreign Policy* (paperback edition, New York, 1973; original edition, 1949), 566–570; Walter LaFeber, ed., *John Quincy Adams and American Continental Empire; Letters, Papers, and Speeches* (Chicago, 1965).

24. Symonds, *Navalists and Antinavalists*, 231–233.

25. Edwin M. Hall, "Samuel Lewis Southard," Paolo Coletta, ed., *American Secretaries of the Navy*, 2 vols. (Annapolis, Md., 1980), I: 131–140.

26. Linda M. Maloney, "The U.S. Navy's Pacific Squadron, 1824–1827," in *Changing Interpretations and New Sources in Naval History*, 180–191; Paullin, *Diplomatic Negotiations of American Naval Officers*, 341–343.

CHAPTER 2

1. James D. Richardson, ed., *A Compilation of the Messages and Papers of the Presidents, 1789–1902,* 10 vols. (Washington, D.C., 1903), II: 437–438.

2. Ibid., II: 459.

3. Richard B. Latner, *The Presidency of Andrew Jackson; White House Politics, 1829–1837* (Athens, Ga., 1979), 207–212.

4. Naval historians have acknowledged that virtually no debate on naval policy occurred during the Jackson administration. For example, see David F. Long, "The Navy Under the Board of Navy Commissioners, 1815–1842," Kenneth J. Hagan, ed., *In War and Peace: Interpretations of American Naval History, 1775–1978* (Westport, Conn., 1978), 63–78; Charles O. Paullin, *Paullin's History of Naval Administration, 1775–1911* (Annapolis, Md., 1968), 159–203; Leonard D. White, *The Jacksonians: A Study in Administrative History, 1829–1861* (New York, 1954), 213–216. Jackson's biographers have also failed to uncover any debate on the subject, and his published correspondence is devoid of substantive comment on the navy, John Spencer Bassett, ed., *Correspondence of Andrew Jackson*, 7 vols. (Washington, D.C., 1935).

5. Branch to Jackson, 14 August 1830, *Correspondence of Andrew Jackson*, IV:

171–172; W. Patrick Strauss, "John Branch," in Paolo Coletta, ed., *American Secretaries of the Navy*, 2 vols. (Annapolis, Md., 1980), I: 143–149.

6. W. Patrick Strauss, "Levi Woodbury," ibid., I: 151–153; Edmund Roberts, *Embassy to the Eastern Courts of Cochin China, Siam, and Muscat* (New York, 1837).

7. W. Patrick Strauss, "Mahlon Dickerson," in *Secretaries of the Navy*, I: 155–163.

8. George Rogers Taylor, *The Transportation Revolution, 1815–1860* (Torchbook edition, New York, 1968; original edition, 1951), Appendix A, 444; Douglas C. North, *The Economic Growth of the United States, 1790–1860* (New York, 1961), Appendix III, 284–285.

9. Ibid, 143, 135.

10. John H. Schroeder, "Rep. John Floyd, 1817–1829: Harbinger of the Oregon Territory," *Oregon Historical Quarterly*, 70 (1969): 333–346; Henry Nash Smith, *Virgin Land; The American West As Symbol and Myth* (New York, 1950), 20–32.

11. For a list of these agreements, see Emory R. Johnson et al., *History of Domestic and Foreign Commerce of the United States*, 2 vols. (Reprint, New York, 1967; original edition, 1915), II: 339.

12. David H. Finnie, *Pioneers East: The Early American Experience in the Middle East* (Cambridge, Mass., 1967), 46–63; James A. Field, Jr., *America and the Mediterranean World, 1776–1882* (Princeton, N.J. 1969), 141–153; David F. Long, *Sailor-Diplomat; A Biography of Commodore James Biddle, 1783–1848* (Boston, 1983), 155–162; Charles O. Paullin, *Diplomatic Negotiations of American Naval Officers, 1778–1883* (Baltimore, 1912), 122–153.

13. Richardson, *Messages of the Presidents*, II: 594; III: 238; Thomas Hart Benton, *Thirty Years' View; Or, A History of the Working of the American Government for Thirty Years*, 2 vols. (New York, 1854), I: 608. See also Paul J. Zingg, "To the Shores of Barbary: The Ideology and Pursuit of American Commercial Expansion, 1816–1906," *South Atlantic Quarterly*, 79 (1980): 408–424.

14. Early American contacts with Indonesia are treated thoroughly in James W. Gould, "Sumatra—America's Pepperpot, 1784–1873," *Essex Institute Historical Collections*, 92 (1956): 83–152, 203–251, 295–348.

15. A detailed account of the whole affair is David F. Long, " 'Martial Thunder': The First Official American Armed Intervention in Asia," *Pacific Historical Review*, 42 (1973): 143–162. See also John M. Belohlavek, "Andrew Jackson and the Malaysian Pirates: A Question of Diplomacy and Politics," *Tennessee Historical Quarterly*, 36 (1977): 19–29; Captain John F. Campbell, "Pepper, Pirates and Grapeshot," *American Neptune*, 21 (1961): 292–302.

16. Charles M. Endicott's Statement, 7 February 1831, *American State Papers; Class VI (Naval Affairs)*, 4 vols. (Washington, D.C., 1834–1861), IV: 154–155.

17. Woodbury to Downes, 9 August, 1831, Ibid., IV: 153. See also, Woodbury to Downes, 27 June 1831, Ibid., IV: 150–152.

18. Long, " 'Martial Thunder,' " 149–150.

19. Jeremiah N. Reynolds, *Voyage of the United States Frigate Potomac . . . in 1831, 1832, 1833, and 1834* (New York, 1835), 95–96. Another first-hand account is Francis Warriner, *Cruise of the U.S. Frigate Potomac Round the World, 1831–1834* (New York, 1835).

20. Downes to Woodbury, 17 February 1832; I. Shubrick to Com. J. Powers (*U.S.S. Potomac*), 6 February 1832, *American State Papers, Class VI (Naval Affairs)*, IV: 156–158.

21. Downes to Woodbury, 17 February 1832, Ibid., IV: 156.

22. *National Intelligencer*, 10 July 1832; also 13 July 1832.

23. *Washington Globe*, 11 July 1832. Newspaper clippings on the whole controversy are in Series II, Box 30 of the Levi Woodbury Papers, Manuscript Division, Library of Congress.

24. Richardson, *Messages of the Presidents*, II: 596; Report of the Secretary of the Navy, 3 December 1832, *Register of Debates*, 22nd Congress, 2nd Session (1832–1833), Appendix, 15; Woodbury to Silas Silsbee, 30 August 1832, Levi Woodbury Papers, Dartmouth College.

25. Woodbury to Downes, 16 July 1832, Letters Sent by the Secretary of the Navy to Officers, 1798–1868, Naval Records, Record Group 45, National Archives, vol. 20 (Microfilm Series 149). (Cited hereafter as Secretary of the Navy Letters to Officers).

26. For accounts of the crisis, see Harold F. Peterson, *Argentina and the United States, 1810–1960* (New York, 1964), 101–120; Paul D. Dickens, "The Falkland Islands Dispute Between the United States and Argentina," *Hispanic American Historical Review*, IX (1929): 471–487; Julius Goebel, Jr., *The Struggle for the Falkland Islands; A Study in Legal and Diplomatic History* (New Haven, Conn., 1927), 434–465. See also Lester D. Langley, "The Jacksonians and the Origins of Inter-American Distrust," *Inter-American Economic Affairs* 30 (1976): 3–21.

27. The diplomatic correspondence related to the incident is contained in William R. Manning, ed., *Diplomatic Correspondence of the Unilted States; Inter-American Affairs, 1831–1860*, 12 vols. (Washington, D.C., 1932), I: 3–17, 65–186.

28. Richardson, *Messages of the Presidents*, II: 553; see also Report of the Secretary of the Navy, 3 December 1832, *Register of Debates*, 22nd Congress, 2nd Session (1832–1833), Appendix, 15–16.

29. Woodbury to Duncan, 15 February 1832, Secretary of the Navy Letters to Officers, vol. 20; Livingston to Baylies, 3 April 1832, *Diplomatic Correspondence of the United States; Inter-American Affairs*, I: 14.

30. Report of the Secretary of the Navy, 3 December 1832, *Register of Debates*, 22nd Congress, 2nd Session (1832–1833), Appendix, 16; New York *Journal of Commerce*, September, 1832, Series II, Box 30, Levi Woodbury Papers, Manuscript Division, Library of Congress.

31. A scholarly account is K. Jack Bauer, "The U.S. Navy and Texas Independence," *Military Affairs*, 34 (1970): 44–48.

32. See, for example, Paullin, *Diplomatic Negotiations of American Naval Officers*.

33. Samuel Eliot Morison, *"Old Bruin"; Commodore Matthew C. Perry, 1794–1858* (Boston, 1967), 121–123.

34. Woodbury to Commodore George Rodgers, 25 January 1832, Secretary of the Navy Letters to Officers, vol. 20. For his first-hand account, see Roberts, *Embassy to the Eastern Courts of Cochin China, Siam, and Muscat*. The correspondence between Roberts and Woodbury on his appointment is in Series I, vols. 11–12, Levi Woodbury Papers, Manuscript Division, Library of Congress.

35. Robert Erwin Johnson, *Far China Station: The United States Navy in Asian Waters, 1800–1898* (Annapolis, Md., 1979), 5–16; Charles O. Paullin, *American Voyages to the Orient, 1790–1865* (Annapolis, Md., 1971), 53–62. This volume is a collection of articles published previously by Paullin in the United States Naval Institute Proceedings. Much of the material is also contained in Paullin's *Diplomatic Negotiations of American Naval Officers*.

36. Roberts' personal accounts of the second voyage are contained in the Edmund Roberts Papers, New Hampshire Historical Society. See also W. S. W. Ruschenberger, *A Voyage Round the World, Including an Embassy to Muscat and Siam, in 1835-1836 and 1837* (Philadelphia, 1838). A biographical sketch of Roberts is in William E. Griffis, "Edmund Roberts, Our First Envoy to Japan," *New York Times*, 6 August 1905.

37. The background to the expedition is treated in two scholarly studies: William Stanton, *The Great United States Exploring Expedition of 1838–1842* (Berkeley, 1975); and David B. Tyler, *The Wilkes Expedition; The First United States Exploring Expedition (1838–1842)* (Philadelphia, 1968).

38. For a collection of correspondence and documents supporting the proposed expedition, see Jeremiah N. Reynolds, *Address on the Subject of a Surveying and Exploring Expedition to the Pacific Ocean and South Seas. Delivered in the Hall of Representatives . . . April 3, 1836* (New York, 1836), 103–241.

39. Ibid., 25, 23, 70–71.

40. Reynolds, *Voyage of the United States Frigate Potomac*, Dedication page and 67–69.

41. *Congressional Debates*, 24th Congress, 1st Session (1835–1836), vol. 12, Part 3: 3473.

42. Ibid., 3556, 3557, 3560; Stanton, *The Great United States Exploring Expedition*, 35-36.

43. Richardson, *Messages of the Presidents*, III: 116, 173.

44. Ibid , III: 161.

45. Ibid., III: 257. Although Harold and Margaret Sprout, *The Rise of American Naval Power, 1776–1918* (revised edition, Princeton, N.J., 1966; original edition, 1939), 105–107 noted Jackson's change of attitudes on the navy between 1829 and 1837, the book attributes the shift solely to the French crisis and the President's anxiety over national defense.

46. Richardson, *Messages of the Presidents*, III: 307.

47. *Historical Statistics of the United States; Colonial Times to 1970*, 2 Parts (Washington, D.C., 1975), II: 1104, 1114–1115.

CHAPTER 3

1. James C. Curtis, *The Fox at Bay; Martin Van Buren and the Presidency 1837–1841* (Lexington, Ky., 1970), 47, 63.

2. Harold F. Peterson, *Argentina and the United States, 1810–1960* (New York, 1964), 124–127.

3. James D. Richardson, ed., *A Compilation of the Messages and Papers of the Presidents, 1789–1902*. 10 vols. (Washington, D.C., 1903), III: 502. Van Buren was even quoted as remarking that the country "required no navy at all, much less a steam navy." *New York Herald*, 23 January 1878, as quoted in Harold and Margaret Sprout, *The Rise of American Naval Power, 1779–1918* (revised edition. Princeton, N.J., 1966; original edition, 1939), 113.

4. W. Patrick Strauss, "Mahlon Dickerson," Paolo Coletta, ed., *American Secretaries of the Navy*, 2 vols. (Annapolis, Md., 1980), I: 160–162.

5. W. Patrick Strauss, "James Kirke Paulding," *Secretaries of the Navy*, I: 165–171.

6. Report of the Secretary of the Navy, 30 November 1838, *Congressional Globe*, 25th Congress, 3rd Session (1838–1839), Appendix, 7.

7. W. Patrick Strauss, "Preparing the Wilkes Expedition: A Study in Disorganization," *Pacific Historical Review*, 28 (1959): 221–232. See also, William Stanton, *The Great United States Exploring Expedition of 1838–1843* (Berkeley, Cal., 1975), 41–72; David B. Tyler, *The Wilkes Expedition; The First United States Exploring Expedition (1838–1842)* (Philadelphia, 1968), 7–27. Documents relating to the preparation of the expedition are contained in *House Executive Document No. 147*, 25th Congress, 2nd Session (1837–1838).

8. Dickerson to Jones, 9 November 1837, Secretary of the Navy Letters to Officers, vol. 24. The commercial primacy of the expedition was reaffirmed in Paulding to Wilkes, 11 August 1838, ibid., vol. 25.

9. Strauss, "Preparing the Wilkes Expedition," 231; *Congressional Globe*, 25th Congress, 2nd Session (1837–1838), 280, 287. See also, Geoffrey S. Smith, "Charles Wilkes and the Growth of American Naval Diplomacy," *Makers of American Diplomacy; From Benjamin Franklin to Henry Kissinger*, Frank T. Merli and Theodore A. Wilson, eds. (New York, 1974), 135–163.

10. James Phinney Baxter, *The Introduction of the Ironclad Warship* (New York, 1968; original edition, 1933); Frank M. Bennett, *The Steam Navy of the United States: A History of the Growth of the Steam Vessel of War in the U.S. Navy and of the Naval Engineer Corps*, 2 vols. (Pittsburgh, 1896); Bernard Brodie, *Sea Power in the Machine Age: Major Naval Inventions and Their Consequences on International Politics, 1814–1940* (Princeton, N.J., 1941).

11. Paulding to Gouverneur Kemble, 8, 16 June 1839, Ralph M. Aderman, ed., *The Letters of James K. Paulding* (Madison, Wis., 1962), 258.

12. Jones to Reynolds, 28 February 1828, and Downes to J. Reed, 21 January 1835, *House of Representatives Report No. 94*, 23rd Congress, 2nd Session (1834–1835), 7 February 1835, 11–12, 7–8.

13. Samuel Eliot Morison, *"Old Bruin"; Commodore Matthew C. Perry, 1794–1858* (Boston, 1967), 124–139.

14. Alexander Slidell [Mackenzie], "Thoughts on the Navy," *Naval Magazine*, II (1837): 5–42. See also [Alexander Slidell Mackenzie], *Popular Essays on Naval Subjects* (New York, 1833).

15. Daniel J. O'Neil, "The United States Navy in the Californias, 1840–1850" (unpublished Ph.D. dissertation, University of Southern California, 1969), 1–41.

16. The standard scholarly study is Curtis T. Henson, Jr., *Commissioners and Commodores: The East India Squadron and American Diplomacy in China* (University, Ala., 1982). An insightful dissertation is James B. Wood, "The American Response to China, 1784–1844: Consensus Policy and the Origin of the East India Squadron" (Unpublished Ph.D. Dissertation, Duke University, 1969). See also Robert Erwin Johnson, *Far China Station: The United States Navy in Asian Waters, 1800–1898* (Annapolis, Md., 1979).

17. Dickerson to Kennedy, 26 January, 2, 7 April, 1835, Secretary of the Navy Letters to Officers, vols. 21, 22.

18. Dickerson to Read, 12 April 1838, ibid., vol. 25.

19. E. Mowbray Tate, "Navy Justice in the Pacific, 1830–1870: A Pattern of Precedents," *American Neptune*, 35 (1975): 20–31. First-hand accounts are Josiah S. Henshaw, *Around the World: A Narrative of a Voyage in the East India Squadron Under Commodore George C. Read*, 2 vols. (New York, 1840): Fitch W. Taylor, *The Flagship;*

Or, A Voyage Around the World in the United States Frigate Columbia . . . 2 vols. (New York, 1840).

20. Early American contact with China is treated in E. Mowbray Tate, "American Merchant and Naval Contacts With China, 1784–1850, *American Neptune*, 31 (1971): 177–191; Stuart C. Miller, "The American Trader's Image of China, 1785–1840," *Pacific Historical Review*, 36 (1967): 375–395; Tyler Dennett, *Americans in Eastern Asia: A Critical Study of the United States Policy in the Far East in the Nineteenth Century* (New York, 1922); Foster Rhea Dulles, *The Old China Trade* (Boston, 1930); Kenneth S. Latourette, "The History of Early Relations Between the United States and China, 1784–1844," *Transactions of the Connecticut Academy of Arts and Sciences*, 22 (1917): 1–209. A brief survey of the literature on the subject is Edward D. Graham, "Early American-East Asian Relations," Ernest R. May and James C. Thomson, Jr., eds., *American-East Asian Relations: A Survey* (Cambridge, Mass., 1972), 3–18.

21. "The Execution of an Italian at Canton," *North American Review*, XL (1835): 58–68.

22. Dennett, *Americans in Eastern Asia*, 86–88; Dulles, *Old China Trade*, 132–135.

23. Charles O. Paullin, *American Voyages to the Orient, 1790–1865* (Annapolis, Md., 1971), 23–32; Dennett, *Americans in Eastern Asia*, 79–80; Dulles, *Old China Trade*, 136–137; Tate, "American Merchant and Naval Contacts with China," 179–181.

24. Master-Commandant Finch's Report to the Navy Department, 14 January 1830," as cited in Paullin, *American Voyages to the Orient*, 37–38; Tate, "American Merchant and Naval Contacts with China," 181–182.

25. Paullin, *American Voyages to the Orient*, 52–73.

26. Jacques M. Downs, "American Merchants and the China Opium Trade, 1800–1840," *Business History Review*, 42 (1968): 418–442; Charles C. Stelle, "American Trade in Opium to China Prior to 1820," *Pacific Historical Review*, 9 (1940): 425–444; Charles C. Stelle, "American Trade in Opium to China, 1821–1839," ibid., 10 (1941): 52–74.

27. American Merchants to Commodore George C. Read, 15 July 1839, *House of Representatives Document No. 119*, 26th Congress, 1st Session (1839–1840), 77; Read to Secretary of the Navy, 23 July 1839, ibid., 74. See also Read to American Merchants, 8, 28 July 1839, ibid., 75–76, 78–80.

28. Snow to Secretary of State, 19 April, 13 May, 29 August 1839, ibid., 24, 61, 68, 69. See also Snow to Secretary of State, 22 May 1839, Ibid., 62–63.

29. Memorial of R. B. Forbes and Others, 25 May 1839, *House of Representatives Document No. 40*, 26th Congress, 1st Session (1839–1840). See also, "Communication From Thomas R. Perkins, and a Great Number of Other Merchants, of Boston and Salem, Mass.," *House of Representatives Document No. 170*, 26th Congress, 1st Session (1839–1840). For his views on the conditions of the early China trade, see R. B. Forbes, *Remarks on China and the China Trade* (Boston, 1844).

30. Read to Secretary of Navy, 23 July 1839, *House of Representatives Document No. 119*, 74.

31. John K. Fairbank, *Trade and Diplomacy on the China Coast: The Opening of the Treaty Ports, 1842–1858* (Cambridge, Mass., 1953).

32. Carroll Storrs Alden, *Lawrence Kearny, Sailor Diplomat* (Princeton, N.J., 1936).

33. Paulding to Kearny, 2 November 1840, Secretary of the Navy Letters to Officers, vol. 30.

34. Kearny to U. S. Consul, or Vice Consul, at Canton, 31 March 1842, Jules Davids,

ed., *American Diplomatic and Public Papers: The United States and China*. Series I: *The Treaty System and the Taiping Rebellion, 1842–1860*, 21 vols. (Wilmington, Del., 1973), 1:5. See also, Wood, "American Response to China," 171–172.

35. Kearny to the Secretary of the Navy, 8 April, 11, 19 May 1842, *Public Papers: United States and China*, 1: 6, 26–27, 29. "Edicts Issued by Governor-General Ke," 6, 16 May 1842, ibid., 1: 25, 28. The correspondence and documents are included in "Correspondence Between the Commander of the East India Squadron and Foreign Powers," *Senate Document 139*, 29th Congress, 1st Session (1845–1846).

36. Kearny to Secretary of the Navy, 23 September 1842, *Public Papers: United States and China*, 1: 59–60.

37. Kearny to Secretary of the Navy, 7 October 1842; Kearny to Governor of Canton, 8 October 1842, ibid., 1: 61–63, 64.

38. Governor-General Ke to Kearny, 15 October 1842; Snow to Kearny, 20 October 1842; Kearny to Secretary of Navy, 15 November 1842, ibid., 1: 65, 67, 68.

39. "Edicts and Memorials," 12, 15, 25 December 1842, Earl Swisher, *China's Management of the American Barbarians; A Study of Sino-American Relations, 1841–1861, With Documents* (New Haven, Conn., 1953), 103–106.

40. Kearny to Secretary of the Navy, 16 January 1843, *Public Papers: United States and China*, 1: 70–71. Sturgis to Kearny, 15 January 1843, Letters Received by the Secretary of the Navy From Commanding Officers of Squadrons, 1841–1886 (East India Squadron), Naval Records, Record Group 45, National Archives, vol. 1 (Microfilm Series 89). (Cited hereafter as the East India Squadron Letters.)

41. Memorial of 18 January 1843, Swisher, *China's Management of the American Barbarians*, 108–111. Kearny to Ke, 13 April 1843, *Public Papers: United States and China*, 1: 77–78.

42. Ke to Kearny, 16 April 1843, ibid, 1: 79.

43. King to Imperial Commissioner Kiying, 28 July 1843, Kiying to King, 29 July, 1, 2 August 1843; King to Secretary of State, 20 September 1843, ibid., 1: 92–97, 105–107.

44. Henson, *Commissioners and Commodores*, 44–45; Dennett, *Americans in Eastern Asia*, 109–111; Alden, *Kearny*, 182–186; Johnson, *Far China Station*, 27–28.

CHAPTER 4

1. "Home Squadron," *House of Representatives Report No. 3*, 27th Congress, 1st Session (1841), 1, 2, 5–6; *House Journal*, 27th Congress, 1st Session (1841), 270–311; *Senate Journal*, 27th Congress, 1st Session (1841), 129–130. See also Edward M. Steel, Jr., *T. Butler King of Georgia* (Athens, Ga., 1964), 36–38. King's notes and a rough draft of the report are in Folder 113, T. B. King Papers, Southern Historical Collection, University of North Carolina.

2. "Home Squadron," 4; *Niles National Register*, 22 May 1841, as cited in Paolo E. Coletta, "George F. Badger," in Paolo Coletta, ed., *American Secretaries of the Navy*, 2 vols. (Annapolis, Md., 1980), I: 174.

3. Claude H. Hall, *Abel Parker Upshur; Conservative Virginian, 1790–1844* (Madison, Wis., 1964), 120–122. *Southern Literary Messenger*, VII (1841), 871; *Army and Navy Chronicle*, 16 September 1841.

4. Hall, *Upshur*, 122–125.

5. Harry Bluff [Matthew F. Maury], "Scraps from the Lucky Bag," *Southern Literary*

Messenger, VI (1840): 233–240, 306–320, 786–800; VII (1841): 3–25, 169–170, 345–379.

6. Frances Leigh Williams, *Matthew Fontaine Maury; Scientist of the Sea* (New Brunswick, N.J., 1963).

7. "Scraps from the Lucky Bag," *Southern Literary Messenger*, VI (1840): 234, 235, 306.

8. Ibid., VI: 239, 238.

9. Ibid., VI: 306.

10. Report of the Secretary of the Navy, 4 December 1841, *Congressional Globe*, 27th Congress, 2nd Session (1841–1842), Appendix, 16–23.

11. Ibid., 22, 20.

12. Ibid., 20.

13. Ibid., 20, 22.

14. *Morning Courier and the New York Enquirer*, 18 December 1841, as cited in Hall, *Upshur*, 130. See also, "Our Navy, Judge Upshur and His Report," *Southern Literary Messenger*, VIII (1842): 89–97; *Army and Navy Chronicle*, 16 December 1841.

15. *Historical Statistics of the United States; Colonial Times to 1970*, 2 Parts (Washington, D.C., 1975), II: 1104.

16. Hall, *Upshur*, 133–136.

17. *Congressional Globe*, 27th Congress, 2nd Session (1841–1842), 501, 498.

18. Ibid., 499. See also, ibid., 498, 500, 506–508, 681.

19. Ibid., 632–633. See also, ibid., 508–509, 513, 521–522, 625–626, 633, 672–673.

20. Ibid., 640, 633. See also, ibid., 498–499, 513.

21. *Historical Statistics of the U.S.*, II: 1115.

22. Report of the Secretary of the Navy, December, 1842, *Congressional Globe*, 27th Congress, 3rd Session (1842–1843), Appendix, 38–44.

23. Ibid. 39.

24. Ibid. 39, 40.

25. Ibid., 42, 43.

26. Charles Francis Adams, ed., *Memoirs of John Quincy Adams*, 12 vols. (Philadelphia, 1874–1877), XI: 277–278; *Congressional Globe*, 27th Congress, 3rd Session (1842–1843), 121.

27. Ibid., 242.

28. Report of the Secretary of the Navy, 4 December 1841, *Congressional Globe*, 27th Congress, 2nd Session (1841–1842), 16–18; Report of the Secretary of the Navy, 25 November 1843, *Congressional Globe*, 28th Congress, 1st Session (1843–1844), 13–14.

29. [Matthew F. Maury], "Direct Trade With the South," *Southern Literary Messenger*, V (1839): 3–12.

30. Williams, *Maury*, 148–156.

31. Charles Wilkes, *Narrative of the United States Exploring Expedition, during the years 1838, 1839, 1840, 1841, and 1842*, 5 vols. (Philadelphia, 1845). See also, William Stanton, *The Great United States Exploring Expedition of 1838–1842* (Berkley, Cal., 1975); David B. Tyler, *The Wilkes Expedition: The First United States Exploring Expedition (1838–1842)* (Philadelphia, 1968).

32. John E. Wickman, "Political Aspects of Charles Wilkes' Work and Testimony, 1842–1849" (Unpublished Ph.D. Dissertation, Indiana University, 1964); Stanton, *Great United States Exploring Expedition*, 281–289.

33. "The United States Exploring Expedition," *Hunt's Merchants' Magazine*, XII (1845), 445; See also W. Patrick Strauss, *Americans in Polynesia, 1783–1842* (East Lansing, Mich., 1963), 142–143.

34. Upshur to Morris, 15 August 1842, 15 February 1842, Upshur to Perry, 30 March 1843, Secretary of the Navy Letters to Officers, vols. 33, 34; Adams, *Memoirs*, XI: 345–346.

35. K. Jack Bauer, "The Sancala Affair: Captain Voorhees Seizes an Argentine Squadron," *American Neptune*, 29 (1969): 174–186.

36. Hooper to Daniel Webster, 7 March 1843, *Papers Relating to the Foreign Relations of the United States, 1894: Affairs in Hawaii* (Washington, D.C., 1894), Appendix II, 46. This volume contains virtually all pertinent correspondence, instructions and documents relating to early U.S. relations with Hawaii. See also Ralph Kuykendall, *The Hawaiian Kingdom, 1778–1854* (Honolulu, Ha., 1938); Sylvester K. Stevens, *American Expansion in Hawaii, 1842–1898* (Harrisburg, Pa., 1945); and Harold W. Bradley, *The American Frontier in Hawaii; The Pioneers, 1789–1843* (Stanford, Cal., 1942).

37. Protest to His Majesty Kamehameha III, 11 July 1843 as cited in Carroll Storrs Alden, *Lawrence Kearny, Sailor Diplomat* (Princeton, N.J., 1936), 194–195.

38. Webster to Agents of the Sandwich Islands, 19 December 1842; Message of the President, 30 December 1842, *Foreign Relations*, 1894, II: 44, 39–40.

39. Upshur to Parker, 26 April 1843; Acting Secretary of the Navy Thomas Smith to Parker, 17 May 1843, Secretary of the Navy Letters to Officers, vol. 35. See also, P. C. Kuo, "Caleb Cushing and the Treaty of Wanghia, 1844," *Journal of Modern History*, 5 (1933): 34–54.

40. Upshur to W. Ramsey, 29 August 1842; Upshur to Perry, 30 March 1843, Secretary of the Navy Letters to Officers, vols. 33, 34.

41. Samuel Eliot Morison, *"Old Bruin"; Commodore Matthew C. Perry, 1794–1858* (Boston, 1967), 173–175; Donald R. Wright, "Matthew Perry and the African Squadron," Clayton R. Barrow, Jr., ed., *America Spreads Her Sails; U.S. Seapower in the 19th Century* (Annapolis, Md., 1973), 80–99.

42. Hall, *Upshur*, 176.

43. Upshur to Jones, 10 December 1841, Secretary of the Navy Letters to Officers, vol. 31.

44. Hall, *Upshur*, 177–179.

45. Upshur to S. Bullus, 2 March 1842; Upshur to W. Salter, 21 July 1842, Secretary of the Navy Letters to Officers, vols. 32, 33. See also, Claude H. Hall, "Abel P. Upshur and the Navy as an Instrument of Foreign Policy," *Virginia Magazine of History and Biography*, 69 (1961): 290–299.

46. An account of the affair is George M. Brooke, Jr., "The Vest Pocket War of Commodore Jones," *Pacific Historical Review*, 31 (1962): 217–233; Hall, *Upshur*, 182–187. See also Charles R. Anderson, ed., *Journal of a Cruise to the Pacific Ocean, 1842–1844, in the Frigate United States* (Durham, N.C., 1937); S. R. Franklin, *Memories of a Rear-Admiral; Who Has Served for More Than Half a Century in the Navy of the United States* (New York, 1898), 49–51.

47. The correspondence and documents related to the incident are contained in Letters Received By the Secretary of the Navy From Commanding Officers of Squadrons, 1841–1886 (Pacific Squadron Letters), Naval Records, Record Group 45, National Archives, vol. 32 (Microfilm Series 89). (Cited hereafter as the Pacific Squadron Letters.)

48. Brooke, "Vest Pocket War," 232–233; Hall, *Upshur*, 186–187; Adams, *Memoirs*, XI: 353.
49. Upshur to Jones, 24 January 1843, Pacific Squadron Letters, vol. 34.
50. Upshur to Dallas, 6 March 1843, Secretary of the Navy Letters to Officers, vol. 34.
51. Ibid.; see also Upsher to Dallas, 20 February 1843, ibid.

CHAPTER 5

1. William Appleman Williams, *The Roots of the Modern American Empire; A Study of the Growth and Shaping of Social Consciousness in a Marketplace Society* (New York, 1969), 77–79; James Christy Bell, Jr., *Opening a Highway to the Pacific, 1838–1846* (New York, 1921), 116–126.
2. The commercial content of Manifest Destiny is treated in Charles Vevier, "American Continentalism: An Idea of Expansion, 1845–1910," *American Historical Review*, 65 (1960): 323–335: Norman A. Graebner, *Empire on the Pacific: A Study in American Continental Expansion* (New York, 1955).
3. *Hunt's Merchants' Magazine*, I (1839), 1, 2.
4. For example, see Daniel D. Barnard, "Commerce, as Connected with the Progress of Civilization"; "The Advantages and Benefits of Commerce"; Charles King, "Commerce as a Liberal Pursuit"; John Sargeant, "Mercantile Character"; Philip Hone, "Commerce and Commercial Character," all in ibid., I (1839): 3–20, 200–202; II (1840): 9–24; III (1841): 9–22; IV (1841): 134–135.
5. Herbert Wender, *Southern Commercial Conventions, 1837–1859* (Baltimore, 1930); John McCardell, *The Idea of a Southern Nation; Southern Nationalists and Southern Nationalism, 1830–1860* (New York, 1979), 91–140.
6. *Senate Document No. 306*, 29th Congress, 1st Session (1845–1846); *Illinois Daily Journal*, 3 November 1849, as cited in Robert R. Russel, *Improvement of Communication With the Pacific Coast as an Issue in American Politics, 1783–1864* (Cedar Rapids, Iowa, 1948), 21.
7. *The United States Magazine and Democratic Review*, VI (1839): 287–307; 413–424; VIII (1840): 289–311; XIII (1843): 3–16.
8. Report of the Secretary of the Treasury, 3 December 1845, *Congressional Globe*, 29th Congress, 1st Session (1845–1846), Appendix, 8–13. James P. Shenton, *Robert John Walker; A Politician From Jackson to Lincoln* (New York, 1961), 70–98.
9. Graebner, *Empire on the Pacific*, 103–149; David M. Pletcher, *The Diplomacy of Annexation; Texas, Oregon, and the Mexican War* (Columbia, Mo., 1973), 291–351, 402–417. See also Norman A. Graebner, "Maritime Factors in the Oregon Controversy," *Pacific Historical Review*, 20 (1951): 331–345.
10. Charles Wilkes, *Narrative of the United States Exploring Expedition, during the Years 1838, 1839, 1840, 1841, and 1842*, 5 vols. (Philadelphia, 1845), IV: 313; See also, IV: 316, 317, 325–326, V: 168, 182–183. William Sturgis, *The Oregon Question. Substance of a Lecture Before the Mercantile Library Association, Delivered January 22, 1845* (Boston, 1845), 27. See also, Charles Wilkes, *Statement . . . of the Survey of the Mouth of the Columbia River* (Washington, D.C., 1846).
11. Daniel Webster to Fletcher Webster, 6 August 1846, Fletcher Webster, ed., *The Writings and Speeches of Daniel Webster*, 18 vols. (Boston, 1903), 16: 465. See also Pletcher, *Diplomacy of Annexation*, 555–568; Graebner, *Empire on the Pacific*, 191–216.

12. James D. Richardson, ed., *A Compilation of the Messages and Papers of the Presidents, 1789–1902*, 10 vols. (Washington, D.C., 1903), IV: 413.

13. Bancroft to Conner, 29 March 1845; Bancroft to Sloat, 24 June 1845, Confidential Letters Sent By the Secretary of the Navy to Officers, 1842–1861, Naval Records, Record Group 45, National Archives, vol. 1. (Cited hereafter as Confidential Letters Sent by Secretary of the Navy). See also Bancroft to Sloat, 17 October 1845, ibid.

14. Richardson, *Messages of the Presidents*, IV: 412; Report of the Secretary of the Navy, 1 December 1845, *Congressional Globe*, 29th Congress, 1st Session (1845–1846), Appendix, 17–19.

15. *Senate Document Nos. 187 and 263*, 29th Congress, 1st Session (1845–1846). The reports were published in the *Niles National Register*, 14 March and 11 April 1846.

16. The standard scholarly study is K. Jack Bauer, *Surfboats and Horse Marines: U.S. Naval Operations in the Mexican War, 1846–1848* (Annapolis, Md., 1969).

17. K. Jack Bauer, "Naval Shipbuilding Programs, 1794–1860," *Military Affairs*, 29 (1965): 29–40.

18. Edward M. Steel, Jr., *T. Butler King of Georgia* (Athens, Ga., 1964), 53–54. The standard work on the subject is the detailed scholarly study John G. B. Hutchins, *The American Maritime Industries and Public Policy, 1789–1914; An Economic History* (Cambridge, Mass., 1941). See also, David B. Tyler, *Steam Conquers the Atlantic* (New York, 1939).

19. Hutchins, *American Maritime Industries*, 350–351, 353–354; Tyler, *Steam Conquers the Atlantic*, 142. See also, L. J. Gulliver, "The Navy and the First U.S. Ocean Mail Ships," *United States Naval Institute Proceedings*, 65 (1939): 1264–1269.

20. *Congressional Globe*, 29th Congress, 2nd Session (1846–1847), 423–424.

21. *House of Representatives Report No. 685*, 29th Congress, 1st Session (1845–1846). A draft of the report in King's hand is in Folder 113, T.B. King Papers, Southern Historical Collection, University of North Carolina.

22. Richardson, *Messages of the Presidents*, IV: 630,633,635,637-638.

23. Report of the Secretary of the Treasury, 8 December 1847, *Congressional Globe*, 30th Congress, 1st Session (1847–1848), Appendix, 9–16; Report of the Secretary of the Treasury, 9 December 1847, *Congresional Globe*, 30th Congress, 2nd Session (1848–1849), Appendix, 11–20.

24. *Philadelphia Pennsylvanian*, 11 December 1847; *Delaware Gazette*, 23 December 1847, in the Robert J. Walker Papers, Manuscript Division, Library of Congress. The extent and intensity of the public response to Walker's reports can be gauged through the press clippings contained in his papers.

25. *Washington Union*, 7 November 1849, 4 October 1851, as cited in Robert W. Johannsen, "Stephen A. Douglas and the American Mission," in *The Frontier Challenge; Responses to the Trans-Mississippi West*, John G. Clark, ed. (Lawrence, Kan., 1971), 127, 114. See also *Congressional Globe*, 31st Congress, 1st Session (1849–1850), Appendix, 365.

26. "The Commercial Age," *DeBow's Review*, VII (1849): 236.

27. Abbott Lawrence to John M. Clayton, 5 April 1850 as cited in Paul A. Varg, *United States Foreign Relations, 1820–1860* (East Lansing, Mich., 1979), 196; *Congressional Globe*, 31st Congress, 1st Session (1849–1850), Appendix, 262.

28. George Rogers Taylor, *The Transportation Revolution, 1815–1860* (Torchbook edition, New York, 1968; original edition, 1951), Appendix A, 444-445, 441.

29. *Congressional Globe*, 30th Congress, 1st Session (1847–1848), 429 as cited in

Reginald Horsman, *Race and Manifest Destiny: The Origins of American Racial Anglo-Saxonism* (Cambridge, Mass., 1981), 242–243. For similar sentiments, see the remarks of Daniel Webster, John Clayton, Jacob Collamer, Samuel Houston, John Dix, and Daniel Dickinson as cited in ibid., 242–244.

30. *New York Tribune*, 27 November 1846. See also *National Intelligencer* 8, 12 June, 18 December 1847, 29 January 1848, 1 January, 9 June 1849.

31. *House of Representatives Report No. 596*, 30th Congress, 1st Session (1847–1848), 10, 16, 17, 18.

32. Clayton to William Rives, 5 July 1850, *Papers Relating to the Foreign Relations of the United States, 1894: Affairs in Hawaii* (Washington, D.C., 1894), Appendix II: 87–88.

33. Louis N. Feipel, "The Navy and Filibustering in the Fifties," *United States Naval Institute Proceedings*, 44 (1918): 767–780, 1009–1029. See also, *National Intelligencer*, 14 August 1849, 13, 14 June 1850.

34. Lester D. Langley, *The Struggle for the American Mediterranean; United States-European Rivalry in the Gulf-Caribbean, 1776–1904* (Athens, Ga., 1976), 98–100.

35. Harold D. Langley, "William Ballard Preston," in Paolo Coletta, ed., *American Secretaries of the Navy*, 2 vols. (Annapolis, Md., 1980), I: 243–255; *Historical Statistics of the United States; Colonial Times to 1970*, 2 Parts (Washington, D.C., 1975), II: 1114. The actual appropriation dropped from $9,787,000 in 1849 to $7,905,000 in 1850.

36. *National Intelligencer*, 17, 26, 29 April, 1 May 1851.

37. Webster to L. Severance, 14 July 1851; Webster to Rives, 19 June 1851, *Foreign Relations, 1894*, II, 99–102, 97–98. See also, Sylvester K. Stevens, *American Expansion in Hawaii, 1842–1898* (Harrisburg, Pa., 1945), 49–54.

38. For example, Richardson, *Messages of the Presidents*, V:88, 132, 176.

39. Harold D. Langley, "William Alexander Graham" and "John Pendleton Kennedy," *Secretaries of the Navy*, I: 257–267, 269–277. See also Max R. Williams, "Secretary William A. Graham, Naval Administrator, 1850–1852," *North Carolina Historical Review*, 48 (1971): 53–72.

40. Maury to Graham, 7 October 1850, J. G. de Roulhac Hamilton, ed., *The Papers of William Alexander Graham*, 4 vols. (Raleigh, N.C., 1960), III: 408–432.

41. Report of the Secretary of the Navy, 30 November 1850, *Congressional Globe*, 31st Congress, 2nd Session (1850–1851), Appendix, 10–15; Report of the Secretary of the Navy, 29 November 1851, *Congressional Globe*, 32nd Congress, 1st Session (1851–1852), Appendix, 18–22.

42. Report of the Secretary of the Navy, 4 December 1852, *Congressional Globe*, 32nd Congress, 2nd Session (1852–1853), Appendix, 7–17.

43. *Senate Document No. 50*, 32nd Congress, 1st Session (1851–1852); *Congressional Globe*, 31st Congress, 1st Session (1849–1850), Appendix, 14; *Congressional Globe*, 31st Congress, 2nd Session (1850–1851), Appendix, 14. See also Maury to Graham, 7 October 1850, *Papers of Graham*, III: 431–432.

CHAPTER 6

1. Vincent Ponko, Jr., *Ships, Seas, and Scientists; U.S. Naval Exploration and Discovery in the Nineteenth Century* (Annapolis, Md., 1974); Geoffrey S. Smith, "The Navy Before Darwinism: Science, Exploration, and Diplomacy in Antebellum America," *American Quarterly*, 28 (1976): 41–55; A. Hunter Dupree, *Science in the Federal Gov-*

ernment: A History of Policies and Activities to 1940 (Cambridge, Mass., 1957); John D. Kazar, "The United States Navy and Scientific Exploration, 1837–1860" (Unpublished Ph.D. Dissertation, University of Massachusetts, 1973.)

2. Ponko, *Ships, Seas, and Scientists*, 33–60, 93–107; Wayne D. Rasmussen, "The United States Astronomical Expedition to Chile, 1849–1852," *Hispanic American Historical Review*, 34 (1954): 102–113. See also, William Lynch, *Commerce and the Holy Land; A Lecture* (Philadelphia, 1860).

3. Kennedy to T. J. Page, 29 January 1853, Kennedy to C. Ringgold, 28 February 1853, Confidential Letters Sent by the Secretary of the Navy, vol. II.

4. Report of the Secretary of the Navy, 29 November 1851, *Congressional Globe*, 32nd Congress, 1st Session (1851–1852), Appendix, 21; Frances Leigh Williams, *Matthew Fontaine Maury; Scientist of the Sea* (New Brunswick, N.J., 1963), 180, 190.

5. Edward L. Towle, "Science, Commerce and the Navy on the Seagoing Frontier (1842–1861)—The Role of Lieutenant M. F. Maury and the U.S. Naval Hydrographic Office in Naval Exploration, Commercial Expansion and Oceanography Before the Civil War" (unpublished Ph.D. dissertation, University of Rochester, 1966).

6. Lt. M. F. Maury, "Great Commercial Advantages of the Gulf of Mexico," *DeBow's Review*, VII (1849): 510–523; Maury, "Direct Foreign Trade of the South," ibid., XII (1852): 126–148.

7. John P. Harrison, "Science and Politics: Origins and Objectives of Mid-Nineteenth Century Government Expeditions to Latin America," *Hispanic American Historical Review*, 35 (1955): 175–202.

8. Harold Peterson, "Edward A. Hopkins, A Pioneer Promoter in Paraguay," *Hispanic American Historical Review*, 22 (1942): 245–261.

9. Ernesto Ruiz, "Geography and Diplomacy: The American Geographic Society and the 'Geopolitical' Background of American Foreign Policy, 1848–1861" (unpublished Ph.D. dissertation, Northern Illinois University, 1975), 9–33.

10. M. F. Maury, "On Extending the Commerce of the South and West By Sea," *DeBow's Review*, XII (1852): 381–399; Maury, "Direct Foreign Trade of the South," ibid., XII (1852): 126–148.

11. Donald Dozer, "M. F. Maury's Letter of Instruction to W. L. Herndon," *Hispanic American Historical Review*, 28 (1948): 219.

12. Graham to Herndon, 15 February 1851, Confidential Letters Sent by the Secretary of the Navy, vol. II. A copy of the instructions is included in Lt. William Herndon, *Exploration of the Valley of the Amazon*, Part I, *The New American State Papers, 1789–1860; Explorations and Surveys*, Thomas C. Cochran, gen. ed., 15 vols. (Wilmington, Del., 1972), 10: 36–38.

13. Dozer, "Letter of Instruction to Herndon," 217, 218.

14. Ibid., 220.

15. Ibid., 225, 228, 221, 223.

16. Herndon, *Exploration of the Valley of the Amazon*, 106.

17. Ibid., 200–202.

18. Lt. Lardner Gibbon, *Exploration of the Valley of the Amazon*, Part II, *New American State Papers, Explorations and Surveys*, vol. 10.

19. *House of Representatives Executive Document No. 43*, 32nd Congress, 2nd Session (1852–1853); *House of Representatives Executive Document No. 53*, 33rd Congress, 1st Session (1853–1854).

20. Herndon, *Exploration of the Valley of the Amazon*, 202–205.

21. Gibbon, *Exploration of the Valley of the Amazon*, 729, 730.

22. Inca [M. F. Maury], "The Amazon and the Atlantic Slopes of South America," *National Intelligencer*, 17 November–3 December 1852; Maury, "Valley of the Amazon," *DeBow's Review*, XIV (1853): 449–460, 556–567; XV (1854): 36–43; Maury, "Shall the Valleys of the Amazon and the Mississippi Reciprocate Trade," ibid., XIV (1853): 136–145; Maury, "Memorial on the Navigation of the Amazon River," February, 1854, *House of Representatives Miscellaneous Document No. 22*, 33rd Congress, 1st Session (1853–1854).

23. Percy Alvin Martin, "The Influence of the United States on the Opening of the Amazon to the World's Commerce," *Hispanic American Historical Review*, 1 (1918): 146–162; Lawrence F. Hill, *Diplomatic Relations Between the United States and Brazil* (Durham, N.C., 1932), 214–238.

24. Harrison, "Science and Politics," 192–194.

25. Peterson, "Hopkins," 245–253.

26. Edward A. Hopkins, "Free Navigation of the River Parana and Its Tributaries," *Hunt's Merchants' Magazine*, XXVI (1852): 147–155; Hopkins, "Navigation of the Confluents of the Rio de la Plata," ibid., XXI (1849): 80–87; Hopkins, "The LaPlata and the Parana—Paraguay," *DeBow's Review*, XIV (1853): 238–251; *National Intelligencer*, 21, 28 April, 12 May 1849; Hopkins, "The Republic of Paraguay; Since the Death of the Dictator Francia," *America Whig Review*, VI (1847): 245–260; Hopkins, "The Natural History of Paraguay; With Some Account of the Jesuits," ibid., VII (1849): 49–69.

27. Hopkins, "Memoir on the Geography, History, Production, and Trade of Paraguay," *Bulletin of the American Geographical and Statistical Society*, I (1852): 14–42.

28. Report of the Secretary of the Navy, 4 December 1852, *Congressional Globe*, 32nd Congress, 2nd Session (1852–1853), Appendix, 10.

29. Kennedy to Page, 29 January 1853, Confidential Letters Sent by the Secretary of the Navy to Officers, vol. II. Clare V. McKanna, "The *Water Witch* Incident," *American Neptune*, 31 (1971): 7–18.

30. Maury to Page, 4 February 1853 as cited in Harrison, "Science and Politics," 197.

31. Ponko, *Ships, Seas, and Scientists*, 108–133.

32. Harold F. Peterson, *Argentina and the United States, 1810–1960* (New York, 1964), 167–169.

33. McKanna, "The *Water Witch* Incident"; O. P. Fitzgerald, "Profit and Adventure in Paraguay," in Clayton R. Barrow, Jr., ed., *America Spreads Her Sails; U.S. Seapower in the 19th Century* (Annapolis, Md., 1973), 70–79.

34. T. J. Page, *Synoptical Report . . . on the Late "Exploration and Survey of the River LaPlata and Its Tributaries," New American State Papers*; *Explorations and Surveys*, 12: 384, 388. See also T. J. Page, *LaPlata, the Argentine Confederation, and Paraguay* (New York, 1859).

CHAPTER 7

1. Merle Curti, "Young America," *American Historical Review*, 32 (1926): 34–55; David B. Danbom, "The Young America Movement," *Journal of the Illinois State Historical Society*, 67 (1974): 294–306.

2. "Democratic Platform of 1852," Donald B. Johnson, ed., *National Party Platforms*, 2 vols. (revised edition, Urbana, Ill., 1978; original edition, 1956), 18.

3. James D. Richardson, ed.,*A Compilation of the Messages and Papers of the Presidents, 1789–1902*, 10 vols. (Washington, D.C., 1903), V: 198–199, 200.

4. Roy F. Nichols, *Franklin Pierce; Young Hickory of the Granite Hills* (Second edition, revised. Philadelphia, 1958), 268–269; William Marcy to David Gregg, 4 April 1854, *Papers Relating to the Foreign Relations of the United States, 1894: Affairs in Hawaii* (Washington, D.C., 1894), Appendix II, 121–122.

5. David M. Potter, *The Impending Crisis, 1848–1861* (New York, 1976), 185; Basil Rauch, *American Interest in Cuba, 1848–1855* (New York, 1948), 262–302; Robert E. May, *The Southern Dream of a Caribbean Empire, 1854–1861* (Baton Rouge, La., 1973), 47–67.

6. Andor Klay, *Daring Diplomacy; The Case of the First American Ultimatum* (Minneapolis, 1957).

7. Lyon to Ingraham, 2 July 1853 as cited in ibid., 94.

8. *Congressional Globe*, 33rd Congress, 1st Session (1853–1854), 2323.

9. Richardson, *Messages of the Presidents*, V: 210.

10. Harold D. Langley, "James Cochrane Dobbin," Paolo Coletta, ed., *American Secretaries of the Navy*, 2 vols. (Annapolis, Md., 1980), I: 279–300.

11. Annual Report of the Secretary of the Navy, 5 December 1853, *Congressional Globe*, 33rd Congress, 1st Session (1853–1854), Appendix, 13–18.

12. Ibid., Appendix, 424, 425. The debate is contained in ibid., 803–809.

13. Ibid., 803. For Benton's position during the French crisis, see Thomas Hart Benton, *Thirty Years' View; Or, A History of the Working of the American Government for Thirty Years*, 2 vols. (New York, 1854), I: 588–600.

14. *Congressional Globe*, 33rd Congress, 1st Session (1853–1854), 807; ibid., Appendix, 509, 510.

15. Ibid., 804.

16. Marcy to Soulé, 3 April 1854 in William R. Manning, ed., *Diplomatic Correspondence of the United States: Inter-American Affairs, 1831-1860*, 12 vols. (Washington, D.C., 1939), 11: 175-178. See also Amos A. Ettinger, *The Mission to Spain of Piérre Soulé; 1853-1854; A Study in the Cuban Diplomacy of the United States* (New Haven, Conn., 1932), 246-247.

17. Marcy to Mason, 23 July 1854 as cited in Nichols, *Pierce*, 343.

18. A copy of the Ostend Manifesto is contained in *House of Representatives Executive Document No. 93*, 33rd Congress, 2nd Session (1854–1855).

19. Potter, *Impending Crisis*, 192.

20. Louis N. Feipel, "The Navy and Filibustering in the Fifties," *United States Naval Institute Proceedings*, 44 (1918): 1219–1240; Ivor D. Spencer, *The Victory and the Spoils; A Life of William L. Marcy* (Providence, R.I., 1959), 309–317. Official documents and correspondence related to the incident are in *Senate Executive Document No. 126*, 33rd Congress, 1st Session (1853–1854).

21. Dobbin to Hollins, 10 June 1854, Confidential Lettters Sent by the Secretary of the Navy, vol. III.

22. Letter of Joseph W. Fabens, 11 July 1854; Proclamation of George W. Hollins, 12 July 1854 in Feipel, "Navy and Filibustering in the Fifties," 1234–1235.

23. May, *Southern Dream of Empire*, 83. See also Charles H. Brown, *Agents of*

Manifest Destiny; The Lives and Times of the Filibusters (Chapel Hill, N.C., 1980), 174–408; Feipel, "Navy and Filibustering in the Fifties," 1527–1545.

24. Gerstle Mack, *The Land Divided: A History of the Panama Canal and Other Isthmian Canal Projects* (New York, 1944), 161–165.

25. Charles C. Tansill, *The United States and Santo Domingo, 1798–1873* (Baltimore, 1938), 176-204. Dobbin to J. T. Newton, 19 June 1854, Confidential Letters Sent by the Secretary of the Navy, vol. III.

26. Dobbin to G. Hollins, 12 December 1853, ibid., vol. III; the expedition is described in Vincent Ponko, Jr., *Ships, Seas, and Scientists; U. S. Naval Exploration and Discovery in the Nineteenth Century* (Annapolis, 1974), 160–177.

27. "Democratic Platform of 1856," *National Party Platforms*, I: 26.

28. Richardson, *Messages of the Presidents*, V: 447.

29. Feipel, "Navy and Filibustering in the Fifties," 1837–1848, 2063–2085.

30. Richardson, *Messages of the Presidents*, V: 466.

31. Report of the Secretary of the Navy, 3 December 1857, *Congressional Globe*, 35th Congress, 1st Session (1857–1858), Appendix, 28–32.

32. Harold D. Langley, "Isaac Toucey," *Secretaries of the Navy*, I: 303–318.

33. Report of the Secretary of the Navy, 6 December 1858, *Congressional Globe*, 35th Congress, 2nd Session (1858–1859), Appendix, 17–21.

34. Ibid., 21.

35. Francis X. Holbrook, "Come, Papillangi, Our Fires Are Lighted," in Clayton R. Barrow, Jr., ed., *America Spreads Her Sails; U.S. Seapower in the 19th Century* (Annapolis, Md., 1973), 112–125; E. Mowbray Tate, "Navy Justice in the Pacific; 1830–1870: A Pattern of Precedents," *American Neptune*, 35 (1975): 25–28.

36. *Congressional Globe*, 35th Congress, 1st Session (1857–1858), 1963, 2546–2547.

37. The most detailed study of the relations between the two countries in this period is Thomas O. Flickema, "The United States and Paraguay, 1845–1860: Misunderstanding, Miscalculation, and Misconduct" (unpublished Ph.D. dissertation, Wayne State University, 1966). For accounts of this affair, see Thomas O. Flickema, "The Settlement of the Paraguayan–American Controversy of 1859: A Reappraisal," *The Americas*, 25 (1968): 49–69; Thomas O. Flickema, " 'Sam Ward's Bargain': A Tentative Reconsideration," *Hispanic American Historical Review*, 50 (1970): 538–542; Pablo M. Ynsfran, "Sam Ward's Bargain with President Lopez of Paraguay," ibid., 34 (1954): 313–331.

38. Flickema, "Settlement of the Paraguayan-American Controversy of 1859," 58–69.

39. Richardson, *Messages of the Presidents*, V: 514–517.

40. For Senate and House debates, see *Congressional Globe*, 36th Congress, 1st Session (1859–1860), 3110–3120; 3172–3177. A detailed account of the affair is Paul J. Scheip, "Buchanan and the Chiriqui Naval Station Sites," *Military Affairs*, 18 (1954): 64–80.

CHAPTER 8

1. Shunzo Sakamaki, "Japan and the United States, 1790–1853," *The Transactions of the Asiatic Society of Japan*, 18 (1939); Helen Humeston, "Origins of America's Japan Policy, 1790–1854" (unpublished Ph.D. dissertation, University of Minnesota, 1981).

2. Porter to J. Madison, 31 October 1815, Allan B. Cole, "Captain David Porter's Proposed Expedition to the Pacific and Japan, 1815," *Pacific Historical Review*, 9 (1940):

61–65; David F. Long, *Nothing Too Daring; A Biography of Commodore David Porter, 1780–1843* (Annapolis, Md., 1970), 173–174.

3. William A. Borst, "The American Merchant and the Genesis of Japanese-American Relations, 1790–1854" (unpublished Ph.D. dissertation, St. Louis University, 1972), 61–101; Charles W. King, *The Claims of Japan and Malaysia Upon Christendom . . .*, 2 vols. (New York, 1839).

4. David F. Long, *Sailor-Diplomat; A Biography of Commodore James Biddle* (Boston, 1983), 209–220; Merrill L. Bartlett, "Commodore James Biddle and the First Naval Mission to Japan, 1845–1846," *American Neptune*, 61 (1981), 25–35. An excellent analysis of the impact of Biddle's action of subsequent American diplomacy with Japan is contained in Long, *Biddle*, 214–219.

5. *Senate Executive Document No. 59*, 32nd Congress, 1st Session (1851–1852), 57–62, 74–78.

6. *House of Representatives Document No. 138*, 28th Congress, 2nd Session (1844–1845); *Senate Executive Document No. 96*, 29th Congress, 2nd Session (1846–1847).

7. *House of Representatives Executive Document No. 84*, 31st Congress, 1st Session (1849–1850); Walter S. Tower, *A History of the American Whale Fishery* (Philadelphia, 1907), 51–53, 59, 129. See also, Elmo P. Hohman, *The American Whaleman; A Study of Life and Labor in the Whaling Industry* (New York, 1928); Alexander Starbuck, *History of the American Whale Fishery From Its Earliest Inception to the Year 1876*, 2 vols. (Waltham, Mass., 1878).

8. Remarks of John M. Clayton, 18 January 1855, Aaron Haight Palmer, *Documents and Facts Illustrating the Origin of the Mission to Japan. . . .* (Washington, D.C., 1857), 5; *House of Representatives Executive Document No. 96*, 29th Congress, 2nd Session.

9. Aaron H. Palmer, *Memoir Geographical, Political, and Commercial, on the present state, productive resources, and capabilities for commerce of Siberia, Manchuria, and the Asiatic Islands of the Northern Pacific Ocean*, Senate Executive Document No. 80, 30th Congress, 1st Session (1847–1848).

10. Palmer to Clayton, 17 September 1849, *Documents and Facts*, 10–18.

11. William L. Neuman, "Religion, Morality, and Freedom: the Ideological Background of the Perry Expedition," *Pacific Historical Review*, 23 (1954): 247–257; Palmer to Fillmore, 6 January 1851, *Documents and Facts*, 18–20.

12. Flynn to Fillmore, 10 June 1851, *Senate Executive Document No. 59*, 32nd Congress, 1st Session 74–78; Graham to Aulick, 9, 31 May 1851, Confidential Letters Sent by the Secretary of the Navy to Officers, vol. II.

13. Webster to Aulick, 10 June 1851, *Senate Executive Document No. 59*, 80–81.

14. Charles O. Paullin, *American Voyages to the Orient, 1690–1865* (Annapolis, Md., 1971), 123–124.

15. Perry to Graham, 3 December 1851, as cited in William E. Griffis, *Matthew Calbraith Perry; A Typical American Naval Officer* (Boston, 1887), 289–291. The preparations and conduct of the expedition are described in detail in Samuel Eliot Morison, *"Old Bruin"; Commodore Matthew C. Perry, 1794–1858* (Boston, 1967), 270–410; Arthur Walworth, *Black Ships Off Japan; The Story of Commodore Perry's Expedition* (Reprint, Hamden, Conn., 1966; original edition, 1943). In addition to his naval personnel, Perry selected various scientists, artists, a bandmaster, and a chef to accompany the expedition.

16. Kennedy to Perry, 13 November, 1852, Conrad to Kennedy, 5 November 1852, Fillmore to His Imperial Majesty, The Emperor, *Senate Executive Document No. 34*,

33rd Congress, 2nd Session (1854–1855), 2–11. These letters are also printed in Walworth, *Black Ships Off Japan*, Appendices B, C, D: 240–251.

17. Conrad to Kennedy, 5 November 1852, Senate Executive Document No. 34, 4–9.

18. Kennedy to Perry, 12 November 1852, ibid., 2–4.

19. Fillmore to His Imperial Majesty, The Emperor, ibid., 9–11.

20. The specifications and individual commanders of the ships which participated are listed in Morison, *"Old Bruin,"* 356.

21. Perry to Kennedy, 14 December 1852, *Senate Executive Document No. 34*, 12–14. Perry's own account of the expedition is F. L. Hawks, ed., *Narrative of the Expedition of An American Squadron to the China Seas and Japan*, 3 vols. (Washington, D.C., 1856).

22. First-hand accounts of various aspects of the expedition include Allan B. Cole, ed., *With Perry in Japan: The Diary of Edward Yorke McCauley* (Princeton, N.J., 1942); Allan B. Cole, ed., *A Scientist with Perry in Japan: The Journal of Dr. James Morrow* (Chapel Hill, N.C., 1947); Henry F. Graff, ed., *Bluejackets with Perry in Japan. A Day-by-Day Account Kept By Master's Mate John R. C. Lewis and Cabin Boy William B. Allen* (New York, 1952); Roger Pineau, ed., *The Japan Expedition,1853–1854. The Personal Journal of Commodore Matthew C. Perry* (Washington, D.C., 1968); George Henry Preble, *The Opening of Japan: A Diary of Discovery in the Far East, 1852–1856*, Boleslaw Szczesniak, ed., (Norman, Okla., 1962); J. W. Spaulding, *The Japan Expedition: Japan and Around the World* (New York, 1855); Bayard Taylor, *A Visit to India, China, and Japan in the Year 1853* (New York, 1855); S. Wells Williams, "A Journal of the Perry Expedition to Japan (1853–1854)," *Transactions of the Asiatic Society of Japan*, 37 (1910): 1–259.

23. Earl Swisher, "Commodore Perry's Imperialism in Relation to America's Present Day Position in the Pacific," *Pacific Historical Review*, 16 (1947): 30–40; "Extracts from the Rough Journal of Commodore Perry, 24 June 1853" *Senate Executive Document No. 34*, 33–39; "Report of an Examination of the Bonin Group of Islands," Hawks, ed., *Narrative of the Expedition*, II: 127–133.

24. Perry to Dobbin, 14 December 1852, *Senate Executive Document No. 34*, 12–14; Perry to Dobbin, 25 June, 3 August, ibid., 29–35, 43–45.

25. "Notes Referring to . . . the preliminary negotiations of Commodore M. C. Perry with the authorities of Japan, in July, 1853," ibid., 45–57.

26. Morison, *"Old Bruin,"* 336; Walworth, *Black Ships Off Japan*, 115; Paullin, *American Voyages to the Orient*, 135.

27. The correspondence between Marshall and Perry as well as Perry's explanations to the Secretary of the Navy are contained in *Senate Executive Document No. 34*, 87–102. For a full account, see Curtis T. Henson, Jr., *Commissioners and Commodores; The East India Squadron and American Diplomacy in China* (University, Ala., 1982), 94–100.

28. Dobbin to Perry, 28 October, 14 November 1853, Confidential Letters Sent by the Secretary of the Navy, vol. III.

29. Perry to Dobbin, 25 January 1854; Dobbin to Perry, 30 May 1854, *Senate Executive Document No. 34*, 108–110, 112–113.

30. Hawks, ed., *Narrative of the Expedition*, I: 350–352. An interesting sidelight

occurred when Americans had to negotiate a burial site on Japanese soil for an American who died on the expedition, ibid., I: 353–354; Morison, *"Old Bruin,"* 369–370.

31. Hawks, ed., *Narrative of the Expedition*, I: 343–392; Perry to Dobbin, 1 April 1854, *Senate Executive Document No. 34*, 145–150.

32. A copy of the treaty is contained in ibid., 174–175.

33. "Extracts from the Rough Journal of Commodore Perry, 24 June 1853," ibid., 39; Hawks, ed., *Narrative of the Expedition*, II: 153–154, 167–170, 173, 180. Volume II of the *Narrative* contains an assortment of reports and articles on aspects of the expedition including "Remarks of Commodore Perry Upon the Expediency of Extending Further Encouragement to American Commerce in the East," 173–183; "Remarks of Commodore Perry Upon the Probable Future Commercial Relations with Japan and Lew Chew," 185–187.

34. Ibid., 175.

35. Ibid., 177, 176, 178, 180.

36. *A Paper By Commodore M. C. Perry, U.S.N., Read Before the American Geographical and Statistical Society . . . March 6, 1856* (New York, 1856).

37. *Congressional Globe*, 32nd Congress, 1st Session (1851–1852), Part 3: xxi.

38. Ibid., 1975.

39. *Senate Document No. 55*, 32nd Congress, 1st Session (1851–1852).

40. Report of the Secretary of the Navy, 4 December 1852, *Congressional Globe*, 32nd Congress, 2nd Session (1852–1853), Appendix 10.

41. Kennedy to Ringgold, 28 February 1853(2 letters), Confidential Letters Sent by the Secretary of the Navy, vol. III.

42. Glynn to T. ap C. Jones, 21 February 1850, Pacific Squadron Letters, vol. 34.

43. Rodgers to Dobbin, August, 1854, Records relating to the United States Exploring Expedition to the North Pacific, 1854–1856. 2 rolls (nos. 4 and 5) Record Group 45 (Microfilm Series 88), roll 4. A collection of these documents is printed in Allan B. Cole, ed., *Yankee Surveyors in the Shogun's Seas; Records of the United States Surveying Expedition to the North Pacific Ocean, 1853–1856* (Princeton, N.J., 1947), 24. Detailed accounts of the expedition are Allan B. Cole, "The Ringgold-Rodgers-Brooke Expedition to Japan and the North Pacific, 1853–1859," *Pacific Historical Review*, 16 (1947): 152–162; Vincent Ponko, Jr., *Ships, Seas, and Scientists; U. S. Naval Exploration and Discovery in the Nineteenth Century* (Annapolis, Md., 1974), 206–230; Robert Erwin Johnson, *Rear Admiral John Rodgers, 1812–1882* (Annapolis, Md., 1967), 101–138.

44. Rodgers to Dobbin, 15 February 1855, North Pacific Records, roll 4.

45. Rodgers to Secretary of State of the Empire of Japan, 7 February 1855, ibid.

46. George M. Brooke, Jr., *John M. Brooke; Naval Scientist and Educator* (Charlottesville, Va., 1980), 115–119. For his first-hand account see J.M. Brooke, "Coasting in Japan," *U.S. Nautical Magazine and Naval Journal* 5 (1856-1857): 196-204, 278-287, 338-347, 411-422; 6 (1857-1858): 25-39.

47. Rodgers to Secretary of State of the Empire of Japan, 7 February 1855; Rodgers to the Governor of Simoda, 20 May 1855, North Pacific Records, roll 4.

48. Rodgers to Dobbin, 11, 19 June 1855, ibid.

49. Rodgers to Dobbin, 29 January 1856, ibid., roll 5.

50. Toucey to Brooke, 24 May 1858, Confidential Letters Sent by the Secretary of the Navy, vol. IV.

51. Brooke, *John M. Brooke*, 159–223.

CHAPTER 9

1. Two detailed scholarly studies on the subject are Curtis T. Henson, Jr., *Commissioners and Commodores; The East India Squadron and American Diplomacy in China* (University, Ala., 1982); and Te-kong Tong, *United States Diplomacy in China, 1844–1860* (Seattle, 1964). See also, Eldon Griffin, *Clippers and Consuls; American Consular and Commercial Relations With Eastern Asia, 1845–1860* (Ann Arbor, Mich., 1938).

2. James D. Richardson, ed.,*A Compilation of the Messages and Papers of the Presidents, 1789–1902*, 10 vols. (Washington, D.C., 1903), IV: 358.

3. John K. Fairbank, "The Early Treaty System in the Chinese World Order," *The Chinese World Order; Traditional China's Foreign Relations*, John K. Fairbank, ed. (Cambridge, Mass., 1968), 257–275. The concept of extraterritoriality also fits within the Chinese conception of how the "barbarians" should be managed. See Tong, *United States Diplomacy in China*, 47.

4. Ibid., 108–113.

5. John K. Fairbank, *Trade and Diplomacy on the China Coast; The Opening of the Treaty Ports, 1842–1854* (revised edition, Stanford, Cal., 1969); Tong, *United States Diplomacy in China* 113–115.

6. Edward V. Gulick, *Peter Parker and the Opening of China* (Cambridge, Mass., 1973), 181–195.

7. H. Marshall to State Department, 26 May 1853, Jules David, ed., *American Diplomatic and Public Papers: The United States and China*. Series I: *The Treaty System and the Taiping Rebellion, 1842–1860*, 21 vols. (Wilmington Del., 1973), 4:160. See also Tong, *United States Diplomacy in China*, 32–33.

8. Parker to Marcy, 12, 27 December 1856, *Public Papers: United States and China*, 13: 71–73, 366–367.

9. Tong, *United States Diplomacy in China*, 196–197.

10. Marcy to Parker, 27 February 1857, *Public Papers: United States and China*, 13: 156.

11. Cass to Reed, 22 April 1857, ibid., 14: 161–163.

12. Marshall to Marcy, 30 May 1853, ibid., 4: 38–44; Abbot to Marcy, 30 July 1855, Joel Abbot Papers, Nimitz Library, United States Naval Academy. (Microfilm Reel 25.)

13. Dobbin to J. Armstrong, 27 February 1857, Confidential Letters Sent by the Secretary of the Navy, vol. III. See also Marcy to Parker, 27 September 1853, 2 February 1857, *Public Papers: United States in China*, 6: 18–24; 13: 347–348.

14. Dobbin to Aulick, 10 September 1853, Secretary of the Navy Letters to Officers, vol. 51. The Marshall-Aulick controversy is discussed in Henson, *Commissioners and Commodores*, 85–89.

15. Chester A. Bain, "Commodore Matthew Perry, Humphrey Marshall, and the Taiping Rebellion," *Far Eastern Quarterly*, 10 (1951): 258–270; Henson, *Commissioners and Commodores*, 92–103.

16. Marshall to Secretary of State, 20 May 1853, *Public Papers: The United States and China*, 4: 271–277; Perry's explanation is provided in Perry to Secretary of the Navy, 6, 16 May 1853 and Perry to Marshall, 12, 16 May 1853, *Senate Executive Document No. 34*, 33rd Congress, 2nd Session (1854–1855), 19–20, 21–22, 23, 27.

17. Marshall to Perry, 22 September 1853; Perry to Marshall, 29 September 1853; American Merchants to Perry, 5 November 1853; Perry to American Merchants, 9 November 1853, ibid., 71–74, 78–79.

18. Perry to Dobbin, 9 October, ibid., 70–71.

19. Perry to Dobbin, 31 August 1853, ibid., 59–60. Marshall's assessment of the secondary importance of the expedition to Japan is contained in Marshall to Perry, 13 May 1853, ibid., 23–26.

20. Marshall to Marcy, 30 October 1853, *Public Papers: United States and China*, 4: 235.

21. Marcy to Parker, 5 October 1855, ibid., 6: 26–38.

22. Graham to Aulick, 31 May 1851, Confidential Letters Sent by the Secretary of the Navy, vol. III; See also, Toucey to C. Stribling, 10 June 1859, ibid., vol. IV.

23. Parker to Marcy, 27 December 1856, *Public Papers: United States in China*, 13: 366–367.

24. George Rogers Taylor, *The Transportation Revolution, 1815–1860* (Torchbook edition, New York, 1968; original edition, 1951), Appendix A, 450, 452.

25. Parker to Marcy, 12, 27 December 1856, *Public Papers: United States and China* 13: 71–73, 366–367.

26. Cass to Reed, 30 May 1857, ibid., 14: 180–184.

27. For example, see Tyler Dennett, *Americans in Eastern Asia; A Critical Study of United States' Policy in the Far East in the Nineteenth Century* (New York, 1922), 305. Dennett likened the Reed mission to that of a man dispatched "to stand under the tree, with his basket, waiting for his associates to shake down the fruit, and . . . to offer mediation in case those in the tree became involved with the owners of the orchard."

28. Tattnall to Nicholson, 7 April 1858, East India Squadron Letters, vol. 12; Reed to DuPont, 19 May 1858, *Public Papers: United States and China*, 15: 16.

29. James D. Johnston, *China and Japan: being a Narrative of the Cruise of the U.S. Steam-Frigate Powhatan in the Years 1857, '58 '59, and '60* (Philadelphia, 1861), 86–87, 71–72.

30. Henson, *Commissioners and Commodores*, 121–122; Fairbank, *Trade and Diplomacy*, 335–346.

31. Sturgis to Abbot, 2 January 1855; Abbot to Sturgis, 2 January 1855, East India Squadron Letters, vol. 9.

32. Parker to Chin Heen Leang, 4 January 1855; Abbot to Parker, 6 January 1855; Parker to Abbot, 6 January 1855, *Public Papers: United States and China*, 7: 89–91. Abbot to My Dear Son John, 8 January 1855, Joel Abbot Papers, Nimitz Library, United States Naval Academy. (Microfilm Reel 25.)

33. Abbot to Dobbin, 9 January 1855, East India Squadron Letters, vol. 9.

34. George E. Paulsen, "Under the Starry Banner on Muddy Flat, Shanghai: 1854," *American Neptune*, 30 (1970): 155–166; W. S. Wetmore, *Recollections of Life in the Far East* (Shanghai, 1894), 1–11.

35. A detailed scholarly account of the incident is David F. Long, "A Case for Intervention: Armstrong, Foote, and the Destruction of the Barrier Forts, Canton, China, 1856," Craig L. Symonds, ed., *New Aspects of Naval History* (Annapolis, Md., 1981), 220–237. See also, Henson, *Commissioners and Commodores*, 128–136; William Maxwell Wood, *Fankwei; or, the San Jacinto in the Seas of India, China, and Japan* (New York, 1859), 415–469.

36. Long, "A Case for Intervention," 224–225.

37. Armstrong to Dobbin, 10, 12 November 1856, East India Squadron Letters, vol. 10; Parker to Armstrong, 11 November 1856, *Public Papers: United States and China*, 13: 41–42.

38. Armstrong to Dobbin, 10, 12 November and 10, 12, 13 December 1856, East India Squadron Letters, vol. 10. The potential for further incidents near Canton was removed later in December when the Chinese burned the houses surrounding the foreign factories and the fire spread and destroyed the entire foreign settlement there.

39. Parker to Marcy, 22 November 1856, *Public Papers: United States and China*, 13: 303–305.

40. Thomas R. Cox, "Harbingers of Change: American Merchants and the Formosa Annexation Scheme," *Pacific Historical Review*, 42 (1973): 163–184; Harold D. Langley, "Gideon Nye and the Formosa Annexation Scheme," *Pacific Historical Review*, 34 (1965): 397–420; Leonard Gordon, "Early American Relations With Formosa," *The Historian*, 19 (1957): 262–289.

41. Nye to Parker, 10 February 1857; Parker to Nye, 10 February 1857; Parker to Marcy, 12 February 1857, *Public Papers: United States and China*, 12: 219–220; 13: 473–474.

42. Confidential Memorandum by Parker, 27 February 1857, ibid., 12: 228; Armstrong to Parker, 23 March 1857, ibid., 12: 256–257.

43. Parker to Secretary of State, 10 March 1857, ibid., 12: 233–234.

44. Edith Roelker Curtis, "Blood is Thicker Than Water," *American Neptune*, 27 (1967): 157–176.

45. Tattnall to Toucey, 4 July 1859, East India Squadron Letters, vol. 12; Henson, *Commissioners and Commodores*, 165.

46. Toucey to Tattnall, 5 October 1859, Confidential Letters Sent by the Secretary of the Navy, vol IV; Frederick Wells Williams, ed., "The Journal of S. Wells Williams," as cited in Henson, *Commissioners and Commodores*, 171.

CHAPTER 10

1. Report of the Secretary of the Navy, 3 December 1857, *Congressional Globe*, 35th Congress, 1st Session (1857–1858), Appendix, 32; Report of the Secretary of the Navy, 6 December 1858, *Congressional Globe*, 35th Congress, 2nd Session (1858–1859), Appendix, 18, 19.

2. *Congressional Globe*, 36th Congress, 1st Session (1859–1860), 3067, 3068, 3098, 3108, 3110.

Notes on Sources

Several basic bibliographies are available for the maritime and diplomatic history of this period. Robert G. Albion, *Naval and Maritime History: An Annotated Bibliography* (4th edition, Mystic, Conn., 1972) contains a detailed annotated list of published and some unpublished works. Kenneth J. Hagan, "The Navy in the Nineteenth Century, 1789–1889," in *A Guide to the Sources of United States Military History*, Robin Higham, ed. (Hamden, Conn., 1975), 152–184 is also useful. For diplomatic history, the standard bibliography is Richard Dean Burns, ed., *Guide to American Foreign Relations Since 1700* (Santa Barbara, Cal., 1983).

The official records of the Department of the Navy in the National Archives provide the basic primary source for naval activity prior to the Civil War. Two series are essential for naval policy: Letters Sent by the Secretary of the Navy to Officers (Ships of War), 1798–1868, 86 vols., Record Group 45 (Microfilm Series 149); and the Confidential Letters Sent by the Secretary of the Navy to Officers, 1842–1861, 4 vols., Record Group 45. The specific activities of the navy are detailed in the Letters Received by the Secretary of the Navy from Commanding Officers of Squadrons, 1841–1886, 300 vols., Record Group 45 (Microfilm Series 89). The records of the East India Squadron and the Pacific Squadron were most essential for this study. Also available are the Records Relating to the United States Exploring Expedition to the North Pacific, 1854–1856, 2 rolls (nos. 4 and 5), Record Group 45 (Microfilm Series 88).

Printed document collections provided another important primary source. *The American State Papers*; Class VI (Naval Affairs), 4 vols. (Washington, D.C., 1834–1861) is especially useful for the period prior to 1830, and K. Jack Bauer, ed., *The New American State Papers; 1798–1860; Naval Affairs*, 10 vols. (Wilmington, Del., 1981) covers the entire period. For the exploring expeditions of the 1840's and 1850's, an excellent collection is Thomas C. Cochran, ed., *The New American State Papers; 1798–1860 Explorations and Surveys*, 15 vols. (Wilmington, Del., 1972). The standard edition of presidential messages to Congress is James D. Richardson, ed., *A Compilation of the Messages and Papers of the Presidents, 1789–1902*, 10 vols. (Washington, D.C., 1903). Although the reporting was uneven and inadequate at times, the only nearly complete records of congressional debates are in *The Debates and Proceedings in the Congress of the United States, 1st to 18th Congresses, March 3, 1789–May 27, 1824 (Annals of Congress)*, 42 vols. (Washington, D.C., 1834–1856); *Register of Debates in Congress: 18th–25th Congress*, 2 December 1823–16 October 1837, 14 vols. (Washington, D.C., 1825–1837); *The Congressional Globe:* 23rd Congress to 42nd Congress, 2 December 1833–3 March 1873, 46 vols. (Washington, D.C., 1834–1873). The annual reports of the Secretary of the Navy are printed conveniently in the *Congressional Globe* with the supporting documentation and reports printed in the Serial Set of the United States Congress. An excellent index to this valuable series is James B. Adler, ed., *CIS US Serial Set Index*, 12 Parts (Washington, D.C., 1975). The various House of Representatives and Senate reports and documents in the Serial Set also contain a considerable amount of records and documents pertaining to the diplomatic and commercial activities of the navy. The treaties of the United States are organized chronologically in Hunter Miller, ed., *Treaties and Other International Acts of the United States*, 8 vols. (Washington, D.C., 1931–1948).

Although unpublished, personal manuscript sources were not essential to this book, several collections supplemented other primary sources. In the Manuscript Division of the Library of Congress, the Levi Woodbury Papers contain pertinent information on Jacksonian naval activities while the Robert F. Walker Papers include excellent material on Walker's dreams of commercial empire while he served as Secretary of the Treasury. In the Southern Historical Collection of the University of North Carolina Library, the Thomas R. King Papers include the drafts of several reports written by King as Chairman of the House Naval Affairs Committee. In the New Hampshire Historical Society, the Edmund Robert Papers and the Levi Woodbury Papers provided useful information on the commercial activities of these two Jacksonian officials. At the Chester W. Nimitz Library of the U.S. Naval Academy, the Joel Abbot Papers contain a diary and personal letters which amplify his official duties as commander of the East India Squadron.

A number of periodicals and newspapers provided additional primary source material. The *Niles' National Register* is a valuable source for the 1822 to 1849 period because of its array of speeches, reports, debates, and newspaper editorials. The two leading proponents of the gospel of commerce were *Hunt's Merchants' Magazine* (New York) for the years 1839 to 1860 and *DeBow's Review* (New Orleans) for the years 1846 to 1860. Partisan viewpoints on various commercial and diplomatic questions were presented in the *Democratic Review* (1837–1859) and the *American Whig Review* (1845–1852). Other useful periodicals were the *Southern Literary Messenger* (1834–1860), the *Southern Quarterly Review* (1842–1857), the *Army and Navy Chronicle* (1835–1842), the *Naval Magazine* (1836–1837), and the *Bulletin of the American Geographical and Statistical Society* (1852–1857).

For specific topics and regions, a number of primary source materials proved essential. On Latin American relations, an indispensable source is William R. Manning, ed., *Diplomatic Correspondence of the United States; Inter-American Affairs, 1831–1860*, 12 vols. (Washington, D.C., 1932). For early relations with China, an excellent collection of official records is Jules Davids, ed., *American Diplomatic and Public Papers: The United States and China. Series I: The Treaty System and the Taiping Rebellion, 1842–1860*, 21 vols. (Wilmington, Del., 1973). A useful collection which includes translations of Chinese documents is Earl Swisher, *China's Management of the American Barbarians; A Study of Sino-American Relations, 1841–1861, With Documents* (New Haven, Conn., 1953). Correspondence and documents dealing with relations between the United States and Hawaii are printed in the *Papers Relating to the Foreign Relations of the United States, 1894: Affairs in Hawaii*, Appendix II (Washington, D.C., 1894).

For the United States Exploring Expedition, correspondence and documents supporting the proposed project are contained in Jeremiah N. Reynolds, *Address on the Subject of a Surveying and Exploring Expedition to the Pacific Ocean and South Seas* (New York, 1836) and *House of Representatives Report No. 94, 23rd* Congress, 2nd Session (1834–1835). On the preparations for the expeditions, see *House of Representatives Executive Document No. 147*, 25th Congress, 2nd Session (1837–1838). The story of the expedition is detailed in Charles Wilkes, *Narrative of the United States Exploring Expedition, During the Years 1838, 1839, 1840, 1841, and 1842*, 5 vols. (Philadelphia, 1845). Two detailed studies of the expedition are William Stanton, *The Great United States Exploring Expedition of 1838–1842*, (Berkeley, Cal., 1975) and David B. Tyler, *The Wilkes Expedition; The First United States Exploring Expedition* (1838–1842) (Philadelphia, 1968).

Three congressional documents which contain valuable information on commercial and naval affairs in early relations with China are *House of Representatives Document Nos. 40, 119, and 170*, 26th Congress, 1st Session (1839–1840). See also *Senate Document 139*, 29th Congress, 1st Session (1845–1846). An excellent study of the navy's role in China is Curtis T. Henson, *Commissioners and Commodores: The East India Squadron and American Diplomacy in China* (University, Ala., 1982). See also Robert Erwin Johnson, *Far China Station: The United States Navy in Asian Waters, 1800–1898* (Annapolis, Md., 1979); Te-Kong Tong, *United States Diplomacy in China, 1844–1860* (Seattle, 1964); and John K. Fairbank, *Trade and Diplomacy on the China Coast; The Opening of the Treaty Ports, 1842–1854* (revised edition, Stanford, Cal., 1969; original edition, 1953).

Primary source materials on the background of the expedition to Japan are contained in *House of Representatives Document No. 138*, 28th Congress, 2nd Session (1844–1845); *Senate Executive Document No. 96*, 29th Congress, 2nd Session (1846–1847); *House of Representatives Executive Document No. 84*, 31st Congress, 1st Session (1849–1850); *Senate Executive Document No. 59*, 32nd Congress, 1st Session (1851–1852). For records and correspondence related to the mission itself, see *Senate Executive Document No. 34*, 33rd Congress, 2nd Session (1854–1855). For Perry's own account of the expedition, see F. L. Hawks, ed., *Narrative of the Expedition of an American Squadron to the China Seas and Japan*, 3 vols. (Washington, D.C., 1856). Detailed accounts of the expedition are Arthur Walworth, *Black Ships Off Japan; The Story of Commodore Perry's Expedition* (Reprint, Hamden, Conn., 1966; original edition, 1943); Samuel Eliot Morison, *"Old Bruin"; Commodore Matthew C. Perry, 1798–1858* (Boston, 1967).

For background on the North Pacific Exploring Expedition, see *Senate Executive Document No. 55.*, 32nd Congress, 1st Session (1851–1852). The expedition's records cited previously have been edited and printed in Allan B Cole, ed., *Yankee Surveyors in the Shogun's Seas; Records of the United States Surveying Expedition to the North Pacific Ocean, 1853–1856* (Princeton, N.J., 1947). An account of the expedition is Allan B. Cole, "The Ringgold- Rodgers-Brooke Expedition to Japan and the North Pacific, 1853–1859," *Pacific Historical Review*, 16 (1947): 152–162. See also, Robert Erwin Johnson, *Rear Admiral John Rodgers, 1812–1882* (Annapolis, Md., 1967); and George M. Brooke, Jr., *John M. Brooke; Naval Scientist and Educator* (Charlottesville, Va., 1980).

For the exploring activities of the navy in the 1840's and 1850's, a detailed account is Vincent Ponko, Jr., *Ships, Seas, and Scientists; U.S. Naval Exploration and Discovery in the Nineteenth Century* (Annapolis, Md., 1974). The official accounts of the Amazon expedition of William Herndon and Lardner Gibbon are contained in *The New American State Papers, 1789–1860; Explorations and Surveys*, vol. 10, while the report of the La Plata expedition commanded by T. J. Page is in vol. 12. See also T.J. Page, *La Plata, the Argentine Confederation, and Paraguay* (New York, 1859).

Representative Thomas R. King's report on the need for a Home Squadron is printed in *House of Representatives Report No. 3*, 27th Congress, 1st Session (1841). Pertinent records on construction of convertible mail steamers are contained in *House of Representatives Report No. 685*, 29th Congress, 1st Session (1845–1846) and *Senate Document No. 50*, 32nd Congress, 1st Session (1851–1852). The lack of naval fitness and preparation in the mid–1840's is detailed in *Senate Document Nos. 187 and 263*, 29th Congress, 1st Session (1845–1846).

A number of other secondary works deserve special mention. Although they are outdated, two general naval histories which proved useful for this study were Dudley K. Knox. *A History of the United States Navy* (revised edition, New York, 1948; original edition, 1936); Harold and Margaret Sprout, *The Rise of American Naval Power, 1776–1918* (revised edition, Princeton, N.J., 1966; original edition, 1939). Paolo Colletta, ed., *American Secretaries of the Navy*, 2 vols. (Annapolis, Md., 1980) is an excellent reference work which proved very useful for this study. See also the essays by David F. Long and Geoffrey S. Smith on the 1815–1861 period in Kenneth J. Hagan, ed., *In War and Peace: Interpretations of American Naval History, 1775–1978* (Westport, Conn., 1978). A traditional account is Charles O. Paullin, *Diplomatic Negotiations of American Naval Officers, 1778–1883* (Baltimore, 1912).

In addition to the squadron and area studies already cited, several others need to be noted. Robert Erwin Johnson, *Thence Round Cape Horn: The Story of United States Naval Forces on Pacific Station, 1818–1923* (Annapolis, Md., 1963) is an operational account, while James A. Field, Jr., *America and the Mediterranean World, 1776–1882* (Princeton, N.J., 1969) is an exceptional work of scholarship which places naval activity in the context of the full American experience in the Mediterranean. Although serious works have been written on the Africa, Brazil, and Home squadrons, full-scale studies of each remain to be done. For a detailed, serialized account of the navy's antifilibustering activities in the Caribbean in the 1850's, see Louis N. Feipel, "The Navy and Filibustering in the Fifties," *United States Naval Institute Proceedings*, 44 (1918). Detailed and extensively researched biographies of two central naval figures in this period are Frances Leigh Williams, *Matthew Fontaine Maury; Scientist of the Sea* (New Brunswick, N.J., 1963) and Claude H. Hall, *Abel Parker Upshur, Conservative Virginian, 1790–1844* (Madison, Wis., 1964). A detailed scholarly study of the maritime industries is John G. B. Hutchins, *The American Maritime Industries and Public Policy, 1789–1914; An Economic History* (Cambridge, Mass, 1941).

In addition to the bibliographic items already cited, a wealth of other sources exists on the naval, diplomatic, commercial, and political history of the antebellum United States. Many printed collections of speeches, writings, and correspondence are available for political and diplomatic figures, but these editions invariably provided individual citations or quotations rather than extensive sources on the navy's commercial diplomacy. For the navy, numerous officers and enlisted men left memoirs, narratives, or diaries of their personal and naval activities. Although these narratives tend to be purely descriptive of places and events, I have drawn on these often fascinating accounts in numerous instances and so indicated in the footnotes. In addition, there are many biographies, monographs, articles, and general histories which treat aspects of the subject covered in this book in detail. A few of these studies have been noted in this brief essay, but most have not, and appear instead in individual footnotes. The footnotes have been constructed to reveal the abundant secondary as well as primary sources on which this book is based. Indeed, the many historians who have produced scholarly studies of the era and its aspects helped make it possible to write a study of this scope on the commercial diplomacy of the antebellum American Navy.

Index

About the Author

JOHN H. SCHROEDER is Associate Professor of History at the University of Wisconsin, Milwaukee. His previous works include *Mr. Polk's War: American Opposition and Dissent, 1846-1848*, as well as chapters and articles in *Captains of the Old Steam Navy, Command Under Sail: Makers of the American Naval Tradition, Encyclopedia of American Political History, Guide to American Foreign Relations Since 1700*, and *The New England Quarterly*.

Recent Titles in
Contributions in Military Studies